RED HIGHWAYS

RED HIGHWAYS

A Liberal's Journey into the Heartland

ROSE AGUILAR

PoliPointPress

For my mom ~
Thank you for your laughter
and for spreading sunshine wherever you go.

Red Highways: A Liberal's Journey into the Heartland
Copyright © 2008 by Rose Aguilar

13 12 11 10 09 08   1 2 3 4 5

Portions of this book appeared in a slightly different form in *AlterNet.org*: "The Blue Tint of Indian Country," October 24, 2005; "Off the Front Lines and Forgotten," August 29, 2005; "One State at a Time," August 23, 2005; "Houses of Right-Wing Worship," June 7, 2005; and "A Journey into Red America," May 23, 2005. *AlterNet*, 77 Federal Street, San Francisco, CA 94107. All rights reserved.

Production management: BookMatters
Book design: BookMatters
Cover design: Charles Kreloff Design, Inc.

LIBRARY OF CONGRESS CATALOGING-IN-PUBLICATION DATA
Aguilar, Rose, 1972–
  Red highways : a liberal's journey into the heartland / Rose Aguilar.
  p. cm.
  Includes index.
  ISBN 978-0-9794822-7-4 (alk. paper)
  1. Presidents—United States—Election—2004. 2. Voting—United States.
3. Bush, George W. (George Walker), 1946– —Public opinion. 4. Iraq War, 2003–
—Public opinion. 5. Public opinion—United States. I. Title.
  JK5262004 .A38 2008
  324.973'0931—dc22   2008035276

Published by:
PoliPointPress, LLC
P.O. Box 3008
Sausalito, CA 94966-3008
(415) 339-4100
www.p3books.com

Distributed by Ingram Publisher Services

Printed in the United States of America

Perhaps travel cannot prevent bigotry, but by demonstrating that all peoples cry, laugh, eat, worry, and die, it can introduce the idea that if we try and understand each other, we may even become friends.

~MAYA ANGELOU

Contents

Introduction

I didn't know it at the time, but the idea for this book began taking shape in September 2004, a year and a half after the United States invaded Iraq. It was a gorgeous Saturday afternoon in Petaluma, California, and I was in the middle of a heated debate at an engagement party with four conservative men my father's age about the Bush administration's justification for the invasion. The more alcohol they drank, the louder they became. "The intelligence may have been wrong, but Saddam Hussein had to go!" screamed the man downing vodka tonics. "You can't honestly believe that our government would lie to us," said the guy holding a Budweiser. These guys were getting their news from Fox, so they believed there was a connection between 9/11 and Iraq, and they'd never heard of Scott Ritter, former UN weapons inspector in Iraq who, before the invasion, had argued that weapons of mass destruction would never be found because they didn't exist. Every five minutes their wives would stop by, but they wouldn't stick around for very long. "This is an engagement party! You're not supposed to talk about politics!" As the party began to wind down, one of the guys gave me his business card before hopping onto his Harley and asked me to add him to my email news list. "We probably disagree on just about everything," he said quietly, "but I respect you because you give a damn." He rendered me speechless.

That conversation got me thinking about how small my bubble really is. As a journalist living in San Francisco, just 40 miles south of Petaluma, I rarely met people who supported George W. Bush or the invasion of Iraq. In my corner of the world, no one could understand how anyone could vote for Bush. "Who are those people and what is happening to our country?" became something of a mantra for despairing citizens, but no one seemed to have any answers.

Even though we have access to unprecedented amounts of information, I wasn't finding many insights about why people vote the way they do. The opinions of average people were glaringly missing from most of the political magazines and books I was reading. And watching the Sunday morning political talk shows and the cable networks, I cringed every time I saw the same dozen hosts and pundits—mostly white men who live in New York or Washington, DC—give the same shallow analysis about horse race issues, and argue about the latest polls and statistics. Where were the in-depth conversations about real issues? Where were the voices of the very people the pundits claim to know so much about? I'd hear them once in a great while, but all I got was a 30-second sound bite and very little context.

The discussion we hear in the corporate—mostly television—media has largely descended into an us-versus-them mentality and thrives on sweeping generalizations about so-called values voters, soccer moms, the white working-class, the "far-left fringe," the antiwar crowd, NASCAR dads—the list goes on. My dad isn't white, but he is a retired sheet metal worker who considers himself working class. He's also a lifelong union member and enjoys a NASCAR race every now and then. Here in "liberal California," we actually have two NASCAR tracks; one is just 45 miles north of San Francisco. According to the pollsters and pundits, my dad's union ties would make him a Democrat, but his NASCAR ties would make him a Republican. Are we dumbing down the electorate by not only simplifying the debate, but also by simplifying each other?

I was especially interested in learning more about Republicans, but other than a few family friends and former colleagues, I don't know many. A week after the engagement party in Petaluma, I decided to join a few conservative newsgroups and discussion boards, including *freerepublic.com*, a site for archconservatives, and *hannity.com*, a site for diehard fans of the conservative talking head Sean Hannity. I spent the first few weeks eavesdropping on the groups' conversations about "liberating Iraq" and the "liberal media." (Just about any news source you can name is liberal, according to these groups.) When I finally joined the conversations, I was attacked. I didn't say I wasn't a Republican; I merely questioned the party's claims of supporting the troops by posting a few articles about inadequate health care for returning veterans. Within seconds of asking members what we could do to convince Republicans to fund the Department of Veterans Affairs (VA), I was banned. I joined another list to discuss big-spending, big-government Republicans. Banned again. The message was loud and clear: don't mess with our president. But by this time, I was addicted.

A month before the 2004 election, I joined ReDefeat Bush, a group that called women in swing states to find out if they were registered to vote and if they were planning to vote for John Kerry, the candidate my fellow volunteers reluctantly supported. "Can we instead ask if they're willing to vote against Bush?" asked one woman. We weren't supposed to talk for very long, but whenever I reached someone who was either undecided or supporting Bush, I couldn't help myself. Talking to a real live Republican was much better than discussion boards. My conversations averaged between 10 and 20 minutes and, yes, they were always civil.

I asked Ursula, an 80-year-old, lifelong Republican living in Eugene, Oregon, why she's a Republican. "Because my family is Republican and Republicans are for the common man," she said. When I asked her to tell me what Bush had done for the common man, she said he passed a tax cut for the middle and lower classes. I responded by sharing the following facts. According to the nonpartisan Congressional Budget Office, the poorest 20 percent of workers, who earned $16,600 annually, got a tax break of $250 in 2004, which was less than two percent of their income. That's about 68 cents a day. By comparison, the richest one percent, with average incomes topping $1.1 million, received $78,460 in tax cuts. That is nearly seven percent of their income.

Ursula also commended Bush for taking care of the military. I pointed out that his 2005 budget called for cutting the VA staff that handles benefits claims. At that time, the VA was receiving 60,000 to 70,000 claims a day from soldiers who had experienced physical injuries and mental problems in Iraq and Afghanistan. Ursula hadn't heard about the budget, and she was furious when I told her that soldiers stationed in Iraq have been forced to buy their own body armor. We went on to talk about education, the high price of prescription drugs, and Republicans who want to privatize social security.

Before we hung up, Ursula told me she'd have to think about our conversation and talk to her best friend about it. "For the first time in my life, I might have to cross party lines," she said ruefully.

The information I shared with Ursula and many others is easy to find online in articles and reports; it's not easy to find if you get your news from the talking heads on television or AM radio.

Most of the male volunteers in the group, including my boyfriend Ryan (who didn't vote for Kerry), weren't as successful. When Julie told him that if John Kerry were in office, Saddam Hussein would still be in power, he yelled, "But Saddam wasn't involved in 9/11!" Her response? Click. Getting self-righteous and yelling was obviously not the way to go. I soon found a more effective, less presumptuous approach: ask people what they think instead of *telling* them what to think.

The man who answered my next call said his wife wasn't home, so I asked him if he was voting for Kerry.

"No, I'm a hardcore Republican and very much in favor of the war; in fact, I'm in favor of World War III," he replied.

"And in favor of killing innocent people?" I asked.

"War isn't easy, but it's our only option," he said.

As we continued talking about Iraq and Republican values, his position gradually became more moderate. He conceded that right-wing fundamentalists had hijacked the Republican Party, but he said he was hopeful it would eventually move back to the center. Before saying good-bye, he thanked me for calling and said while he didn't agree with me, he hoped ReDefeat Bush kept up the good work.

I was at a loss for words. I wanted to hang up on him, but he was willing to listen and seemed sincere in his desire for people with different opinions to engage in respectful conversations. I then looked down at my call sheet and realized I had called the wrong number.

On the day before the 2004 election, Ryan and I decided to go to a swing state to knock on doors and meet voters in person. We could have driven to Reno, but we couldn't pass up the possibility of celebrating under the Eiffel Tower, so even though we don't gamble, we booked a deal we found at the Paris Las Vegas Hotel. We spent two days knocking on doors in residential areas and met a number of people who were still undecided. We couldn't believe it. How could anyone still be undecided? Based on the conversations I had, they either didn't have access to substantial information or were being misled by the news they read. For example, most of the women I met truly believed that Afghan and Iraqi women were being liberated. Very few were familiar with Bush's anti-abortion and anti–birth control policies. A handful said they were voting for Bush because their husbands liked him. I was horrified.

Back at the hotel, after it became clear that Kerry would concede, Ryan wiped my tears, turned off the television, and convinced me to leave the room to get a bite to eat. *Fox News* was on at the busy hotel bar downstairs, but the volume was turned down. On our way out, we passed chain-smoking gamblers shoving dollar coins into slot machines. Outside, we saw scores of people running across the street to watch the Bellagio Hotel's man-made water and light show with Celine Dion blaring in the background. I was in hell. It was as if the election had never happened. No one was talking about it. Did any of these people vote? Did they realize what was in store for the next four years? As much as I couldn't wait to leave Paris, I dreaded going back to my San Francisco bubble.

As expected, back home the air was thick with depression and utter confusion. I realized that I couldn't continue life as usual, but I wasn't sure what that meant. I loved my job as a radio reporter and producer, but I was tired. I was tired of covering some of the largest marches in recent history, including the March for Women's Lives on April 25, 2004, in Washington, DC, only to watch the corporate media all but ignore them. I was tired of spending endless hours watching documentaries and reading books and articles about the folly of the Bush administration. I was tired of staying up until the wee hours of the morning reading political blogs. I was tired of feeling hopeless about our current state of affairs. And I was tired of listening to the left try to figure it out. How could anyone vote for a guy who called himself the "war president"? Where did we go wrong? Where do we go from here? The problem was, we were asking each other.

I believed we needed to look for answers outside of San Francisco, a city unlike any other in the United States. Here, antiwar protests are essentially outdoor celebrations. In November 2005, voters approved the nation's toughest ban on handguns by making it illegal for city residents to possess them and they voted against allowing military recruitment on public school campuses. Women run more public safety agencies, including the fire and police departments here, than in any other major city in the country. When the antichoice group, Walk for Life, announced plans to march in San Francisco on January 22, 2005, the city's Board of Supervisors quickly designated that day as "Stand Up for Choice Day."

In November 2003, we had a mayoral runoff between Gavin Newsom, a Democrat, and Matt Gonzalez, a Green. Republicans don't run for office in San Francisco. Newsom won by only 11,000 votes after outspending Gonzalez 10 to 1. In fact, Mayor Newsom, the man who made international headlines after issuing marriage licenses to gay couples in February 2004, is considered moderate by San Francisco standards. We have one of the highest minimum wages in the country ($9.36 per hour in 2008), and we are the only city in the country requiring employers to give their workers paid sick leave. As the debate about health care continues at the national and state levels, the city of San Francisco has decided to go it alone and try something new. Healthy San Francisco is the first initiative in the country to offer health care to the city's 82,000 uninsured residents. And finally, even though San Francisco is one of the most popular destinations in the world, George W. Bush has never graced us with his presence. He's the first president not to visit since Calvin Coolidge, according to the *San Francisco Chronicle*, and only the second in more than a century. To say I live in a bubble is putting it mildly.

One night, after spending several hours online, sending articles to friends who were probably sick of me barraging them with emails, and practically falling over piles of political books and magazines I had yet to open, I realized that it was time to leave my comfort zone. I needed to turn off my computer and get out into the streets to find out why people vote the way they do and find out if we're as divided as we're led to believe. But I wanted to get past the superficial sound bites and engage in real conversations, hopefully respectful conversations. For example, I'd never had an in-depth conversation with ardent anti-choice activists. I'd briefly interviewed people at antichoice rallies, but it was almost impossible to get past the talking points. I also wanted to find out what people think when they hear the words "liberal" and "conservative." How many times have you heard a talking head on television or the radio scream about the "far left" or the "liberal agenda"? What exactly does that mean? I didn't want to ask people who are regularly interviewed; I wanted to ask average, everyday voters and nonvoters (it's easy to forget that more than 100 million Americans don't vote) living in states that tend to lean Republican. And I wanted to do it in person. I decided I would need six months.

My family thought I was crazy. "I really don't want you going to rural Texas to try to change people's minds," said my concerned mom. "You work way too hard. Maybe you need a break from the news. Can't you go back to Sri Lanka or India and volunteer?" I told her my goal wasn't to change hearts and minds. If it were, I probably wouldn't get very far.

Ryan loved the idea of taking a road trip to meet "those people." A month or so after discussing the idea, he called me from work and excitedly said, "I just gave my notice. Let's look for a van!"

The next month was chaotic, but the plan came together quickly. Up until a few days before we left, I was producing radio shows and writing about military recruiters, California's shrinking arts budget, peak oil, and homeless veterans. I took a leave of absence from my radio job, got rid of stuff I no longer needed through *Freecycle.org*, found someone to rent my room in my apartment, set up the website for the trip, searched for a van to buy on Craig's List, and put together a silent auction at a café to raise money for the trip, which I funded myself.

The theme of the auction was, "Everyone is sick of politics, so my friends are sending me to the red states." Family, friends, and even strangers who found out about the trip through word-of-mouth donated massages, career counseling sessions, jewelry, books, a website with server space, artwork, and wine. The turnout was incredible and we managed to raise over $2,000. We used the money to buy a brown 1984 Toyota van in relatively good condition. We spent a thousand to rebuild the engine. The mechanic offered to fix the air conditioner for another thousand. I was warned about oppressively hot Southern summers before we left, so it was tempting, but I couldn't justify the expense.

We decided against following a fixed itinerary, but we did choose the states we wanted to visit. I wanted to visit places I knew little to nothing about. We chose Texas, Mississippi, Oklahoma, Utah, and Montana.

Before we left, we made two rules: no political bumper stickers on the van and no political T-shirts on Ryan, which would prove to be a challenge since most, if not all, of his shirts express his views. He brought his political shirts, but promised he would either wear them to bed or cover them up if he wore them out.

Political awareness was encouraged and prevalent in Ryan's household. He grew up in an East Coast secular Jewish-Irish family with strong connections to the social justice movement. His father (a doctor) and mother (a former nurse and Planned Parenthood activist) were children of the 1960s. They took their kids to protests and were involved in the folk music scene and the "No Nukes" movement. Like millions of immigrants, Ryan's great-grandfather came to the United States from Poland with only the clothes on his back. He eventually opened a store and raised a son who became a lawyer. Ryan was expected to go to graduate school after college and pursue a professional career like his father and grandfather; but as an iconoclast, he wasn't interested in a nine-to-five structured life, so he decided to travel instead. After three years in India, he went to art school, and then he took off for Australia, where he lived in a van and worked on fruit farms for a year. His experiences of living in a van and traveling came in very handy on our trip.

I, too, have been fortunate enough to travel to many countries overseas, but unlike Ryan's, my family never discussed political issues, and I was never pressured to follow a specific career path. In fact, I'm the first person on both sides of my family to graduate from college. My mother comes from a traditional Serbian family that still believes in arranged marriages and traditional roles for women, leaving little room for education and independence. One of eight children, she decided to break the rules by marrying my father, an American Indian. They eventually divorced, and my mom raised my brother and me, encouraging us to go to college and take advantage of the opportunities she never had.

I was drawn to journalism because it has the power to make a difference and create a more informed citizenry, at least that's the hope. To this day, I'm still amazed at what can be accomplished by giving people a voice, focusing on issues that don't get the attention they deserve (such as inequality and poverty), and starting a conversation. The goal of this trip was to do just that.

Once everything was in place, we packed up the van, I glued a few plastic dolphins to the dashboard for good luck, and we made our way to Texas.

I

WELCOME TO TEXAS

My First Taste of Fear, Hope, and Hospitality

BEFORE WE LEFT, I read that we could get from San Francisco to Houston in just two days. We drove eight-hour shifts with little sleep, but the van could barely push 60. It took three full days. What's another day when you have no itinerary? I've done road trips before, but always as a tourist with a particular destination in mind. I usually had a specific goal to see a national park or monument, and then I had to get back to work. On this trip my goal was an idea, and I had six months to get there.

As we passed the "Arizona: The Grand Canyon State Welcomes You" highway sign, I stuck my head out the window, took a few deep breaths, and watched life go by with a smile on my face. At that moment, I realized I was no longer passing through. For six months, I would be living among people who also call the United States their home—the middle-aged man who whizzed by with his family in the black Cadillac Escalade, the elegant woman driving the red Jaguar, and the young guy wearing what looked like a shirt from a fast-food joint in the beat-up white Toyota truck. We breathe the same air, we live under the same political system, we've probably seen the same television and news shows, and most of us grew up going to public schools; yet because we might vote differently once every four years, we find ourselves stereotyped in the national media and separated by red and blue borders.

As we continued driving along Highway 10, we were struck by the new subdivisions and strip malls we saw, each hauntingly similar to the last. We preferred the desolate stretches of wild dry land covered in cactus and unique red rock formations. I wondered how the descendants of the Native Americans who once lived on this harsh but stunning landscape feel about the changes and overdevelopment. How has the environment changed over the years? We didn't have time to stop and find out because Ryan wanted to make it to Houston in time for dinner with his aunt and uncle.

We did, however, have plenty of time to get used to our newfound freedom and fiddle with our iPods. On long stretches of road, I preferred to blast rock music because it kept me awake. Pearl Jam, System of a Down, and old Metallica were a few of my driving favorites. The louder, the better. Ryan preferred the Grateful Dead, Danny Barnes, and Billy Bragg. Luckily, we didn't mind compromising. Our theme song for the trip was the Who's "Going Mobile." We also made a point of regularly flipping the radio dial to hear the local stations. The farther we drove, the more Spanish, religious, and conservative programming we heard.

We also counted "Support Our Troops" ribbons and Wal-Mart signs, the two most common icons we found on the highway. It seemed like the yellow ribbons were on almost every car and SUV that sped by. After 100, I stopped counting. We passed four Wal-Marts in one hour. We also passed several homemade signs along the highway that said: "Pro-Life Vineyard," "Polygamy is Abuse," and "Christ + His Holy Bible = Solutions to All Life's Problems."

We tried to stop at Chevron stations whenever possible because they're almost guaranteed to have a clean bathroom and soap—a luxury on a road trip. Most stations cater to truck drivers and road trippers, offering a random assortment of items, including switchblades, DVDs, and toys. We found dolls you might see a toddler carrying, but they were as tall as a three-year-old. I asked a cashier if they sell. "Sure, they make good driving companions," he said laughing. At a gas station near the New Mexico–Texas border, a variety of knives and confederate-flag wallets were in a glass case next to an ice cream freezer.

Ryan regularly indulged in mini-mart junk food and almost always had chips and Reese's Peanut Butter Cups within reach. I'm vegan, so the only thing I ever bought was bottled water. We wanted to buy bottled water only when necessary, but the heat was already unbearable. I assumed finding food on the road would be difficult, so before we left we stocked up on rice, beans, canned soups, soy milk, cereal, dried fruit, trail mix, and granola bars. We had a few large plastic tubs of food in the back, along with two boxes of books, a spare tire, a rechargeable jumper device, a club for the steering wheel (we were told the van was easy to break into), a few duffle bags of clothing and toiletries, computer equipment, a printer, a box of wires and plugs for our equipment, and a cooler. It was liberating to know that everything we needed for the next six months was in the back of the van.

After two days on the never-ending highway, we were greeted with a sign that said, "Welcome to Texas: Drive Friendly—The Texas Way." The change in scenery as we entered Texas through El Paso was astounding. The highway was lined with every chain store you can imagine, loud fluorescent signs, and endless advertisements. We were used to such long stretches on the road, so driving from the western to the eastern part of the state—745 miles—didn't seem like such a big deal. After more than 10 hours of driving, we arrived in Houston. We were too tired to come up with an actual plan, so we ate dinner and crashed for the night.

A Day at the Mall

The next morning, I made a few phone calls to let my friends and family know we had made it safe and sound. My brother, who isn't very political, yelled at me, saying I was naive for thinking I could go to rural Texas and change people's minds. "Ryan isn't a big guy. You're going to get your asses kicked!" I was taken aback and realized that my own family still didn't understand what I was doing. After we hung up, I stared out the kitchen window and wondered if *I* knew what I was doing. Had I made the right decision? What really was my goal?

I had left my job to spend six months talking to strangers about the two topics you're supposed to avoid in mixed company: politics and religion. Not to mention the fact that Texas is the second-largest state in the country with just over 23.5 million residents. Houston is the largest city in the state (population 2,144,491) and the fourth largest in the United States.

I spent a few days trying to come up with some sort of plan, but I had more questions than answers. Where should I begin? Will strangers want to talk? Or will they view me as an outsider with an agenda? What if we run out of money? Ryan and I spend a lot of time together at home, but we have our own interests and value our own space. What if we fight? I paced back and forth for what felt like hours asking myself these questions. In the meantime, Ryan was lounging on the couch happily watching mindless television, something we never do at home. What if he becomes a TV addict?

This was becoming ridiculous. I had to leave the house. But where would I find a diverse group of people on a hot April afternoon in Houston, Texas? After doing some searching online, I stumbled upon the Galleria Mall, the number-one shopping and tourist destination in Houston, with over 24 million annual visitors. According to the mall's website, with 2.4 million square feet of retail space and more than 375 restaurants and stores, it's a "city within a city."

"Grab your stuff," I said. "We're going to the mall."

The parking lot was packed. We rushed past the shops and made our way to the food court to buy cold drinks. Ryan said he probably wouldn't be able to contain himself if someone I interviewed said something he disagreed with, so he sat down and grabbed Mahmood Mamdani's *Good Muslim, Bad Muslim: America, the Cold War, and the Roots of Terror* out of his bag. When Ryan studied in India, his program director recommended he always have a book handy because trains and buses are never on time, and it's nice to have something to read while you're waiting. He never went anywhere without at least one book, always nonfiction, and usually about politics or the Middle East. He was content for hours as long as he had something to read.

I pulled my digital recorder and microphone out of my bag and thought about what I was going to say. I decided to approach two casually dressed, friendly looking gray-haired men eating lunch. "Excuse me," I said, "I'm a journalist from San Francisco and I'm traveling around the country talking to people about their communities and issues they care about. I'm also curious to learn why people vote the way they do. Would you mind if I ask you a few questions?"

They looked at each other and chuckled, "Welcome to Texas."

John proudly told me he's a Republican, but his mother and siblings are all Democrats.

"So how did you end up Republican?" I asked.

"Because of the platform and the issues they stand for, like gay marriage and abortion. The more conservative issues. I'm 100 percent against gay marriage."

"You must have heated conversations with your family."

"Oh, all the time."

A former pastor, John opposes abortion and gay marriage because of his "biblical understanding." He knows gays, but because he lives in a sheltered area, he "tries to keep them in the closet."

"If a family member said they were gay, would you still love them?" I asked.

"I would still love them. I would embrace them, but they would know where I stand on the issue."

John's friend Ron chimed in to say that God loves everyone!

As long as they stay in the closet?

"I've gone over this in my mind," Ron said with a serious tone. "What if it were my grandchildren or children? I would tell them, I love you, but just because I love them doesn't mean I approve of what they're doing. I've met some gays who've been very nice."

Ron usually votes Republican, but most of his relatives, including his mom, are Democrats. "But she goes to church," he said taking a bite of his rice dish. "She considers herself a Christian."

"A lot of Democrats go to church and a lot of Democrats are Christians!" I said. They laughed.

John then asked me for my opinion on gay issues, specifically gay adoption. I felt the spotlight on me and I wasn't sure what to say. I only offer my personal opinions during interviews if I'm asked, which is surprisingly rare. People enjoy talking about themselves, but because I was looking for more than a sound bite and was asking such personal questions, I had a feeling I'd be asked to share my views on occasion.

"Well," I said nervously, "my aunt is lesbian, and she and her partner are raising a young son together. They absolutely adore him." I told John that I used to mentor a young girl whose mom often forgot to feed her. "She has a handful of siblings from different dads. Her dad took off when she was a baby, and she hasn't heard from him since. When I used to pick her up to take her out for the day, her mom never bothered to ask where we were going or when we would return. Shouldn't a loving, healthy environment be more important than whether a parent is gay or straight?" John stared ahead and didn't answer.

I stood up to thank John and Ron for their time, and we shook hands. John didn't let go. He looked me in the eyes and wished me well. I'll never know what was running through his mind when I shared my story, but I could tell that it got him thinking. His views on social issues couldn't be more different from mine, yet for a moment we connected. I realized this project would generate conversations with real people, sometimes real *different* people. If I wanted them to let me into their lives, I was probably going to have to let them into mine.

I decided to approach five heavily made-up women wearing black suits and pearl necklaces, who looked like they were taking a break from the makeup counter at Nordstrom's. I went up to the woman wearing the least amount of makeup.

Caroline is a rep for Mary Kay Cosmetics. She usually votes Republican but isn't tied to the party. She told me the Texas legislature is obsessed with gay marriage. If it were up to her, gays could marry in

City Hall, but not in a church. "I'm really conflicted on this one. Marriage is marriage. In my heart I would love to follow the Bible, then again, I know God loves everyone," she said. "But I do believe that marriage is sacred between a man and a woman. I believe consenting gay couples can have a lot of the rights of a heterosexual marriage, but marriage in the eyes of God is between a man and a woman."

"What about gay adoption?"

"There are so many kids that need love," she said. "If the gay couple is loving and offers them a home, then why not? It doesn't mean they're going to be gay, but it is confusing to them. There are also a lot of whacko heterosexual couples who shouldn't have kids, but you always wonder. What's the long-term effect? I'd rather the child be loved than be neglected."

I spent the rest of the afternoon having similar conversations with Republicans about the topics of their choice: gay marriage and abortion. A 20-something woman on her lunch break told me Texans are afraid of change. "I work in this mall, and my gay friends can't be gay at work unless they work at a salon. Around here, especially in Houston, if you're gay and they know it, they won't hire you. That's why my friend turns off his 'gayness.' He acts more macho at work than he does when he's not at work."

She doesn't vote because she hasn't made time to go register. I suggested she print out the form online and send it in. She didn't know that was an option.

Not So Red

The following day we looked at the Texas political map to decide where to go next. Other than the southern tip, it's a huge sea of red. In passing conversations, I'd heard that southern Texans usually vote Democratic because they're poor Latinos. That tiny blue spot on the map was too enticing to pass up, so we decided to head toward Laredo, the fastest-growing city on the Rio Grande. More than 90 percent of Laredo's population is Latino, and most residents are bilingual. According to our *Lonely Planet Texas* guide, Immigration and

Naturalization Service—now ICE—officers are forbidden to pursue Mexicans trying to enter Laredo via the Rio Grande because the river is so contaminated.

It took just over five hours to get from Houston to the Mexican border, where it finally felt like we had escaped "Chain Store USA." The narrow streets were filled with taco carts, "Guns & Ammo" shops, and independent stores selling all kinds of cheap trinkets made in Mexico and China. Five minutes later, we entered the newly developed area of town and saw the usual suspects: Best Buy, Target, Radio Shack, Old Navy, and Bed Bath & Beyond. Both areas were equally packed.

The next day we stopped for lunch at a local Mexican restaurant with dozens of somber-looking deer heads, boar heads, snakes, and a variety of other creatures I couldn't identify hanging from the wall. There was nothing I could eat on the menu and even if there had been, I've always had a hard time eating with dead animals staring at me, so I watched Ryan happily devour greasy tortilla chips and a meaty burrito dripping with cheese. Before we left, I asked our waiter where we could find wireless Internet access. "There's a Starbucks up the road and two Wal-Marts in town!" he said enthusiastically. Morning, noon, and night, the Wal-Mart parking lots we passed were almost always full.

We continued along the sea of blue in south Texas. A few hours later, we stopped in Crystal City, a small town (population 7,190) whose two main roads reveal its slow decline. The shops on the main drag near the movie theater, where "House of Wax" was showing for four dollars, were empty and dilapidated. We drove by a piñata party at Pizza Hut and spotted a Dairy Queen sign touting the virtues of its rancheros plate. Ryan thoroughly enjoyed the authentic Mexican food, but the beans were cooked in lard and the rice was cooked in chicken stock, so my only option was the veggie sandwich at Subway.

At three in the afternoon very few people were on the street. We drove by an outdoor flea market where a handful of women and children were selling bottled water, candy apples, and used clothing hanging from a metal fence. We decided to stop. As I was explaining the project, they stopped what they were doing and glanced back and forth between my microphone and me. They were clearly skeptical. It's not every day that a journalist stops by a flea market in Crystal City, Texas, to ask questions. I tried to break the ice by asking them what the locals do for work.

"I am a cook for early Head Start and I'm a labor contractor in the fields, and then I work as a part-time cook in a taco stand," said Sofia Munoz, a 50-something Crystal City native with red-orange wavy hair and tired-looking light brown skin.

Did I hear that correctly? "You have three jobs?"

"Yes, three jobs to support myself."

Sofia works 64 hours a week. She makes $5.00 an hour at the taco stand; $5.15 an hour picking cabbage, onions, and melons; and $6.76 an hour at Head Start, a national organization that focuses on assisting children from low-income families. That's about $1,433 a month.

Sofia said she barely makes ends meet but rarely complains about her one percent annual cost of living raise—not when the unemployment rate in Crystal City is fourteen percent, one of the highest in Texas.

Several times during our conversation, Sofia said that if she can work, anyone can. "There are a lot of people out there who depend on welfare and shouldn't. They give Mexicans a bad name. We work hard for our money. It's not easy when there are no opportunities available."

Crystal City is one of the poorest towns in Texas, and 98 percent of the city's inhabitants are Hispanic. All the women at the flea market, including Sofia, had no idea they live in the most Democratic constituency in Texas, but they're not surprised. "Democrats give more opportunities to low-income and minority people," said Maria Alvarez, another woman selling clothes who also works as a teacher in a local Head Start program.

When I asked them if they vote, Sofia practically shoved her fist in the air. "Yes! We fought hard for the right to vote!" She votes for Democrats, but she's not happy with the party. "The politicians only come around during election time. They should always be there for the people. We put them there. They should be working for the people."

"What message would you send politicians?"

"Please don't be an opportunist. Please fight for our rights. A lot of people here are being hurt by the economy. Over here in the small town, they think we don't have anything to say, but we do."

Sofia was fired up. "I always keep in touch with everything that's going on. I graduated from high school, and we never had the means to go to college. But I ask questions because I need to know what's going on. Some of us get in trouble for asking questions, but it's important to know the facts."

Before I left, Sofia gave me a bottle of water, a candy apple, a big hug, and a scrap of paper with her name and address on it. "Would you do me a favor? Send me magazines, newspapers, anything. We need more information." Those of us who regularly visit political blogs are guilty of assuming that we all have access to the same information, but working three jobs leaves little time to stay informed about the latest scandal in Washington, DC. These women weren't reading *The Nation* or *Mother Jones*—in fact, they'd never even heard of these publications. They could barely afford a magazine subscription, let alone a computer, and there was no library in town.

Before we drove off, Sofia ran over and told us we should meet city manager Diana Palacios to talk about the high school walkout. She scribbled her number on the scrap of paper. I called Diana, and she agreed to meet me at her office, just a short drive away.

She told me that Crystal City's staunchly Democratic tradition dates back to 1969, when more than 1,700 high school students staged a walkout to protest a high school rule that allowed only one Hispanic on the cheerleading squad.

"Cheerleading may not sound significant now, but thanks to that walkout, everything changed," she said. The issues at stake now were much larger: bilingual education, Hispanic teachers, college preparation, and representation in the curriculum. Following the walkout, activists formed La Raza Unida Party (the Unified Race Party) to advocate for the Mexican-American community.

"Today, every member of the school board is Hispanic. Back then, they were all white," she said. "We couldn't even speak Spanish and had no one to look up to."

It was a proud moment in Crystal City's history when this small town became a catalyst for similar protests around the country. The walkout did not, however, change the town's fortunes, and it has since languished, as a neglected outpost of progressive America.

Palacios considers herself a lifelong Democrat because "our efforts for equality have always been more supported by the Democrats than the Republicans. That's why they get our votes."

Self-Described Poor Republicans

As we continued driving on the town's main road looking for a meal and a place to stay, we saw a large, faded red and blue "Viva La Bush!" sign in someone's backyard. Ryan and I looked at each other and without saying anything, he took a right and stopped in front of the house. "You have to interview them!"

"What, knock on their door and say, 'Hi, what's with the sign?'" The truth is, I was tired and hungry, but this was too good to pass up.

I knocked on the front door and gave my spiel. "Hi, sorry to bother you. I'm a journalist from California and I'm traveling around the country talking to people about current events and politics. I saw the sign in your backyard and I'm wondering if I can ask you a few questions."

Without even asking me for a business card or proof that I'm actually a journalist, Diana Guerrero invited me in, offered me orange juice and Mexican pastries from a local bakery, and introduced me to her husband, Jesus. "He's the one who likes to talk politics." He was sporting a "Support Our Troops" T-shirt.

Jesus proudly told me he was the town's first Hispanic to run as a Republican for the city council, and he is now Crystal City's municipal judge. He advertises his politics in his backyard because his neighbor and former governor George W. Bush removed Saddam

Hussein from power. When I raised questions about the reasons for invading Iraq, he brought the conversation back to 9/11. "We're just lucky it never happened in our neck of the woods because we're not populated."

I asked him if he believes there was a connection between 9/11 and Iraq.

"From what I hear, no, but al Qaeda was still active. They needed to get Osama bin Laden."

"But we were told bin Laden was in Afghanistan, not Iraq."

"Yeah, but he has a lot of money and certain connections."

"I don't know too much about the details of the war, but I do support any military person that signs up and wants to keep us free," added Diana. Her cousin served in Iraq for a year.

Diana, a self-described "poor Republican," voted for President Clinton twice, but said he was "too busy with Monica Lewinsky to pay attention to bin Laden." Like many voters, Diana isn't devoted to a specific party. "Since the age of 18, I have always split my ticket. I look at my ballot and if I see a woman, whether they're Republican or Democrat, I'm going to give them my vote because I feel women can handle more than men."

Jesus then left the room, and I asked Diana about women's issues. She's anti-abortion but believes contraception should be widely available because there are far too many unwanted children and teen pregnancies in the community. "I think we should educate our families about the responsibilities of being a parent. I don't think we've touched on that."

"Do you believe in sex education?"

"Yes. There are so many diseases out there that our children can contract by having sex, and I think if we want to save our children, we need to educate them and tell them."

I told her that I visited a Planned Parenthood in Houston and met a number of Hispanic women who said if it weren't for the clinic, they'd have 10 or more children by now, yet the state's Republican lawmakers are on a mission to slash funding. Diana said she supports Planned Parenthood and the services it provides. "To become a par-

ent, you should want a child. I work in public housing, and I see 15-
and 16-year-olds having babies, and grandma is taking care of them. A
lot of support is at local churches, but you have to ask for help."

Diana's daughter then walked in to get ready for her high school
dance. Jesus returned and invited me to stay for dinner, but we needed
to find a place to stay for the night. "Come back and visit anytime,"
he said.

I walked out and found Ryan sleeping. We were both exhausted,
and I was famished. That night, we couldn't find a campground, so we
looked for a motel. We had two options: an old one that reminded us
of the Bates Motel in *Psycho* or a place that charged $75 a night. The L
in the Bates Motel sign was faded and blinking and the only car in the
parking lot looked abandoned, so we took the $75 room and made
beans and rice for dinner.

Camping in Kerrville

A woman I met at a gas station in Crystal City suggested we visit
Kerrville, a predominantly Republican community just two hours
north. Kerrville is part of the Texas Hill Country and is said to be
one of the nicest places in the country to retire. It's also home to an
annual 18-day folk festival.

The drive through the Hill Country's gently rolling terrain was
stunningly beautiful. Large open fields, billowing trees, and pictur-
esque lakes were a nice change from Wal-Marts, fast-food joints, and
strip malls. After passing sprawling ranches protected by high fences
and wrought-iron gates, it was clear we were entering a prosperous
area. I could've sworn we passed a zebra kissing a horse. Ryan said
I was daydreaming, but I later spoke to people who said the locals
began importing a wide range of exotic animals over 60 years ago and
more than a few wealthy ranchers have their own herds of zebras.

The weather was nice, so we decided to camp at the Internet-
friendly KOA campground for $19 per night. *Koa.com* proudly boasts
that the Kerrville campground is "just three short miles from the Su-
per Wal-Mart." Once we finished setting up camp, we found ourselves

surrounded by huge RVs decorated with American flags, red, white, and blue lights, and "Support Our Troops" ribbons. It was May, but it felt like the Fourth of July.

During check-in, I met John, an unassuming, soft-spoken guy who runs the place. After I casually mentioned my project, he proudly told me he's a liberal Democrat but is a registered Republican because there are never any Democrats on the ballot in local elections. "I wouldn't be able to vote as a registered Democrat," he said.

John rarely talks politics and would never wear a shirt or put a bumper sticker on his car revealing his views because it "wouldn't be to my advantage." John said the area was predominantly Republican because the residents were retired, and many were full-time RVers, meaning they'd condensed their entire lives into one vehicle. I decided to knock on a few doors. How could you not be outgoing and open if you choose to wake up to a new neighbor every few days and spend your life on the road?

The first RV I approached belonged to Jane, 73, and Bill, 75. Jane answered the door with a huge smile on her face and three flying butterflies on her bright pink T-shirt. A large green heart pendant dangled from her neck. Without blinking, she invited me into her wallpapered and nicely decorated RV, complete with a chirping bird clock, a floral couch, Internet access, two televisions, and two bedrooms. Jane and Bill got married in 1950 and have been happily living in their house on wheels since 1992. They live in Kerrville for seven months of the year and northern Arizona for five, but Jane said they're home wherever they are. They have church groups in both places and vote in the KOA campground's recreation room. The issues they follow closely are Medicare and prescription drug plans.

Do they think the Bush administration did a good job on those issues?

"Oh, I don't know," said Jane. "I'm not seeing much progress. It seems to me there is never any unity in our government. I would not want to be president. I think his hands are tied."

"Are you a fan of the president?"

"Yes, I like him."

"What do you like about him?"

"He's just a friendly, outgoing person, and I like the fact that he does admit that he has faith in God. We have turned from what our country was founded on, and we have gone to the other extreme as a country."

"Which is?"

"To just whatever anybody wants to do. There are no guidelines; there are no rules. We have a friend in Arizona who was appointed a federal judge several years ago, and he was criticized for being an active Christian, and I think that's wrong. I think we should be allowed and not be criticized for our faith."

"Do you think politics should be brought into the church?" I asked.

"No, and religion should not be brought into politics," Jane said with certainty.

"Are you a Christian, Rose?" asked Bill.

I knew I would get that question, but I didn't expect it so soon. "Well, I was raised Catholic, but we didn't go to church . . . "

"Have you allowed the Lord Jesus Christ into your heart?"

Smile. Slowly nod.

"Praise the Lord," said Bill.

Three seconds of silence felt like an hour.

"So . . . Have you ever voted Democratic or do you always vote Republican?"

"We voted Democrat when we were young. As a matter of fact, our parents would probably have just been horrified if they ever knew we changed and voted Republican," said Jane. "The part of Texas we were in, mostly everybody was Democrat."

"Why did you change and when did you change?"

"Forty years ago at least," said Jane.

"We had what we called 'Yellow Dog' Democrats," added Bill. "If a yellow dog was running, they would vote for him."

"We tried to vote for the person and what they stood for and that's really when we switched more to the Republicans," said Jane.

"What was it about the Republican Party that made you switch?"

"Conservatism," said Bill.

"What does that mean? And what does 'liberal' mean to you? Those terms are always being thrown around."

"Liberals believe that everybody oughta be equal," said Bill. "There's nothing wrong with that. They're more, I think, communist. In other words, they think the government oughta divide everything up. They believe in a strong central government, whereas the conservative is less government and I think that's what we need. We need to be able to take care of ourselves," he said.

"What do you think about the amount of money being spent overseas versus the money spent here at home? The Bush administration has spent billions in Iraq."

Jane jumped in, saying the government needed to be more conservative with its money. "When we see the conventions, we see the money they're spending that they could be putting to better use and especially the money they spend on these campaigns and yet they say we need more money for this and that and they aren't willing to cut their lifestyle. The government is too well paid. They could take that money and spread it around and help more people."

"You sound like a liberal!"

"The Republicans can spread it around too, now," she said laughing. "There are a lot of well-to-do people here, but there are a lot of children on the school lunch program because wages aren't that great."

Before I left, I asked Jane if she would be open to voting for a Democrat in the future.

"We would consider the issues and the party. We're not tied to the [Republican] Party," she said.

As I was about to get up, Bill and Jane softly grabbed my hands and asked me if they could say a prayer for the rest of my journey. "God, thank you for bringing Rose into our home. Please watch over and protect her as she continues her journey. Amen."

I was eager to knock on more doors, but we wanted to check out the town and grab a bite to eat before it got dark. We unknowingly drove toward the 24-hour Wal-Mart Supercenter and passed an endless array of churches along the way. I counted 14 churches within a three-mile radius. There was First Baptist, Zion Lutheran, St. Paul's United Methodist, Impact Christian Fellowship, and Kingdom Hall of Jehovah's Witnesses. Ryan spotted a BBQ joint and practically screeched to a halt. He rarely eats meat around me, but that rule didn't seem to apply on this trip. I was curious about the churches, so while he ordered, I borrowed the phone book and found 72 houses of worship listed in Kerrville alone.

Mary, the owner of the 23-year-old restaurant, asked me what I was looking for.

"I'm just visiting and was surprised to see so many churches. I'm curious to see how many there are."

"A lot. And they're all packed on Sundays," she said.

Ryan grabbed his plate of ribs and beans and we found a seat in the back room. A loaf of Wonder Bread was on every table and Fox News was blaring in the background. The walls were covered with deer heads, photos of people showing off the kill of the day, guns, and old newspaper articles. I wrongly assumed the owners were Republican. Mary was a lifelong Democrat, but like our friend at KOA, she never talked politics with her Republican customers.

Later that afternoon we found the only vegetarian restaurant in Kerrville just a short drive away. The Italian and German couple who ran the place said the locals had yet to embrace the healthy lifestyle and believed their family was a "bit wacky." Over the course of an hour or so, a few people walked by, looked at the menu, and moved on.

After returning to KOA, I decided to knock on a few more RV doors. The man with the "W '04" sticker on his truck sternly said he wasn't interested in talking. I think I interrupted his dinner. The man with the "God Bless Our Troops" ribbon on his truck was more than happy to talk. I got a thrill out of approaching people in Kerrville because, unlike the Bay Area, I never knew what I was going to find. John Waters, a 74-year-old full-time RVer, used to vote Republican. "I've become more interested and more aware and sought more information and considered things more carefully than I did before. I used to vote based on family traditions."

John gets most of his news from the *NewsHour with Jim Lehrer* and

Lou Dobbs on CNN. Like so many political junkies, he said he's fed up with the two-party system and special interests. "I shall not vote again until such a time when the elections are totally government funded."

"When did you make that pledge?"

"Just recently. The parties have polarized people and I think that polarization comes about more from the Republicans than the Democrats, but neither one of them really are as good as they should be."

John said he'd love to talk politics with his neighbors, but most of them are set in their ways. "From what I've seen, that'd be like trying to swim up a waterfall."

Blessed Are the Peacemakers

From Kerrville, we drove to Austin, one of the most liberal cities in Texas, and spent the week trying to get used to the heat. Ryan's friend Chris was kind enough to offer his couch, which saved us around $300. The central part of the city is full of bars, restaurants, tattoo parlors, and an endless array of live music. The outlying areas are more conservative. Austin is in Travis County, where John Kerry won 56 percent of the vote in 2004, but despite its liberal leanings, I'm told Republicans still have a great deal of influence.

Because megachurches and evangelicals have become so influential in American politics, I wanted to visit churches as often as possible to see for myself whether pastors spoke about politics from the pulpit.

I was baptized and took communion, but my family never went to church on a regular basis. On the Christmas Eve after 9/11, my mom asked me to go to midnight mass to hear what she hoped would be a positive, uplifting message. A few days earlier, we had heard that one of the church's priests had had a few too many drinks at a bar and picked up one of my aunt's friends. He began the Christmas Eve service by telling us we were all sinners. I haven't been back since.

After doing a quick online search, I found the Shoreline Christian Center, a 47-acre facility with 5,000 seats. We arrived just a few minutes after the 11:00 Sunday service had begun and found the parking lot almost filled to capacity with cars sporting "Shoreline" stickers.

The building itself could pass for a large auditorium or high school in an upscale neighborhood. We rushed past a Starbucks in the foyer and entered what looked like a concert hall. A blaring 13-piece band and 32-person chorus was on stage, and a big screen was on either side. A man wearing a permanent smile greeted us at the door and took us to our stadium-like seats. It sure didn't feel like church. It felt like a bad rock concert. The fiery crowd was dancing with their hands high in the air and Bibles on their chairs. The women to my right jumped up and down screaming, "Jesus wants us to get to the summit!"

I stood up and tried to fit in. Ryan, who enjoys deconstructing the Bible (he majored in religion in college), sat with his arms crossed. Because we arrived late, we were already receiving a few stares. After 20 minutes of singing and dancing, Pastor Rob Koke stormed the stage in jeans and a casual button-down shirt, received a rock-star welcome, and began preaching about the importance of valuing peace. "I want you to be a peacemaker! The world needs peacemakers," he said with conviction. The people around us nodded approvingly. Koke spoke about conflict at the global and local level but never specifically mentioned Iraq or the Middle East. Black-and-white photos of Mother Teresa and Martin Luther King, Jr. flashed on the big screens. Another band then took to the stage, the light show began, and as if on cue, the crowd jumped out of their seats.

When the music faded, first-time guests were welcomed, and we were asked to greet our neighbors. I shook many hands and looked around to see couples and families of all ages and colors. I saw more diversity in that church than I see in many San Francisco neighborhoods. There was also an announcement about the addition of a third service on Sundays. If it's as well attended as this service, that amounts to 15,000 people every Sunday!

During the second half of the service, I felt like I was at a self-help retreat for people seeking tips to improve their relationships and communication skills. Koke told stories about life at home with his wife and three kids and encouraged the attentive crowd to "say no" more often, discipline your children, reach your goals, and carve out more time to spend with your spouses. I could feel the thousands of people around me hanging on his every word. Many feverishly took notes.

As the service came to a close, we filed out and made our way to the new worshiper reception in the foyer. The Christian gift store was packed with people buying books and CDs, ceramic crosses, cross jewelry, and Koke's past sermons. The information booth was full of flyers announcing a variety of activities for couples, singles, men, women, and youth.

We spotted Koke at the reception and introduced ourselves. He agreed to do a quick interview. He told me that between 7,000 and 10,000 people from all religious backgrounds call this interdenominational church their home. Not bad considering he and his wife started it in their home in 1987. I asked him to explain the philosophy behind his church's teachings. "I choose messages that will hopefully impact people's lives on Monday morning," he said. "It's not just about theology or pie-in-the-sky type of information; it's practical because the Bible is a very practical book and helps people to live the Christian life productively and positively on Monday morning."

"The word peace came up many, many times, which is rare these days. Has your church taken a stand on the war?"

"We try to be as sensitive as we can on that issue. We're not a political organization; we're a spiritual-focused organization," he said. "We have people from every walk of life that attend our church. If you look around, it's an incredibly diverse multicultural congregation, which is very unique. Whites are worshiping with African Americans and Hispanics. There are Republicans and Democrats and all different types of folks that worship together in this environment, so we don't strive to make a strong political statement; we strive to make a strong spiritual statement."

Koke, a Republican, agreed to answer my questions about Iraq, as a citizen, not a pastor. "When you talk about war, there is a just defense. What I mean by that is if someone came into my home and wanted to rob my home, I'm going to put up a defense for my wife and children, and that is biblically supported. You'd have to understand the motivation behind Iraq and Afghanistan. If you believe that the motivation was a lie and that there were no weapons of mass destruction and that it was all manipulated because of oil, then I think the net result of that would be you would feel that it was wrong. But if you really sincerely believe that this is a defense of our nation and our values as a nation, that we'll be safer as a nation after this process is over and we extend to the nations of the world a commitment to peace through strength and security, that's where that element comes in from our perspective. We think it's justified."

"So you didn't support the war because of the weapons of mass destruction?"

"I think that's correct. The reality of it, personally for me, is, do I believe that our world will be safer with Saddam gone? I say yes, wholeheartedly, and I think our congregation would agree with that."

"Questions are often raised about the pro-life statement you made. Why doesn't war fall under the pro-life platform?"

"I'm pro-life, but if somebody wants to kill me, that's where it stops."

I could tell that Ryan wanted to jump in. Instead he shook his head in disgust and stormed off. I pretended not to notice. "So, basically, you're in favor of the war because Saddam was a dictator?"

"Well, yeah."

"Should we get rid of every dictator in the world?"

"When the dictator affects our national security."

"Terrorism has increased since the invasion. Do you feel safer?"

"Yeah, absolutely."

At this point, a line was forming behind Koke. Before I let him go, I asked him if he'd heard of the Downing Street Memo.

"The what?"

"The Downing Street Memo, the document that said the intelligence and facts were fixed around the policy."

He said no and began shaking hands with the adoring crowd.

That night, we spent a few hours at Kinko's making copies of the Downing Street Memo; a synopsis of the Duelfer Report, which concluded that Saddam Hussein did not possess or have plans to develop nuclear, biological, or chemical weapons; reports about the number of

Iraqis who've been killed since the 2003 invasion; various mainstream articles about veterans who weren't getting the care or support they needed upon their return; and the voting records of politicians who claim to "support the troops." We did this because we were meeting people who believed that the weapons had been found, that there was a connection between 9/11 and Iraq, that the planes that hit the towers on 9/11 were flown by Iraqis, that the U.S. government is taking care of the troops upon their return, and the list goes on. Most people refused to believe us when we'd say, "Actually, the weapons haven't been found," or "Iraqis had nothing to do with 9/11," so we decided to try giving them articles and reports instead. We stuffed them into an orange plastic folder we called our fact folder. At that point, I still believed the facts actually mattered.

Progressive Religion

To get a slightly different perspective from Shoreline, we went to St. Andrew's Presbyterian in Austin, a much smaller and more traditional church. Crosses are on the walls, the setting is intimate, Minister Jim Rigby is wearing a black robe, and he speaks the word of God.

We immediately knew we were in for a different experience after seeing the word "progressive" on the church's program. Minister Rigby began his service by focusing on the importance of humor and laughter to get through bad times. "After the bombing in Iraq began, I went home and watched the *Daily Show* and somehow it saved my life," he says. We couldn't believe we were hearing references to the *Daily Show* in church! I assumed St. Andrew's was full of liberals, but I was wrong.

Bruce Palmer, a 52-year-old writer, says he attends St. Andrew's because the people are friendly, open-minded, and inclusive. "I do not agree with many of the beliefs here, but that's OK. We agree to disagree," he says. Bruce says he's a conservative because he comes from a Republican family, but he no longer votes because the system is corrupt.

I found a few more people with similar sentiments. They love the church and Minister Rigby's overall message, which is decidedly antiwar and proudly liberal, yet they vote Republican. Bob Bartlett, a 50-something, has been attending this church for 10 years. "It's such a friendly church," he says. "We don't care what nationality, race, or creed you are. We don't care how you dress or undress. We have open hearts, open minds, and want everybody to feel welcome."

"I noticed that this is a progressive church. What does that mean exactly?" I ask.

"It means we're open to everybody's thoughts and we're open to everyone no matter what your nationality is or what your religion is or what your sex is. We like all of it."

CNN or MSNBC should send a reporter here to challenge stereotypes by doing a segment about religious Republicans who attend progressive churches in conservative-leaning states. This one wasn't hard to find. There must be others.

We sat down with Minister Jim Rigby, a self-described advocate for social justice, reproductive rights, and gay rights, and I asked him to describe the area.

"We're right above Austin's city limits. In a typical election, there will be three signs in row: the first says, I'm a Republican; the second says, I'm more Republican; and the third says, you're wusses, I'm even more Republican," he says laughing. "There's not even a vestige of Democrats up here."

He says the backlash is extremely difficult and takes its toll. "People get really tired of being shouted at and being called things. People just hunker down after a while."

He says several Shoreline members have attended his services because "they would say things about the liberal church over there and out of curiosity, people would come over."

"And they keep coming back?"

"Yes, but we've had bomb threats. It depends on what's happening. If there are abortion laws at stake, and I get in the newspaper, then there will be bad phone calls and letters."

"The pastor at the Shoreline Christian Center says he keeps politics out of his service, but he encourages people to get involved in politics."

"I think, what it is—not speaking about a particular church—it's all politics," he says. "When you think you're the chosen people, when you think that you have this mandate to control everything, what's more political than that?"

"After hearing your sermon, I assumed everyone here is a Democrat."

"We have some conservatives. They have a conservatives anonymous group," he says laughing. "Usually though, people leave. They feel like they're being attacked. We lose a lot of rich white males thinking they're being attacked by being put on the same plane as everybody else."

From Rigby's perspective, it's all about principles. "If you believe a woman is a person, then she has the same rights over her body that a male has over his firearms, so you kind of look at it with that Second Amendment zeal. I'm not sure if that's been established in the Constitution, that a woman is a person. When we struggle with fetal issues, does it have will, does it have integrity? Well, does a woman? I was sitting in when they [Texas politicians] were doing a lot of the debates, and there wasn't a woman on the panels talking about a woman's most personal issues and there wasn't a woman there. How do you call that a democracy? If women aren't even in control of their own persons, it's not a democracy. If workers are wage slaves, then it's democracy in name only. The corporations choose the two puppets we vote for. The Democrats, on some of the most important issues, have sold us out a little less badly than the Republicans. They're not different enough."

"What message would you send to progressives who write off states like Texas and make sweeping statements about the people who live here?"

"There are some really good people down here. We have universities and some libraries," he says smiling. "It's one country, and what people have done is divide and conquer us. What the powerful elite has been really good at doing is getting us to turn on one another."

"How do you deal with everyday frustrations and political challenges?"

"The work just seems so important to me. It seems like the harder it is, or the fewer people that are doing it, the more important it is. The people who are attracted to prophetic issues need to realize that you're going to lose most of the time. When you start winning, the struggle is over. If you're really trying to build a habitual future, you're going to lose more than you're going to win, but that's so much more important. I'd much rather be in the company of the Martin Luther Kings and the Gandhis and lose, than be with the politicians and win. If people don't have hope, if nobody is saying the truth, then the future doesn't look very bright. Politically we have to compromise on what's doable, but I don't think you should ever compromise your principles and values."

Sex Sells in Dallas

From Austin we drove to Dallas, a sprawling metropolis with the slogan, "Live Large. Think Big." Dallas is the second-largest city in the state of Texas (population 1.2 million) and the ninth largest in the United States. Although the nearby suburb of Plano is ranked as the fifth most conservative city in the country, Dallas, like most major cities, is full of surprises and many firsts. In November 2004, Dallas County voters elected Lupe Valdez, the first Democrat to win a countywide race in 25 years and the first lesbian Hispanic sheriff of Dallas County.

The other unexpected surprise we found were the images of scantily clad women on billboards lining the highway. On one side were ads for strip clubs and smut shops; on the other were ads for churches. We couldn't get over the contrast. I later learned that at least 8,000,000 people a year patronize the state's 150 strip clubs for a lap or pole dance. I wondered if the men driving solo were struggling to decide which exit to take: the one for the Northway Church at 7202 W. Northwest Highway or the one for the Men's Club at 2340 Northwest Highway. In February 2004, NetAccountability, a software company whose mission is to confront the "secret sin" of pornography, put up billboards offering men a blunt suggestion: "Her gift for Valentine's? Stop looking at porn." Tough advice to follow when you're surrounded by it. Even harder when you're addicted. According to a nonscientific poll on XXXChurch.com, 70 percent of Christians struggle with porn.

After a few minutes of driving, I spotted a sign with uppercase, bright red letters screaming "CONDOMS TO GO." I thought it was a joke.

I grabbed the sleeve on Ryan's T-shirt and screamed, "Take this exit!"

"What's wrong?"

"I think I just saw a condom shop!"

He quickly changed lanes and took the exit. We pulled into the parking lot next to a CONDOMS TO GO van, whose back door featured a cartoon penis wearing a blue baseball hat. I got out and stared at the red condom sign. I had seen more smut in the past ten minutes in Dallas than I had in the past year in San Francisco, yet San Franciscans are the ones ruining the so-called traditional family structure and tearing apart America's moral fabric.

I walked into the condom store and told the woman behind the counter that I was surprised to see so much soft porn on display in Dallas. "And I've never heard of a condoms-to-go store! Have any of the state's pro-family Republican politicians ever placed an order?"

"There are four shops in Dallas and just under 10 in Texas," she said with a hearty laugh. "The store in Plano, the one with all the 'W '04' stickers in the parking lot, has the highest sales." Just as I was about to pull my recorder out of my backpack, a woman, probably the manager, appeared. "Can I help you?"

"I'm just passing through and had a few questions about your store."

"You'll have to call my boss."

"Oh, that's OK." On my way out, I passed shelves of plastic sex toys. China supplies 70 percent of the world's supply of adult toys, according to the *Guardian*. The women who make them work eight hours a day for $25–$33 per month.

We left the shop and continued driving. I scanned the radio and found a wide array of religious shows, including Radio Xavier, a Catholic program. After the "Pro-Life Update," which includes news about abortion, stem cell legislation, and judicial appointments, the male and female hosts began a segment on natural family planning with guests Marc and Christina Sanders of St. Ann Parish in Coppell, Texas. Christina described natural family planning as "a way for the couple to monitor their fertility naturally without using any barriers or chemicals, so they can either achieve or avoid a pregnancy."

The female host asked, "So what are the benefits of this?"

"One of the major benefits to practicing natural family planning is that the divorce rate for married couples is almost nonexistent," said Marc. "When we use artificial contraception, then we fall into this trap of denying the life-giving aspect of love and simply seeking after the pleasure aspect."

The male host said his experience with natural family planning was an "awesome, awesome thing." His friends who converted to Catholicism "were contracepting, then they changed, and they've got five kids now!"

Back at our motel, I ran to call Radio Xavier. I reached Dave Palmer, the host who described his awesome natural family planning experience, and told him about my project. I asked him if he was free in the morning. We were planning to attend an 11:00 service at the Cathedral of Hope, the largest gay and lesbian Christian church in the world. I had no idea the largest gay and lesbian church in the world was in Dallas, Texas. I found it online. Dave suggested we meet at 9:00 at a Starbucks near the church.

Anti-abortion Radio

At a quarter to nine the next morning, I sat in Starbucks waiting for Dave to arrive. Ryan drove, but he decided to rest in the van because he can't sit still during these kinds of interviews. Plus, he stayed up late watching *Miami Ink*, a TV show about tattoo artists and the meaning people attach to their works of art. When you're living in hotel rooms

with more than 50 channels you've never seen, shows like *Miami Ink*
can be addictive.

I sat there nervously shuffling through articles and reports about
teen pregnancy, abortion, and poverty. I was tense. I've never had a
conversation with a man—or a woman for that matter—who not
only opposes abortion, even in cases of rape and incest, but also opposes all forms of birth control. Even though the air-conditioning was
on full blast, I was sweating.

Then Dave walked in. I recognized him from the photo on his
website. He held the door open for three people—two women and
a man. I took a deep breath, stood, and motioned for them to come
over. They walked as if in procession to my table. All but one wore
black polo shirts emblazoned with the Radio Xavier logo. The woman
without the polo shirt wore a long black skirt and a fitted white top.

I shook Dave's hand. Before I could introduce myself, he said, "I
searched for your name online last night and found your articles."

I was wondering when that was going to happen. A Google search
for my name brings up articles I've written about women's issues, Iraq,
poverty, and a host of other social issues. I also posted excerpts from a
few of the interviews I had conducted so far on my blog. I wondered
if that was why he brought three people with him.

I was pleasantly surprised he didn't cancel. I looked him in the eye
and said, "I appreciate you showing up. Thank you for coming."

"It seems like you're trying to get out there and report things and
not force your views on others."

"That's the goal."

Dave introduced me to the others, but only one woman, Suzette
Chaires, co-host of Radio Xavier and director of a youth ministry at
a nearby church, said hello. The other two were silent.

With that, they ordered something to drink, and we sat down. I
began by telling Dave about a meeting I had a few days ago with a
few representatives of Texas Right to Life, an anti-abortion state organization. I told him the conversation never went anywhere because
they refused to talk about prevention or about strategies to decrease
the increasingly high number of unwanted pregnancies, other than

making abortion illegal, of course. I asked Dave how he feels about prevention.

"What kind of prevention?"

"Preventing women who don't want to have children from getting pregnant."

"When you talk about prevention, I prevent illnesses, I prevent car accidents. I prevent something bad. You don't prevent something good. A baby that's born is always good. It doesn't matter if it was out of rape, if it was out of incest, if it was out of extramarital sex. It's always good. You don't prevent something that's holy and sacred. You gotta change the language and say why are we preventing something that's holy. Ideally you accept life into the world. I have a daughter and I tell her, anytime you have a baby, that's a wonderful event and we will celebrate that birth."

He didn't answer my question. I tried again. "Would you acknowledge that women have unwanted pregnancies?"

"No pregnancy is unwanted in my opinion. It may be that the mother doesn't want it, but when you talk about life and the baby as being an evil thing—"

"In terms of rape and incest, clearly the woman did not want to get pregnant."

"But that's not the baby's fault."

We were beginning to sound combative. I took a deep breath. "I'm sure you're familiar with Planned Parenthood. They offer free prenatal care and yearly exams to low-income women. Republicans are trying to cut their funding. I went to the clinic in Houston and interviewed women in the waiting room. I asked them, 'Why do you come here?' Most of them had at least three kids with them. They said, 'I don't want to get pregnant again. I'm here for prenatal care and birth control. I already have two jobs and I can't afford another child.' How can you argue with that? Why would you want to take away their birth control?"

"Is abstinence not an option? Catholic priests are asked to live their entire lives without having sex. That is an option," said Dave.

"I probably wouldn't use Catholic priests as a shining example for chastity," I said. "I'm trying to deal with reality here. Why would you want these women to have children they can't afford?"

Dave went on to tell me about his personal experience with natural family planning. If it works for him, it should work for everyone. "There are times when we say, 'Honey, if we're not able to bring in life, we're going to have to abstain for a week or so.' You're not giving these women enough credit. Just ask them to have a little bit of self-control and to communicate with their husbands so they can plan their fertility using God's cycle rather than contraception or abortion."

"That works for you and that's great, but what about the women who don't want to follow their cycle? Is it fair to tell them that this works for me so it should work for you?"

"It's in line with the truth."

When I asked them about the smut billboards and the CONDOMS TO GO store, they refused to acknowledge that they send mixed messages to children and teens. In November 2004, the Texas State Board of Education chose new health textbooks that say abstinence is the only effective way to prevent pregnancy or sexually transmitted diseases. From 2005 to 2006, Texas slashed its family planning budget by 32 percent, yet it has the fifth highest teen pregnancy rate and the highest teen birth rate in the country—63 births per 1,000 girls ages 15 to 19 in 2004, the most recent year for which statistics are available. Despite the sobering reality, Dave and company believe all forms of birth control should be banned. In fact, I had a hard time getting them to admit there's even a problem.

They usually vote Republican because they are one-issue voters, but unlike most "pro-life" Republicans, they're actually consistent. They're against the death penalty and, because Pope John Paul II opposed the invasion of Iraq, Dave said it "wasn't a great idea."

I tried, once more, to make it personal. "I have a close friend who has three kids. Her husband has a good job, and she's lucky enough to stay home with her kids. She takes the pill because she doesn't want any more children. What is the logic behind taking that away from her?"

"I want to take something away from them that is dangerous to her well-being. Why do I take a gun away from a teenager? Why are drugs illegal?"

"We're talking about unwanted pregnancies here, not drugs."

Dave changed the subject and said abortion should be illegal. That would solve everything.

"Abortion is illegal in a number of countries, and women still have them," I said. "If a woman wants an abortion, she's going to do whatever it takes to get one. Do you want women and girls to have back-alley abortions and die in the process? Let's say you get your wish and abortion is illegal. What's the penalty for women who have them? Jail time?"

Silence. Suzette changed the subject. "The lady that you mentioned that has three kids, why doesn't she learn about natural family planning?"

"She tried it and got pregnant," I said.

"I'm not saying that women won't go to a back alley and die and that's tragic," said Dave. "Make it illegal and I guarantee you that you'll see a 90 percent drop. Let's pray to make that happen. You were a fetus once. Praise God that you are alive."

"And I was a wanted child," I said. "What about the women who can't say no in a marriage? There is such a thing as rape in marriage."

"You have to educate the husband, too, because sometimes it's a macho thing," said Dave.

"Do you ever think about all of the poor women who would be forced to have unwanted children in the world you want to create?" I asked. "Do you acknowledge that this is connected? Wealthy women will still be able to pay for safe, underground abortions, but poor women won't. Do you work on poverty issues?"

"My parents do," said Suzette nervously. "I'm probably going to shock everyone here, but my parents are Democrats." Dave grabbed his drink and took a sip.

Suzette paused. "Poverty is one of the reasons why my dad votes for Democrats. Just in Dallas alone, about 60 percent of the Hispanic kids drop out of high school. That's pretty significant. Who is helping these young people? Well, Republicans and poverty don't always go hand in hand. You were talking about different Catholics. Well, I think there's a place for everyone in the Catholic Church. My dad's calling is to help the people who do not have a voice. Ultimately, you can say it's the unborn child who does not have a voice and we try and speak for all of those people. We all have a different calling. Some people have the pro-life calling. I see both sides. I am definitely pro-life, but being Hispanic, I see how minorities get stuck in this poverty cycle and who is trying to help them? That's why I appreciate what you're asking about Republicans. More needs to be done about poverty so these women will have a greater chance and not experience such fear and have to go to Planned Parenthood. I totally get where you're coming from and I think there's a place for everyone in the church. My father is a saintly man, and he's trying to help people who need to eat. That is a significant issue and these do go hand in hand."

Suzette rendered me speechless. She admitted that abortion isn't as black and white as Dave would like it to be. Curiously, the other two Radio Xavier Catholics rarely chimed in. In fact, the other woman in the group never said a word.

Service at the Cathedral of Hope was set to begin soon, so we had to leave. When we walked outside, Ryan put his book down and got out of the van. He was polite, but didn't say much, which was probably a good thing. Suzette asked him to take a few group photos. Dave and Suzette put their arms around me and I smiled nervously. Suzette grabbed the camera and asked Ryan to take her place and smile. I gave them a few reports about family planning overseas; then they hugged me good-bye.

I wanted to like them, but the policies they advocate from the comfort of their radio studio and church are literally killing women around the world. The United States has funded international family planning programs since the 1960s, but in 1984 the Reagan administration passed the Global Gag Rule, which denies U.S. Agency for International Development (USAID) funding to overseas organizations that provide legal abortions with exceptions for rape and incest or to save a woman's life, provide counseling and referrals for abortion, engage in abortion-related public policy debates, or lobby to make abortion legal or more available in their own country.

The Clinton administration ended the Global Gag Rule in 1993 by executive order; President Bush reinstated it on his first day in office in January 2001, halting an estimated $15 million per year in funding to the International Planned Parenthood Federation (IPPF) after it refused to sign the rule.

As a result, community-based health services have been curtailed, and contraceptive supplies have drastically decreased. The United States stopped giving Zambia donated condoms after it refused to sign the Gag Rule, and several family planning clinics across Africa and Asia have been forced to close.

Every year 19 million women face serious injury, illness, or death as a consequence of abortions performed by unskilled people under unsanitary conditions, according to an IPPF report, *Death and Denial: Unsafe Abortion and Poverty*. Nearly 70,000 die. Virtually all of those women live in the poorest countries in the world, and almost every one of those deaths and injuries could easily be prevented.

Everyone's Welcome at the Cathedral of Hope

I didn't expect the Cathedral of Hope service to be so grandiose and formal, complete with a procession of robed clergy. Then again, I didn't expect the largest gay and lesbian church to be in Dallas, Texas. Unlike the megachurch in Austin, this high-ceilinged, stone-walled sanctuary actually had pews, as well as a big-screen TV on either side of the pulpit, a 32-foot-high cross, and eight panels of stained glass spelling out "hope" in English and Spanish. If I brought you to this service, you wouldn't realize it was a gay church until same-sex couples rose from their pews, grabbed hands, and formed long lines to receive communion.

After the service, I met Michael Magnia, a 38-year-old who became a member in 1998 after many years in a traditional Southern Baptist Church. "They never were direct about being gay. It was an unspoken no-no. You just didn't do that," he says. "When I approached my youth minister about a 'gay friend' of mine, his response was, 'Well, you don't hang around those kinds of people because otherwise you'll get infected, too.' People here in Texas take the Bible and thump you across the head with it and say, 'You're going to hell. You're going to hell.' That's not the message of Christ."

As a result, Michael spent nearly a decade as far away from church as possible. He was pulled back after his younger conservative brother began seminary school. Then he found the Cathedral of Hope.

"I came here a long time after being agnostic, bordering on being an atheist, and I came to this place, and all of a sudden I can question what I read in the Bible. I can question my own faith and not be branded a heretic," he says.

But the first time he attended a service, he left early because the reverend repeatedly said the word "gay" from the pulpit.

"It disturbed me so much," he says looking down at the ground. "That was not a part of my life I was comfortable hearing in church. We here in the South are very good at compartmentalizing. We can be smokers and drinkers and just be tramps on the outside, but when we go to church on Sunday we're all proper and prim and holier than thou, and the preacher loves us. Here, we worship with our whole being. That was a shock to me, to hear that my sexuality was being brought out in such a frank manner in front of God. It was a learning process, and I had to convince myself to go for four Sundays. I've been here ever since."

It took three years for Michael's mother, a church-going Southern Baptist conservative, who was shocked to learn her son was gay, to accompany him to his church. "I told her to dress casual, and she wears stereotypical lesbian attire. And my mother is not a lesbian!" he says laughing. "She comes out in this plaid outfit and denim pants. And she just got her hair cut really, really short. I'm like, 'Mom, I want you to look like my mom, not one of the other members of the church. Go put on something pink or white. Not plaid!'"

After the service his mother was speechless. Shortly after we arrived, a member of the staff told me that an antigay reporter for a local religious television station recently came by to do a segment and, before she left, she told him that she couldn't deny God's presence. Michael's mother said the same thing. "She didn't know what to do," he recalls. "I counter the religious mentality through my family. At their Baptist church, they are now very vocal. 'Yes, we have a gay son and we love him and we're not going to judge him.' She's now totally opposed to the government going after gays when there are so many other problems to deal with."

As far as politics go, Michael says there's no way preachers can avoid the subject because it's become such a significant part of everyday life, but he says the reverend doesn't tell people who to vote for. "It's never, 'This is how you will think.' We've never gotten that. It's, 'What do you think? Oh, you don't know. Well, go figure it out.' You can't sit here and just be a consumer. You must be an activist."

"What's the political makeup of the congregants?" I ask.

"We have some very conservative folks here. We don't all agree about the Iraq war. The reverend knows that when he criticizes the war, his inbox on Monday is going to be filled with people who say it's the absolute right thing to do."

Even though "liberal" is a "big dirty word" in Texas, Michael prefers to be in the company of people with opposing views. Being surrounded by like-minded people was foreign to most of the Texans I met. They usually asked, "Aren't you bored being around so many like-minded people in San Francisco? There are no opportunities to reach out and find consensus."

Although 90 percent of Cathedral of Hope congregants are gay, lesbian, bisexual, and transgender, Michael says it's important to reach out to heterosexuals. "I love seeing new straight faces. I saw a straight couple here with their kids the other day, and I went up and welcomed them and told them about the youth ministry. To be honest, I'm tired of talking about being gay! I'm done with it! I can't decorate. I don't have that gene. I own more power tools than most lesbians in this church combined. We struggle with this church changing and being more inclusive."

Lynn and Scott Walters, a straight married couple, have been attending since 2003. "I'm sure people are shocked that we have thousands of members here in Dallas, but it's one of the very few churches in this area that actually speaks to the gospel's teachings and tries to live it out. God is obviously here. They don't have to manufacture that feeling," says Lynn.

Scott says he attends because the message is progressive, and he feels like he has a voice about current events, especially Iraq. "We shouldn't be sacrificing our lives for fictitious reasons. The other churches we went to basically said, 'God's on our side. We're going to win,'" he says. "Obviously I'm not gay, but I feel welcome here in a way that I don't feel welcome at other churches."

Scott and Lynn are involved in a variety of causes and consider themselves activists, but it's draining.

"What strategies do you personally take? What's most effective?" I ask.

"Letters to the editors are very effective. The *Dallas Morning News*, for all its faults, does try to print different points of view. Before the war started, we went to a protest, and there were 4,000 to 5,000 people there, and we were mentioned on the back page. We were saying, 'Let the weapons inspectors do their work,' but that message never got out. Sometimes we listen to conservative radio and call in to express our views. We get cut off mid-sentence, but we try."

On our way out, Lynn and Scott invited Ryan and me to spend the night at their place to save money on hotels. We accepted their generous offer and stayed up late playing with their kids and talking about the challenges they face in Dallas. When Michael Moore's *Fahrenheit 9/11* was released on DVD, they hosted viewing parties, but their neighbors were afraid to attend. "They were afraid the outspoken conservatives down the block would find out and hold it against them," says Lynn.

I didn't expect to find such a thick layer of fear and isolation in Texas, especially in a metropolitan city like Dallas.

Green Republicans

Jackie Wayman, a self-described feminist, opposes drilling in the Arctic National Wildlife Refuge (ANWR) and believes the United States should sign on to the Kyoto Protocol, an international treaty that requires participating countries to cut their emissions of greenhouse gases.

Don Waldman believes overconsumption is ruining the planet. Because his neighborhood doesn't have curbside recycling, he goes to the library to recycle his newspapers and drives five miles to recycle his cans. He's planning to trade in his Honda for a hybrid and he brings his own shopping bags to Whole Foods. "Sometimes, I'll buy a cookie and I'll sit there for a half hour. I never see anyone else who brings in their own shopping bag. I worry about that." He says he's not your typical Texan.

Bob DeJean, an architect who encourages developers to build sustainably, is a member of the Sierra Club, the Audubon Society, and the Nature Conservancy. He also donates to Greenpeace. He gets most of his news from PBS and NPR because he says he prefers in-depth reporting to sound bites. The environment is his top issue.

Jackie, Don, and Bob all believe George W. Bush will go down in history as the worst environmental president ever. They're all members of Republicans for Environmental Protection (REP), a national grassroots organization with chapters in 10 states, including Texas. When I found REP's website, I wondered why I'd never heard of them before. Why aren't they ever in the news?

The site says, "We possess 4 percent of the world's known oil reserves, yet we consume over 25 percent of all the oil produced around the world." They slam Republican efforts to drill for oil in ANWR while giving tax breaks of up to $100,000 to corporations that purchase the largest, heaviest, most gas-hungry vehicles on the market.

Formed in 1995 as a grassroots national organization, REP's mission is "to resurrect the GOP's great conservation tradition and to restore natural resource conservation and sound environmental protection as fundamental elements of the Republican Party's vision for America. Conservation is Conservative!"

"It probably will surprise you to hear what I'm about to say come from a Republican. But then, who better than a Republican to hear it from?" said REP president Martha Marks in a keynote speech at the Minnesota League of Conservation Voters annual dinner in St. Paul, Minnesota, on October 21, 2003. "Those men and women in Congress and the White House who advocate such a drill-and-waste policy are not conservatives. They're not interested in conserving anything. They are, in truth, squanderers. They are literally—and liberally—wasting our resources and jeopardizing our future as a nation. They ought to be ashamed of themselves."

After I found the website, I contacted Martha Marks and she connected me with members in the greater Dallas area. I met Jackie for lunch at the Dove's Nest Restaurant in Waxahachie, a quaint little town 30 miles south of Dallas, with a historic town square surrounded by antique shops, an old-fashioned drug store with a working soda fountain, the White House Barber Shop, and a beautiful red sandstone courthouse.

When we met, Jackie told me her family couldn't believe she agreed to be interviewed by a journalist from San Francisco. "I try to keep an open mind," she said. Jackie used to be a radical feminist. Today she's a conservative Republican. Her views on feminism haven't really changed since her college days, but she stopped voting Democratic when Bill Clinton was elected because she believes Republicans are stronger on defense. "I will vote for national security and hope to God the rest of the stuff doesn't fall apart in the process," she said.

Jackie got involved in environmental issues in 1978, when she was working for a crop-dusting business. "Of course, the government said the chemicals were safe. I ended up with a severe neurological reaction to any kind of chemical. Now I can't go a lot of places. I can't go to church or the theater. You never know who you're gonna sit next to. I don't trust the government," she said. "Within 20 miles or less of where you're sitting, 11 chemical plants and cement plants are spewing pollution into the Dallas–Fort Worth metroplex."

Jackie believes the Bush administration turned back the clock on 30 years of environmental progress, but she still voted for him. Both times.

"God only knows how long it will take to fix," she said. "I think in my lifetime I will never be able to vote *for* a candidate. It will be who I vote *against*."

Don Waldman voted for Bush in 2004. Bob DeJean didn't vote.

Who Supports the Troops?

By this time, we had been on the road for just over a month, but "Support Our Troops" ribbons were already getting on my nerves. In February 2005, I had written an article for *AlterNet* about the lack of government-funded programs to deal with problems facing returning troops, such as health care, post-traumatic stress syndrome, housing, and employment. At the time, Linda Boone, executive director of the National Coalition for Homeless Veterans, told me, "The message our government is basically sending our troops is, 'Once you take off that uniform you're on your own.' To say the Department of Defense isn't doing an adequate job of preparing the military for civilian life would be an understatement."

I had to find out if anything had changed, so I visited the local chapter of Paralyzed Veterans of America, which is connected to the VA Hospital in Dallas. The parking lot was filled with SUVs and trucks sporting ribbons and flag stickers. On the way in we passed a young guy with a missing leg and a bandaged head struggling to get into a van, a wheelchair-bound man whose gray hair stuck out of his Vietnam Veteran baseball cap, and a young woman, who didn't look old enough to serve, hobbling on crutches.

It was worse inside. More than 10 young men looked like they'd been in the waiting room for days. A few nodded off as they attempted to find comfortable positions in their chairs. The rest either looked at the TV screen or stared ahead as if in a painful trance.

We passed the main desk, where hospital staff members answer phones, take names, and shuffle files. On our way to the Paralyzed

Veterans area, we passed nurse after nurse pushing solemn-looking men in wheelchairs. Legislative director Jack Richardson greeted us at the entrance to his office. "Glad you found us. This place is pretty chaotic these days." A heavyset man with a graying mustache and dark, slicked-back hair, he, too, is in a wheelchair. Stacks of paper, articles, and reports about veterans' health care were on his lap and scattered on his desk. As we sat down, he wheeled over to his desk and a magazine fell off his lap. I reached down to pick it up. "This is *PN Magazine*. One of the magazines Paralyzed Veterans puts out," he said, flipping through the pages. He put on a pair of eyeglasses and looked at it. "This is what I said in Congress. Our guy read it. You can see the [budget] numbers. Here are they are. They're gonna have to close down hospitals. If you read the content of this, you'll see." He reached for another pamphlet. "I keep each book to compare what they've taken out from one year to the next, and each year they take stuff out." Jack was speaking so fast and throwing out so many numbers about veterans' health care, I could barely keep up. He moved the paper from his lap to the desk, removed his eyeglasses, wheeled around to the right, and looked me in the eye.

"Remember he [Bush] said he was gonna give all the troops free medical care? Ninety-nine percent of what he says on TV is all bullshit."

A few times a year, Jack drives to Washington, DC (a 20-hour trek with no stops) to urge Congress to find the money needed to take care of veterans.

He said that strategy has largely failed, so he's resorted to regularly contacting the national media. He turned his wheelchair around to face his computer and pulled up the lengthy emails he has sent to CNN, MSNBC, and Fox. His frustration is expressed at the end of each letter: ANSWER ME IF YOU DARE. He has never been contacted for an interview.

Jack served in Vietnam from January 1966 to June 1968. But that's not where he had his accident. "Can you believe it? I flew in from Vietnam and got in a car wreck driving home from the airport," he said, shaking his head. I asked Jack questions about his experience in

Vietnam and his injury, but he didn't want to talk about himself. He wanted to talk about the 30 vets who depend on the center for the basics. "We take vets out of the hospital and to the movies or out to eat. I often take breakfast to them. Biscuits and gravy. They don't like the hospital food here," he said.

"We got a guy here who's trying to live on $800 a month. He's paralyzed and he's in a wheelchair. He's a vet. He's not 65. He don't get Social Security. He begs for money to buy gas to come in for therapy. He doesn't have enough money for gas. Do you buy food or medicine or gas? Or do you get kicked out of your apartment? Mike over there arrives with me and I take him home. He has no car. He has no money. Social Security is gonna be a lifesaver for him. At one time, he was a business owner and made tons of money. His divorce wiped him out and now he lives in an apartment and has a few pair of clothes. That's it. Once a year we have a program where all the homeless vets come in and we feed them, clothe them, and cut their hair. We check their teeth, their eyes, give them backpacks and sleeping bags. We get about a 100 of 'em. These guys come in looking like hobos and they don't live inside. These are the trash left over from Vietnam and Desert Storm. Then they all have a big turkey dinner and get fed. Then they put their stuff on their backs and walk off into the night."

"What do the guys who come here for treatment say about the war?" I asked.

"They agree with Afghanistan. They think Iraq is a personal thing for Bush. For the man. They felt they should have stayed after bin Laden."

"Have you seen the effects of depleted uranium?"

"My personal opinion on that is you're gonna see leukemia. I don't think the government knows and I don't think they care about the effects of depleted uranium. This group just don't seem to care. To them, the military is a nonentity. Cheney said one day, 'Well, it's all volunteer.' What does that mean? They're nothin'? So they volunteer, so they don't mean anything to the country? So they're cattle? They can just go out and shoot 'em and kill 'em and it's no big deal. Of course, they had deferments because they had better things to do."

Soon after Jack got involved with veterans' issues, he changed his party affiliation. "Let me confess. I donated lots of money to the Republican Party, and I'm so damned ashamed of it, I can't see straight."

"Were you raised Republican?"

"No, my dad was a Democrat and my mom was a Republican. My dad was in World War II. He got shot three times. He was for the little guy. He was for the worker. He taught me how to weld before I could do anything else. When I got out of the air force, I went to work as a welder in California, building freeway signs and handrails. I welded 5,000 miles of damn handrail. I can't even believe it," he said, laughing. "I'm serious. You gotta keep the people working in order to grow the economy and keep the stock market healthy. I have money in the stock market. That's why I can do this. I spend over $200 a month out of my pocket coming here to work," he said passionately.

Jack began volunteering in 2001, but because funding is so tight, it turned into a full-time gig. "I get in here at about six in the morning, every day, five days a week, and I usually leave around 3:30. I open up, make coffee, deliver it to the patients, and get their breakfast orders. If they need something from the store, I'll go buy them things."

I asked Jack how he feels about Iraq disappearing from the front pages.

"The news media doesn't want to talk about it. They oughta be ashamed. Why do you think Walter Cronkite came out of retirement and started writing commentaries in the newspaper? Because he was sick and tired of only seeing half the story. Half a truth is also half a lie. I don't feel the media is honest. I had a guy come in here one day who was hollering about that damn liberal media. I said, 'Do you know the definition of liberal?' He said, 'Well no.' I said, 'Why are you cussin' the liberal?' I said, 'You get out of here and read the definition of liberal and you come back in here and tell me what it is.' Same thing for conservative. I took the dictionary and pulled up the definition of liberal and conservative and typed 'em up and gave copies to everybody. I said, 'Now let's see, what's the problem with being a liberal?' I've had people here tell me they believe Iraq had something to do with 9/11. I stand there and argue with them. I gotta get the map out and show people. Look at that tiny country there. What are you scared of?"

"How do people respond when you share your information?"

"They've all come back here and agreed. They didn't realize until they started reading and paying attention. They just watch TV. Mike, out there, voted for Bush. Now he can't believe he was conned by just watching TV. It's all deception," he said. "They [the soldiers] really shouldn't have been there in the first place. The dead really shouldn't have been there. What about the maimed? You can see them out here with their arms blown off. They're trying to figure out how to use their arms. Their legs are blown off. PTSD [post-traumatic stress syndrome] is hitting these kids years faster than it hit the Vietnam vets. The vets that came back from Vietnam didn't know what PTSD was. They crawled in alcohol bottles. They crawled in whiskey and marijuana and anything they could do to eliminate their minds. They wound up here 30 years later. We have a wing of them on this floor. You'll see them wandering around here saying, 'Where am I?'"

"How are your injuries?"

"My spinal chord is smashed. I'm almost 67 years old. I'm way beyond getting well, but I've had a great life. I've been in this chair over 30 years, and I've been to Paris, Nice, all over the world. I've been to Hawaii seven or eight times. I've been on cruises. It doesn't stop me from going anywhere. I saw my grandson graduate from high school last Saturday. I got 10 grandkids. One called me up the other night and read a book to me. He likes to read. I've had a lot of fun. My problem with this bunch [the Republican Party] is I've got 10 grandkids who are going to live in this world, and it scares me thinking about what they have to look forward to if this gang don't get kicked out. That is the bad part. They're not gonna have the shot I had. I come off a dirt farm. I come off the cotton fields. I retired as a VP of engineering. I was making six-figure salaries for the last 15 years of my job. I didn't mind paying $30,000 a year income tax because it paid for the infrastructure. It paid for the roads, the streets, the lights. That's what it's all about. That's my whole objection about trying to get some honesty up there. It's for my grandkids."

Houses of Right-Wing Worship

The sun was blistering hot, and we were at a ceremony that felt more like a Sunday afternoon church service than a political event. Governor Rick Perry decided to sign anti-abortion and antigay legislation inside the gym of the Calvary Christian Academy, an evangelical school in Fort Worth. The ceremony was filled with religious references and praise for "pro-family, pro-life" groups.

"I don't get confused about where God is," Perry said righteously from the podium. "He's everywhere! He's over there, he's here. Matter of fact, we could be doing this in the parking lot of Wal-Mart and God would be there." The diverse crowd of about 1,000 smiled and nodded in agreement. After he signed the bills, the crowd practically screamed "God Bless America."

I needed to take a break from this bizarre mix of religion and politics, so I headed outside where over 300 protesters held signs reading, "Hate Is Not a Family Value," "I'm a Tolerant Christian," "Don't Ruin God's House," and "Separation of Church and State."

Many of the protesters I met said Texans who live in small towns were beginning to speak out and get involved in peaceful demonstrations for the first time. "There have been three special sessions to fix education finance, and all they've managed to do is get a bill passed to eliminate gay marriage that they can sign in a church," said Lisa Earley, a fifth grade teacher from Grand Prairie, Texas. "I happen to be straight. I'm out here because this is wrong."

In addition to educators, nursing home advocates were speaking out against Governor Perry's priorities. Cheryl Killian, owner of three small nursing homes and administrator at the Sycamore Care Center in Fort Worth, told me Texas nursing homes haven't had a rate increase since 1999. "We're about 22 percent underfunded right now, per patient, per day," she said. "People are dying right now in Texas because of the underfunding. They're getting bedsores and lying in their own waste because we can't afford to keep on going. I've been doing this for 30 years and it's never been this bad."

Killian was one of the few protestors I could find who actually voted for Perry. She said her fellow Republicans would rather sit in a church than face reality. "It's not their issue. Maybe they're afraid of speaking out."

After a few hours of interviewing people, I was about to collapse from heat stroke, so I decided to look for Ryan. I found him arguing with a 40-something guy wearing a long-sleeved, white button-down shirt with a stars and stripes tie. The sun was shining on his bald spot and sweat was dripping down the sides of his face.

They were standing in front of a liberty bell between two slabs of concrete engraved with the Ten Commandments. The blue banner under the bell said, "Let Freedom Ring!" It looked like a high school float.

"Do you know how many Iraqis have died so far from this invasion?" Ryan asked.

"Far less from our side than theirs. The insurgents have done a lot more damage than we have."

"Studies have shown that the majority of the casualties are from U.S. forces," said Ryan. Paper was falling out of the fact folder, and he was becoming flustered.

"They're gonna say that, just like in Vietnam," said the man flinging his arm in the air like an angry preacher. He was holding a Bible that was so worn out, it looked like it belonged in a glass case in a museum.

"Do you know how many Vietnamese were killed?" Ryan asked.

"No."

I wondered if Ryan's new friend realized he was defending the bombing of innocent people in front of a monument that says, "Thou Shalt Not Kill."

"Do you know how many Americans were killed during Vietnam?" Ryan tried a different question.

"No, I don't, but I know how many were killed in the Gulf War."

Ryan pulled out a study about Iraqi casualties. "Here's a study by Johns Hopkins University. Read this."

"You know universities are opposed to war. They always have been."

"No, they went to Iraq and did a door-to-door survey. You haven't even read it yet, and you're already criticizing it," said Ryan.

"I already know. They lie."

"You don't know," said Ryan. "Actually you know who lies? Your government."

Ryan then pulled out a copy of the Downing Street Memo. "Have you seen this? It's about a meeting in the UK that proves the facts were being fixed around the policy."

"I'm not buying into your propaganda."

Ryan was so frustrated he read a section out loud. I couldn't help but laugh.

" ... reported on his recent talks in Washington. There was a perceptible shift in attitude. Military action was now seen as inevitable. Bush wanted to remove Saddam, through military action, justified by the conjunction of terrorism and WMD. But the intelligence and facts were being fixed around the policy. The NSC had no patience with the UN route ... "

I took out my camera to take a photo. The man smiled as Ryan continued reading.

The Dallas Divide

I spent the next few days interviewing people about Governor Perry's grandstanding photo-op in Highland Park Village, an upscale outdoor mall with stores like Chanel, Jimmy Choo, Hermes, Calvin Klein, and Escada. Two-story brick-and-glass neighborhoods with two or three Hummers and other snazzy SUVs in the driveway are the standard in Highland Park, one of the wealthiest areas in Dallas. Our van was parked between a BMW and a Land Rover. By this point, I was certain we were driving the only vehicle in the entire state of Texas without air conditioning. We never saw anyone else driving with the windows down.

I was having a difficult time getting interviews because it was

90-plus degrees outside, and most people were in a rush to get from the air-conditioned stores to their air-conditioned cars. The few who were kind enough to sweat with me for a few minutes asked me not to use their names, for fear their opinions might hurt their reputations and job prospects.

"You have to be very careful about what you say here. Depending on what circle you're in, it could come back to haunt you. Even though we're supposed to live in a free country and a free society, the government can still make life unpleasant for certain people," said a 60-something pro-choice Republican woman putting shopping bags in her Range Rover. She said she was bothered by Governor Perry's event and the "stranglehold the Christian Right has on the party."

A 40-something Libertarian woman who was job hunting said she's lived in other countries and different states but has never experienced anything quite like the political climate in Texas. "There's a conformity here that's beyond belief. The party-line thinking comes out of the religious culture, and I would hate to see the whole country go that way because we would become a fascist state. It would really scare me," she said. "You do learn to conform. It's very common. You learn the hard way. I consider it a rabid form of Republicanism. It's not like the East Coast Republicanism of the first Bush administration. That was completely different. Those Republicans don't recognize these Republicans, but these Republicans are the ones who are dominating."

The next day that woman left me a message saying, "I just got a job interview with a company whose CEO has strong ties to the Bush family. Please don't use my name."

The Democrats I met that day—and there were quite a few—whispered, "I'm one of the only Democrats in this area." Perhaps if they weren't so afraid to paste their politics on their cars in the manner of their proud Republican neighbors, they would begin to realize they were not alone.

A 30-year-old Democratic attorney said the Perry event was a slap in the face for people who believe in separation of church and state. "I think he showed blatant disregard for that, especially considering the bills he signed."

I asked her what it's like living in a predominantly Republican area.

"It gets pretty nasty around election time. I'm one of the few Democrats at my law firm. Everyone laughs about it, but around election time, especially when judges are up for reelection, I'll get a bunch of propaganda in the mail from fellow attorneys about Republican judges, but none about Democratic judges. They'll also bring judges by your office to shake hands with you and campaign for your votes, but they're all Republicans. They don't bother to bring in the Democratic judges. A lot of Republicans tend to be sympathetic to the gay struggle, but when it comes down to it, it's something they don't really like to talk about."

I spent another hour talking to people about Iraq. Most of the pro-war Republicans I met said the United States should "stay the course" and continue fighting for "freedom and democracy." Significantly, not one has any personal connections to Iraq.

I needed to escape the heat, so I decided to meet Ryan at a nearby bookstore, where he had spent the afternoon reading. He regularly encouraged me to stop working for a few hours and relax with a cold drink, but by this time, I was obsessed with interviewing anyone who would talk. After five minutes of sitting, I walked outside and met B.W., a 23-year-old who was preparing to graduate from Southern Methodist University (SMU), Laura Bush's alma matter. "It costs $40,000 a year to go here. Most of the kids drive BMWs and Range Rovers. It's kind of intimidating when you don't have a lot of money, but I'm used to it by now."

B.W. told me that in 2003, a black family bought a home in Highland Park and the *Park Cities News*, the local paper serving the area, ran an article called, "Area's First Black Family Welcomed." The first line of the article read, "Guess who's coming to dinner—and staying awhile?" That was a startling reference to the 1967 movie, *Guess Who's Coming to Dinner*, starring Spencer Tracy and Katharine Hepburn as the wealthy white parents of a daughter who brings her black boyfriend, Sydney Poitier, home for dinner.

You can't miss the class and race disparities in Highland Park.

With the exception of B.W., the only other African Americans I saw in three days all work in Highland Park stores. Out of nine checkers and baggers I saw at the main grocery store in the area, seven were black. "The only blacks that you're going to see here either work here or go to this school," said B.W. "When I first came here, it was culture shock. I hated it. I just felt out of place. During spring break, people would ask, 'Where are you summering?' Summering, what is that? I'm going home. I knew it was a rich school, but I didn't realize it was this rich. They have two names for this school: the Harvard of the South and Southern Millionaires University. For the most part, I still feel out of place."

"I interviewed a guy who works at the bookstore yesterday and he said he experiences racism on a regular basis here. Do you?"

"I wouldn't say racism, but I do experience stereotyping and profiling. A lot of students live in a bubble and don't realize what they're saying. They don't think racism exists. We can drink out of the same fountains so everything is fine. You're at SMU just like I am, so everything is equal. I hear that a lot. The thing is, their parents will get them jobs when they graduate. I've always had roommates whose parents owned a business or had lots of connections. People in my family have good jobs, but no one owns businesses or has connections."

"How have you changed after going to a predominantly white, upper-class school?"

"I've learned a lot. I've learned how my potential future employers think. When I get out in the corporate world, it won't be mostly black, it'll be mostly white. I've learned how to be quiet. I know it sounds weird. After reading a book about slavery, the teacher asked us how we felt. One girl said, 'I think it's kind of harsh.' My teacher said, 'Well, yeah, slavery was pretty harsh.' He was one of the few black professors at the school. I've learned that a lot of these people don't really understand racism the way I understand it. They've heard about it, but I can ask my mother about it and hear first-hand accounts. My mother was born before the Civil Rights Act. In their world, there's no more racism. I've learned when it's appropriate to talk about these kinds of issues and when it's not."

B.W. suggested we get a different perspective by doing interviews at the Southwest Center Mall in South Dallas, about a 25-minute drive from Highland Park. The change in scenery was striking. As we crossed the line to the south side, we saw roads in disrepair, older tract homes, worn-out bungalows that didn't look habitable, and several beat-up cars.

The mall itself had no coffee shops or bookstores, and sold mostly discounted clothing; there were also plenty of empty storefronts and 90 percent of the shoppers were African American. Despite my best efforts, I couldn't find a single person who supported the war in Iraq. Yet, also in sharp contrast to Highland Park, every person I interviewed knew at least one person serving there. "My daughter-in-law's brother was one of the first who was killed there," said Cooter Rivers. "He was 19 years old, just out of high school and had no training. They had him missing for a long time. They didn't even ship his whole body home. The war isn't necessary. We should leave that country and bring our boys and girls home."

Cooter said the area was hurting from job losses and low wages. I asked him what message he would send to politicians.

"On election day, I picked up people to take them to vote. When I was in line voting, I saw people who didn't know how to vote and the volunteers didn't show them. I stopped filling out my paper and helped people in line. They were like, 'How do you do this?' I said, 'You've never voted?' 'No.' And no one helped them. That was right here in this area. I'd like to tell Democrats to get more volunteers down here when voting time comes around. Show people how to vote. Go door to door. Do whatever it takes."

"Where do you get your news?"

"I read the newspaper and go online to Yahoo. I like to keep up with Arnold Schwarzenegger in California."

"Why?" I said laughing.

"I don't understand how he could become a governor in our country. It's amazing," he said shaking his head.

D. W. Awane, a 31-year-old who works for a liquor company, believes the United States invaded Iraq for money, power, and oil.

"People should know the truth. Stop lying to people. Tell them the truth. Our brothers and sons and cousins are out there fighting and losing their lives. For what?"

"Do you know anyone over there?"

"I have a cousin who is a Navy SEAL. My other cousin is a sergeant. Another cousin from New Orleans is a captain. I know about six or seven people over there. I tell them I love them when I talk to them. I say, 'I appreciate what you're doing, but I wish you were doing it for the right reasons.' I don't like our people going to fight over something that doesn't belong to us. We've been fighting for things that aren't ours forever. It started with the Indians."

"What's life like in this area? What's needed most?"

"Guidance. In order to keep people off the streets and reduce crime, they need guidance. When people don't have anything, what happens? Crime goes up. People gotta eat and survive. There's so much negativity knocking people down."

"A lot of Republicans I interview say people need to take responsibility for their actions and they shouldn't rely on government handouts. Everyone has the opportunity to pull themselves out of poverty. How do you respond to that?"

"How would they know everybody has a chance unless they're out here? It's easy to say that when you have a job and a nice place to call home. I challenge all politicians to come and live out here. Leave Washington, DC and see life for what it is. Go out and communicate when it's not election time. You'll learn about starvation and homelessness. Just go downtown and sit there. They think people aren't trying? People are trying. If you live way up north, you have no idea what's it like down here. Come on down. I'll show you around."

The Blueberry Festival

We needed an afternoon off, so we decided to go online to find something fun to do, something that didn't involve politics. We chose a blueberry festival in Nacogdoches. "Set deep in Texas Forest Country in the Oldest Town in Texas, the Texas Blueberry Festival is a delightful day of the America you dreamed still existed."

As soon as we arrived in town we saw churches on almost every street corner. With over 65 churches listed in the Nacogdoches Yellow Pages, the town of almost 30,000 lives up to its reputation as the "city of churches."

We got to the festival at one in the afternoon, and the sun was out in full force. Within minutes of walking, I grabbed a tissue out of my bag to wipe the sweat off my face. Little bits of paper stuck to my forehead. When Ryan was with me, he'd remove them. When I was on my own, I'd usually spot them in a mirror at the end of the day. For some reason, no one else would ever bother to tell me they were there.

At the festival we passed face-painting booths, blueberry pie-eating contests, blueberry pancakes, live bands, and a pet parade. I saw a man handing out bottled water and picked up the pace, which made me sweat even more. It was a booth for the First Baptist Church. Next door was God's Open Door to Eternal Life, a mission for homeless people. Ryan and I looked at each other and smiled. That's code for, "I'm outta here." He took off, and I gladly accepted a deliciously cold bottle from Pastor Allen Reed. I wrapped my fingers around it and placed my cold hand on the back of my neck. After taking a big swig, I noticed the label. "If anyone thirsts, let him come to me and drink."

"It's 90-degree weather and people get thirsty," he said.

"I'm from San Francisco, and I'm not used to such intense heat. Thanks for the water."

"What brings you to East Texas?"

I was tempted to say we were just passing through, but I decided to tell him about the project and ask him a few questions. In the 24 years he's lived in Nacogdoches, he's seen only two major changes. The Hispanic community has grown significantly, and East Texas became Republican. "It didn't matter who was running for what, you'd vote Democrat. If Uncle Sam or Mickey Mouse was runnin', you'd still vote Democrat. That's changed a great deal."

"Why?"

"The ethical and moral issues that face our country are more in line with the conservative party." He said he and his fellow Republicans "cannot accept a lot of the liberal politics."

I knew the answer, but I asked anyway. "Like what?"

"Abortion. Homosexuality."

Like most of the pastors I've met, he said he doesn't tell his congregants who to vote for, but he does say, "As Christians, this is what we believe and you go vote your convictions and your conscience." That's code for, "Vote Republican."

I told him that one of the safest, nicest neighborhoods in San Francisco is the Castro, the predominantly gay neighborhood.

"That's what I understand."

"I'm posting a bunch of my interviews on my blog, and I received an email from a gay man this morning who said the interviews I've done with people opposed to homosexuality made him cry. He said he doesn't understand why there is so much hate in this country. What would you say to him?"

"Don't hate the person. Hate the sin. Homosexuality is an abomination to the Lord. It's a sin, but all of us are sinners. I don't hate the homosexual, but I certainly don't agree with the lifestyle. It's unnatural."

Don't hate the person. Hate the sin. I've heard this at least a dozen times from people like Reed.

"Do you have any gay friends?"

He looked away and handed out a few more water bottles. "Two of my family members were gay. One was my brother, a Vietnam vet, and the other was my niece. Both of them are deceased now."

His brother was gay? I was dumbfounded. "Sorry to hear that. Did you maintain a good relationship with them?"

"Yes, I conducted the funerals for both of them. It's in everybody's family these days. They knew I loved them and that I didn't agree with their lifestyle. It's a sin. Let's agree to disagree."

"So you take the Bible literally? The Bible says a woman must marry her rapist. The Bible says women should be silent. The Bible also says divorce is a sin."

"That's true. I would like to ban divorce now that you brought it up." He said he marries divorced people as long as they marry "believers." He stopped short of saying women should be silent.

"Do you think more time should be spent on other issues and less time on gay marriage, especially since gay marriage here is already illegal?"

"It's crucial to stop the gay agenda."

I kept hearing about this so-called gay agenda, but it seemed like the only agenda people like Reed had was to talk about gays. So many of the religious Republicans I met were obsessed with gays. "What is the gay agenda?"

"They're trying to cram it down our throats. In the school system, they're teaching, Sammy has two mammas or George has two daddies. It's being forced on us. They're saying, this is a lifestyle you're going to accept one way or the other."

"What would you say to gays who are just trying to live their lives?"

"We're all entitled to our opinions, but their lifestyle is wrong."

I had to change the subject. "Does your church ever work on poverty issues? Do you help the poor?"

"We have ministries, like the one next door here. We support them financially. We have HOPE, Helping Others Practice English. We have about 250, mostly Hispanic, but all kinds of people who live here. We teach them English. We use the Bible as a textbook."

"You use the Bible as a textbook?"

"Yes, and a curriculum manual. We have volunteers from several churches in the community. They come together and meet once a week for two or three hours to help them learn English so they can get jobs. When people have needs, whether it's for food or utilities, medicine, a doctor's bill, we do have some resources to help with that. We have an organization called Love Inc., Love In the Name of Christ, that we support."

My water bottle was empty. I was dripping in sweat. I was hungry. And I was becoming irritated. People were lining up for water and information about the gay agenda, so I thanked Reed for his time. "Great talkin' to ya," he said with a big smile.

I bought a cool drink and sat on a curb in the shade. I wondered if the families walking by with blueberry stains on their flag T-shirts made in China thought it was normal to use the Bible as a textbook.

A woman wearing a permanent smile sat down next to me. She removed her red visor and wiped her sweaty forehead. She was wearing red shorts and a white T-shirt that screamed "Freedom!" above a waving flag. She had curly blonde shoulder-length hair, and her checks were covered in bright pink blush. "Excuse me, I notice that your shirt says freedom. What does that word mean to you?" I couldn't resist.

"My nephew was just shipped over to Japan with the army for two years," she said. "You don't realize how you take your freedom for granted until you know someone who's sent away to fight for it."

"What will he be doing in Japan?"

"I'm not really sure what's he doin', but he's fightin' for our freedom."

More than 40,000 United States troops are stationed on approximately 91 bases throughout mainland Japan and Okinawa. According to Chalmers Johnson, author of *Blowback: The Costs and Consequences of American Empire,* there are American military bases on every continent, 737 in over 130 countries.

"What does freedom mean to you?"

"Freedom means I can practice my religion openly," she said, flashing her pearly whites.

A young child pulled on her arm. "Mommy, I want cotton candy."

"Sorry, gotta run."

I was ready to leave. After 10 minutes of wandering around, I found Ryan happily eating some kind of meat on a stick. "I found meat. I found meat!" he said smiling. He was in a playful mood, and I was irritated. "Let's get out of here."

"We traveled all this way. We're at a blueberry festival. We can't leave without having the blueberry ice cream. You haven't even tried the blueberries. Please. Pretty please. I'll throw the meat away."

How could I say no?

He tossed his plate in the trash, and we made our way to the Heart of Texas, a quintessential country store selling everything from flow-

ery tea towels and birdhouses with the Texas star on the roof to homemade blueberry jam and ice cream sundaes. We sat at the ice cream bar
and ordered an ice cream sundae and a bowl of fresh blueberries. Because we were lugging around so much equipment in our fairly large
backpacks, people usually asked if we were from out of town.

"Let me guess. Y'all aren't from around here," said the woman behind the counter.

"No, we're visiting from San Francisco," I said without going into
my usual spiel.

Much to my chagrin, Ryan did it for me. "We're traveling around
the country talking to people about politics. Feel like answering a few
questions?"

"Sure. But this isn't Bush country," she said proudly while putting
the final touches on an ice cream sundae.

I almost fell off my chair. Gerry grew up in nearby Lufkin and
opened the country store in 1992. She said she rarely talks politics
because "Republicans act like you're ignorant if you say you're a Democrat. A lot of times we just keep our mouths shut. I've always been a
liberal. We've got to take control again. I believe in stem cell research.
I believe in a woman's right to choose. I believe in so many of those
things that they are trying to take a giant step backward on. That really aggravates me."

"Do you talk about these issues with Republicans here?"

"No. We do what we can to get local officials elected. Their political party really doesn't come into play. It's really about their agenda.
I've got a lot of friends that are Republicans. Rather than get into
arguments, we just don't talk politics."

"Do your friends know you're a Democrat?"

"Well, we don't talk about it, but I think they know. Some will say,
I know you're a Democrat, but . . . And my husband has a ponytail, so
that's a good giveaway here. It's not a problem with my friends. We try
to look beyond that. I forgive them for being Republican, unless they
cram it down my throat."

"What do you think about the war?"

"It's time to leave Iraq. My nephew is over there working for a private company guarding ammunition dumps. We've wasted a lot of money over there. We have a health care issue here. There are so many people without health care, myself included. My health care went up to $1,000 a month. I can't pay $1,000 a month for insurance. If we could take all that money that we've blown up in smoke over there, we'd have fewer problems here, but that's not gonna happen. Bush's agenda is anything but taking care of the home front."

"You said you've always been a liberal. What does that mean to you?" I asked.

"Live and let live. If people are not hurting me or my family and they're happy, I'm OK with it."

"Where do you get most of your news?"

"CNN. My husband watches Fox, and it drives me insane. I read the daily newspaper here. The Internet takes up too much time. We watch a lot of news on television. My favorite place for news is the *Daily Show* with Jon Stewart."

"Do you think this area has a chance of becoming Democratic again?"

"No, I don't see it happening."

Ryan then shared with Gerry a few stories about his misadventures, and I got to thinking about how this trip has pulled me in directions I have never been before. One minute I feel like I'm in the middle of *The Handmaid's Tale*, talking to people like Pastor Reed, and the next, I'm in blueberry heaven talking to people like Gerry.

It was hard to believe that we had four and a half months to go.

Diversity in East Texas

Before heading to Mississippi we decided to visit one more Texas town. After asking for a few recommendations and reading the local papers, we decided to drive two hours north to the Piney Woods region of Linden (population 2,000). The town's motto is "Where the Music Never Ends!" Scott Joplin, founder of Ragtime Jazz; Aaron "T-Bone" Walker, Daddy of the Blues; and Don Henley, cofounder of the Eagles, are just a few of the musicians who called Linden home.

The drive was peaceful and smooth. On the way we passed a huge sign for Vacation Bible School called B.O.O.T. CAMP—Biblical Outlook & Outreach Training. An hour later, we reached downtown Linden. It felt like we were driving around an old-fashioned movie set complete with a historic courthouse that looked like a mini White House, mom-and-pop shops, benches, and trees lining the sidewalks. It was early, so it wasn't too hot, and the mood was calm and quiet.

I struck up a conversation with a woman taking a cigarette break near her store. She asked me not to use her name because speaking out isn't advisable. "As a business owner in a small town, it's not a good thing to do. Don't talk religion and don't talk politics. Not town politics, not any kind of politics. They [the locals] are very loyal. They'd be more loyal to someone outside of town that agrees with them than they would their own neighbor," she said.

"What do people do for work around here?"

"Most people either work for the city government or work in factories just outside of town," she said. "There's International Paper nearby. There's another one 30 miles from here. There's the Red River Army Depot. That's pretty much where everybody works."

She took a long drag of her cigarette, turned her head to blow out the smoke, and turned back to face me. She said she's not very political but never misses an election. "I read the paper and every day something different amazes me. The federal laws like medical marijuana. If people don't have cancer, who in the hell are they to say you can't use marijuana? Our priorities are all messed up. If God can't help us now, we're in big trouble."

A self-described Democrat who grew up poor, she said making ends meet in Linden is becoming increasingly difficult, and the local poverty rate is increasing. "Most people don't have insurance 'cause it's not affordable. I talk to these people every day. Some people can't feed their kids or afford their medicine. The whole United States is all messed up."

She insists she's not political, yet she reads anything she can get her hands on, and she spends many evenings watching documentaries about 9/11, electronic voting machines, and the invasion of Iraq. And they're making her angry. "I don't like knowin' it, but I keep up with it. For years and years I didn't. But once you do, it's hard to turn your back on it," she said. "I don't trust the elections. Why in the hell do they have so many problems with punch cards? This government has gotten away with so much. If they can get away with this war, they can get away with anything. Even if you can get everybody to vote, it won't matter."

"What message would you send to Democrats?"

"Take a stand. Get a clue."

Ryan was repacking the van, so I approached a guy wearing a cowboy hat who had just gotten out of his truck. Bob Vernon, 67, is spending his retirement on his family farm just outside of town. "It's an absolutely idyllic place to live." After 9/11 Bob decided to leave Massachusetts, his home for 20 years, to return to Linden. "I actually retired a few months early. I don't think anyone is going to bother to bomb 300 acres of piney woods."

Bob's family is Democratic, but he's "more right-wing" than he lets on. He has no faith in U.S. intelligence, is mostly concerned about immigration issues, believes most Republicans in DC are RINOs— Republicans in Name Only—and would love to see Condoleeza Rice in the White House. He gets most of his news from *freerepublic.com,* the archconservative site I spent so much time perusing.

"You're a freeper?" I said with astonishment. I've never met a freeper in person before. I told him that I tried to take part in a discussion about veterans' issues on the site, but got kicked out just minutes after asking why the government wasn't spending more on health care. "If you criticize Republicans, you get kicked off!"

"Hey, now, people characterize us as being a bunch of right-wing wackos," he said. "You'd be amazed how many times people come on and say, 'I need prayer.' They aren't cold, noncompassionate people. They're just Americans. They have discussions on everything from creationism to you name it."

I had an interview in 30 minutes with a radio station in Dallas, but I couldn't find a cell phone connection, so we had to take off to find a pay phone. Before I left, Bob told me that liberals are "dummies." All I could do was laugh and shake my head.

I grabbed a granola bar from the back and hopped in the van. "You made another friend?" Ryan asked laughing.

"That guy is a freeper!"

"You're kidding."

Just as we were about to take off, Bob walked over to Ryan's side. "Hey, I just want you to know she was talkin' to a real Texas redneck." He pulled a pistol out of his back pocket and put it in his palm so Ryan could get a good look. Bob gave him an evil grin, put the pistol back in his pocket, turned around, and began walking toward the courthouse.

After driving around for 10 minutes or so, we found a pay phone in front of a local grocery mart. I had some time to spare, so I decided to approach the next person walking by. I introduced myself to a man wearing jeans, cowboy boots, a cream-colored cowboy hat, a nicely pressed button-up jean shirt, and a pale yellow tie covered in horseshoes and small imprints of the Lone Star state. A jovial, polite man with a sincere smile, 56-year-old Charles McMichael is a Democratic judge in Cass County. He was born and raised in the area and told me he's been attending the same church for the past 52 years. "It hasn't changed a great deal. The pace is slow. We don't have things like traffic jams. Sometimes it's a little harder to find jobs here, so it's not necessarily good livin', but it's a good life." He said the population usually stays the same.

"What makes you a Democrat?"

"Well ma'am, I've always had to work for a livin'. I don't like the war. I'm afraid it's turnin' into another Vietnam."

"What issues do you care most about?"

"The economy is the most important. High gas prices. I'm not in the service, but if we're goin' to send these boys overseas, we need to pay them well."

"What message would you send to Democrats in DC?"

"Don't get into gun control. Work on real issues. Our priorities are all messed up."

"What do you think of George W. Bush?"

"He's a wannabe cowboy. I know a man who lives near him and it's all a front. I was born like this myself," he said with a smile.

"I was hoping to meet an authentic cowboy before leaving Texas. Thanks for your time."

"No problem, ma'am. Be safe now."

As he went on his way, a guy with unruly long hair in a beat-up yellow truck loudly asked me what I was interviewing people about. After I told him I'm from San Francisco, he said he left California because he got sick of hearing Hispanics speak Spanish. Over the course of a two-minute conversation, he told me he doesn't have a Social Security number, believes the government took down the planes on 9/11 via remote control, and is in favor of shooting all politicians. I think he was drunk.

Then it was time for my radio interview. The pay phone was to the right of the entrance door, so there was no privacy. The hosts asked me general questions about why I took the trip and my church experiences. A large burly man wearing jean overalls slowly walked by as I told them about a few of the interviews I had done about religion and the separation of church and state. He stopped and stared. All of a sudden, he started screaming. "There should be no separation of church and state. I'm not a Democrat! I'm a Republican!" I was afraid he was going to charge me. Instead, he loudly cleared his throat and spat on the ground. It landed near my left foot. I gasped and tried to answer a few more questions. The man walked toward his car but looked over his shoulder a few times with an angry look on his face. The radio interview ended, I ran across the parking lot, jumped in the van, and locked the door. It was time to say good-bye to Texas.

Pro-War Vegan

That night, we splurged. Since we were planning to be on the road for another four-and-a-half months, we stayed in a Holiday Inn Express in Shreveport, Louisiana. Staying at a Holiday Inn Express usually meant we were guaranteed to get a fast Internet connection, a comfy bed, and thick bath towels, luxuries we take for granted at home. Because it was too hot to camp, we were spending a lot more money than we expected on hotels, so we'd put a "donate" button on our blog and when we checked email that night, we were pleasantly surprised to find a number of donations from complete strangers. A woman in Elgin, Illinois, sent $20, a woman from Los Angeles sent $60, a woman from Oklahoma City sent $40, and a woman from Bell County, Texas, sent $10 with a short note that said, "Thanks for all these stories of my homeland." It was nice to know that people were willing to help fund this kind of project.

By this time, we had our routine down. Ryan lugged in two plastic crates, one full of food and dishes and the other full of gadgets and wires, and I brought in the duffle bags with our toiletries and clothing. Ryan usually cooked dinner while I transcribed interviews and updated the blog. A little olive oil and hot sauce does wonders for rice and beans, especially when that's the main course. Other than Subway and an occasional Mexican or Thai restaurant, I wasn't finding much to eat, but I was trying not to think about it.

If anything, the lack of food choices made me appreciate all the vegan options I have in San Francisco. When we did find a vegetarian restaurant on the road, I felt like a kid in a candy store. I was elated when I found a black bean burger on the menu at Chili's! In Shreveport I was pleasantly surprised to find Healthy Planet, the only vegetarian restaurant in town. It's actually a vegan restaurant, but the owner calls it a vegetarian restaurant because "most people aren't even familiar with the term vegan." Jim Rosso has been a vegan for 13 years. He opened Healthy Planet about 12 years ago. "As you can see, we're still very small," he said. We were his first customers of the day, and it was close to 2:30.

After we ordered sandwiches and fresh carrot juice I chatted with Jim about animal rights and the benefits of veganism. Ryan grabbed his book and moved to a table in the corner. He's heard this conversation many times before (yet he still eats meat).

A half hour into the conversation, it became clear that I was talking to a pro-war Republican vegan. It was a first.

Ryan started listening when the conversation turned to Iraq. He walked over and handed Jim a copy of the Downing Street Memo. "This came out in July 2002. It's a memo from British intelligence." Jim spent a few minutes reading it, and then the debate began.

"There were a lot of statements that were made. I don't think the UN held up its end of the bargain."

"In what sense?" asked Ryan.

"These other countries didn't experience 3,000 people dying."

"Iraq had nothing to do with that."

"But it did."

"No, it didn't. It had nothing to do with 9/11," said Ryan.

"It's tied in."

"It had nothing to do with it. Sorry, but it makes me want to bang my head against the wall. Their PR campaign makes you think that. That was the point."

"I don't think it was because of the PR campaign."

"It certainly wasn't reality. Bush himself has said they had nothing to do with it. Bush himself said it."

"That doesn't mean anything, just 'cause Bush said it."

My sandwich and juice arrived, so I decided to try to enjoy lunch at a different table. I was exhausted and didn't have the energy for another debate. Twenty minutes later, they were still going at it.

"Why haven't there been any more problems with terrorism in the United States?" asked Jim. "We don't have a problem anymore."

"We don't have a problem anymore? American soldiers and Iraqis are being slaughtered every day, but it's not our problem?"

"Not on our ground."

"So if it happens over there, it's OK?"

"At least there haven't been any more terror attacks on our soil."

"Terrorism has increased around the world."

"Well, I hate to say this, but I don't care about that."

"Then why do you expect the rest of the world to care about you?" asked Ryan.

"I care more about the USA than I care about Iraq. I'm sorry. You don't care more about Americans than others?"

"No, I don't think that an American life is any more valuable than an Iraqi or a British life, and it's racist to assume it is."

"I care more about this country. That's why I'm here."

"If you care about the U.S. you should do things that ensure its safety. Blowing up other countries does not increase our safety."

Ryan then read statements by American soldiers serving in Iraq who've said the insurgency can't be stopped by military action.

"A lieutenant colonel named Frederick Wellman said, 'We can't kill them all. When I kill one, I create three.'"

"Where'd you read that?"

"Knight-Ridder."

With the exception of fair and balanced *Fox News,* Jim, like so many of the Republicans we've met, doesn't trust the media.

Ryan raised his voice as he began a brief history lesson about sanctions and U.S. support for Saddam Hussein, but he tried to sound polite by calling Jim "sir." I wasn't sure if Jim was trying to appease him or was actually interested in what he had to say. He listened without interrupting, then stood up and said, "Don't lose your train of thought. I have to go to the restroom." Ryan grabbed the fact file and rummaged through articles and reports as if he was reloading a weapon. The papers and reports covered the table.

Jim returned and a cordial conversation continued for another 25 minutes.

"So what's the answer?" demanded Jim.

"We have to leave Iraq."

"OK, you've had your turn. Now it's my turn." Then Jim gave Ryan his version of history, which he learned from the Bible.

I gave Ryan the "we don't have time for you to deconstruct the Bible" look, so he calmly listened while I paid for lunch. Ryan left a number of articles and reports on the table, Jim filled my cup with more carrot juice, they called a truce, and we went on our way.

II

MISSISSIPPI

A Lesson in Listening

AFTER MORE THAN SIX WEEKS of spending virtually every day together, we decided we needed some other company, so we stopped at a Goodwill store on the way to Mississippi and bought a bunch of plastic toys to add to the dolphins on the dashboard. I filled my side with animals, trees, and fish. Ryan's side was covered with Native Americans and colonial occupiers embroiled in a bloody war. He's a peace activist, but he's still a guy. As you can imagine, it grabbed the attention of passersby when we stopped for gas or a bite to eat. People who would have otherwise ignored us smiled and stopped to take a look. Some even brought their kids over; others gave us recommendations for places to visit next.

Three and a half hours later, we were in Jackson, the capital and the most populous city in Mississippi. I chose Mississippi because of its rich history and because most of the attention the state receives is negative. I also wanted to visit the only clinic in the entire state that still provides abortions.

After checking into our hotel I went out to get some fresh air and met Robert Earl Turner, the security guard on duty. After I told him about the project, he asked me to find positive people to interview. "We're trying to break the stigma that we're a state of hate. If we can get the rights that we won 40, 50 years ago, we'll be fine. We're moving forward. Mississippi is a great state," he said, nodding his head.

Robert became a security guard after losing his job at a cardboard box factory three years before. He's 58. "After 30 years of working for the same company, they walked in and shut us down. That left me struggling for a job. So many plants are closing in the state of Mississippi and right here in Jackson. I'm doing the best I can until retirement in 2010."

Robert said just about everyone he knows is worse off than they were a decade ago. "People might not want to hear this, but war creates more problems. We need to focus on other things besides the war."

"Are you a Democrat?" I asked.

"Yes."

"What makes you a Democrat?"

"I'm a Democrat because I believe in freedom of speech. I work every day and expect a paycheck. I'm against taking from the poor and giving to the rich."

"Why do you think Mississippi is so Republican?"

"The Republicans convince people that we're gonna get people off welfare, but really in Mississippi, you can't get off welfare if you're not working. People want to work. I've been in Mississippi all my life and all I wanted was an opportunity to work. We need to find a solution to solve our problems."

"You've lived here all your life? You must have many memories and stories to share."

"A lot of 'em. Some of 'em good, some of 'em not so good. The only way we'll be successful is to look forward and not backward. We're tryin' to moving forward."

With that, Robert had to get back to the job he said he has grown to love. "I get paid to meet and greet strangers like yourself. Be safe now and be sure to interview people who show you the positive side of Mississippi."

Domestic Violence Changed My Politics

Lifelong Republican Michele Carroll became a Democrat after she started working as director of the Mississippi Coalition to End Domestic Violence in Jackson. I met with Michele to find out why Mississippi is ranked as the worst state in the country for women, according to the Institute for Women's Policy Research.

Michele joined the coalition in 1996 after many years working at a substance abuse counseling center at the state's Department of Education. Even though she's spent most of her adult life in the social work field, she had no idea domestic violence was so pervasive. Even more shocking, she learned that the victims could be anyone.

"I was stunned. A lot of my good friends came to me when I got this job and said, 'This is either happening to me now or this has happened to me in the past.' A lot of times these abusers are very smart and good at brainwashing. They know what they're doing. Anybody can be a victim. We had a past Miss Mississippi come forward. For years, she had been abused. We've had lots of people like that come forward. We did have one lady who came into one of our shelters who made $300,000 a year and she didn't have a dime to her name. Everything was in his name. She was 52. She came to us cause she didn't have anywhere else to go." That woman was lucky. She got out of the relationship, kept her job, and moved on with her life.

"What do people need to know about domestic violence?"

"It affects everybody. You can't just turn your back on it. One in four women will have a severe beating in their lifetime. One in four. It's scary. And if we don't do something about it, it's going to get worse."

"How does politics impact your work?"

"Bill Clinton did more for women's rights than any president. He is the one that got the Family Violence Prevention Act passed. He set up the Violence Against Women Act. He set up the Victims of Crime Act, which established the monies for state domestic violence coalitions and state sexual assault coalitions. I'm sure Hillary was behind him."

Michele said that convincing Washington, DC politicians to set money aside for domestic violence programs became extremely difficult almost immediately after George W. Bush took office in 2001. I told her that the majority of the Republicans I've met on my trip believe the government is spending too much money on social programs.

"A-ha. OK. Well." She sat up straight, pulled her shoulders back, and put on a serious face. She's clearly heard this before. "We are on a shoestring budget. It's nothing. They're giving us a Band-Aid to take care of something that needs an Ace bandage as big as Texas. That crap about we're just in it for the money. Please. I have a master's degree in family therapy. Do you honestly think I'm doing this because I want to make money? My heart is in this. When I go to the legislature, I often hear, 'Well, what does the director make?' I can assure you she's not in it for the money. And it takes a very strong woman to do this work. The only monies that shelters get is that federal money. They can go to the Board of Supervisors and they're almost always male. They can go to mayors or the city councils. Literally, shoestring doesn't even begin to describe these budgets. If domestic violence went unchecked, we'd have more snipers. We'd have more men going up in places and shootin' everybody in sight. They get away with it at home. Why can't they go over here and get away with it? It's going to spill out until we hold them accountable. That's all there is to it."

"What would you say to Republicans who believe everyone has the ability to pull themselves up by their bootstraps? It's all about personal responsibility. I'm hearing this a lot."

"When I started here, I was a Republican. I was. Now I'm not."

"What changed?"

"Look, I get chills just thinking about it," she said, tearing up. "My family is Republican. I'm the black sheep of the family now. It's tangible. I see what is happening. I didn't vote for Bill Clinton the first time around. The second time I did because I saw what he did. Read the Violence Against Women Act sometime. It is amazing. Bush's budget called for shutting down half of the shelters in the entire state. Under Bush, every year, the shelters got on average, a $10,000 cut."

"I assume you have a lot of Republican friends? Do you tell your friends about these issues and how you've been so affected?"

"Yes. It's really funny. I was just talking about that the other day with my very best friend who I've had since I was like 15 years old. I was aggravated because we were arguing over this. I thought, 'I can't believe how she's changed.' Then I thought, 'She hasn't changed, I have.'"

The Last Abortion Clinic in Mississippi

A simple sign on a small hill in Jackson's Fondren District announces the Jackson Women's Health Clinic, the only clinic in the entire state of Mississippi that offers safe and legal abortions. Antichoice groups are on a mission to shut it down. The unassuming white building could pass for a local library. A black metal gate separates the women entering the building from the protestors on the sidewalk. On any given day, a handful of protesters hold signs and plead with the women going in to rethink their decisions. The loud ones grab the bars on the gate tightly as if they are trapped; the quiet ones recite passages from the Bible as if they are speaking directly to their God. When we pulled into the small parking lot, two protesters—an older woman and possibly her daughter—made eye contact with us, quickly grabbed their Bibles, brochures, and signs, and took their places. They were ready for a confrontation.

They thought we had an appointment. I asked Ryan to refrain from saying anything. Just walk past them. I've seen and heard these kinds of protestors before but have never been on the receiving end of their anger and outright hostility. As we got closer to the building, they started screaming. "Your baby doesn't deserve to die! Mommy, don't kill me! Please mommy, don't kill me!" It really was intimidating. Even Ryan was shaken up. For all they knew, I had an appointment for an annual exam or needed birth control pills, but my personal story didn't matter because as far as they're concerned, the clinic is nothing more than an abortion factory. I wondered what this experience was like for young women who come alone. What about the staff? They have to deal with this every day, and in a small town like Jackson, it can't be easy. A tall security guard dressed in a dark blue uniform with a solemn look on his face escorted us through the front door.

Five young African American women sat in the waiting room. Two were with their partners. The security guard stood watch near the front door, Ryan took a corner seat, and I introduced myself to the woman behind the front desk. A few minutes later I was taken to a back room to meet with Betty Thompson, the clinic's administrator and former counselor. She was wearing a silky orange top, gold hoop earrings, and eyeglasses. Her short black hair was pushed behind her ears. I began by telling her about the protesters.

"I've never experienced anything like that at home. Is it safe to say you're in hostile territory?" I ask.

"Without a doubt. When I first started, I recall my insecurities. Not because this was the Bible Belt, but I always wondered what my friends thought. It was such a pleasure to realize that they didn't care one way or the other. They were still my friends. That was eye opening for me. Those that disagreed with me are still my friends. As far as the hostile environment, we've been lucky in Mississippi as far as no bombings and no things of that nature. We've been able to disagree with each other for the most part."

"What's it like for you personally?"

"You're getting up coming to work every day looking over your shoulder. You have to remain vigilant. You never know. Early one Saturday morning, I remember one particular incident. A protestor climbed up on the fence and his head was hanging over the gate and it just so happened that I had a friend with me and he said, 'I cannot believe you are hanging over this gate,' and the protestor said, 'I'm looking for my cat.' And you have to laugh, but to hang over that gate is very frightening. On Mother's Day or on the anniversary of *Roe v. Wade*, we become more in tune to being safe. So, yes, it is a hostile environment. Legislatively, it's very hostile and that's most unfortunate."

"The antichoice people that I've met are opposed to sex education and contraception. Completely getting rid of birth control. How do you deal with that?" I ask.

"They call it abstinence-only. I call it ignorance-only. When you don't tell young people that they have birth control and condoms, then you're promoting ignorance. And Mississippi is usually at the bottom of everything."

"Do you ever have meetings with them?"

"Many of them. I can have a good dialogue even though we disagree. But at least it's not threatening in any way. It certainly doesn't appear to be threatening."

"Do you ever get anywhere?"

"Of course not. Nowhere. Many of the physicians that are in the pro-life movement do not offer contraceptives to their patients, and I think they're wonderful physicians, but I think it's the women's choice. I listened to one of the older doctors talk about when abortion first came to Mississippi. When they first started the contraception program, particularly in the Delta, they did it to handle the growing population. Women learned that they could get an education while they weren't having babies and they could have a life while they weren't having 10 babies. And they didn't have to go to the fields every day and take 10 babies with them. It was a good time for education. Some of the abortion clinics were a result of that initiative. Now the Republicans want us to get away from abortion and contraception and that's detrimental to women."

"Pro-Life Mississippi says their mission is to close this clinic. What would happen if it closed?"

"We would be back in the dark ages. Women would not have contraception available. We pass out contraception daily. Condoms. Pills. We teach them about contraception. We teach them about STDs [sexually transmitted diseases]. One of the most recent studies I've seen says young people may be abstaining from breaking the hymen, but they are partaking in other risky behaviors, what they call different kinds of sex."

"Do you find that with your patients here?"

"Yes, unfortunately we do."

"Do you see any connection between the high poverty rate and the number of abortions in Mississippi?"

"I can speak a lot about poverty. I came from there. Certainly, it has a lot to do with it. That ties right back into education. It ties right back into health care. Poverty is directly related to that."

"What happens to the kids who have kids? Are there services in place to take care of these children?"

"Not a lot. The pro-life people will tell you that there are. They are working on some initiatives, but there aren't a lot of resources available anymore."

"The antichoice activists I've met said they felt empowered when George W. Bush took office in 2000. What changes did you see?"

"Protestors outside felt very powerful. You could see it in their stance. You could see it in their screams. You could see it in their numbers. National leadership makes a difference. The protestors are here every day."

"Does any one story stick out in your mind?"

"There are lots of stories. We get stories every day. When I was counseling, I got my first very, very young girl. She was 11 years old. She came in with her teddy bear and did not have a clue. And most unfortunately, her mother did not have a clue. She had been an early mother herself. And I said, 'How did this happen?' And she said, 'Well, she just came up pregnant.' And I knew that there was a lot of work here to be done in the way of education and awareness. It was powerful. She was just a baby."

"Do you know how she got pregnant?"

"She went back and started investigating and found out that the daughter had spent the night with her boyfriend's family, and some youngster had come in the room while the child was sleeping. I asked her about pressing charges and she refused. I'm sure that grew that young lady up in a hurry."

"Does that happen often?"

"It does. It happens a lot."

"On a personal level, what does this work mean to you?"

"It's important to me. I'm passionate about it. My son was a security guard here. My nieces work here. And I let them know and I let my boys know, there are choices. My family supports me because they love me. I'm kind of outspoken and overbearing, but I get lots of good support. I feel empowered by working here and being involved in these issues. I think women that don't feel empowered are missing out."

The clinic serves 60 women per week. The women out front are waiting for their first counseling session. In 1991, Mississippi passed a law requiring a woman seeking an abortion to first receive, in person, information about the fetus and alternatives to abortion. She must then wait 24 hours before having the procedure and return the following day for a checkup.

Betty said most patients don't like to talk to reporters. I could ask if anyone was interested in being interviewed, as long as I respect their privacy. Out of the five women in the waiting area, two agreed to briefly answer a few questions.

Keira, 27, got pregnant after recently going off the pill. She drove three hours to get to the clinic. Because she doesn't have friends in Jackson or money for a hotel, she has to drive back tomorrow for the procedure and then again on Wednesday for her checkup. If it weren't for this clinic, she and her partner would be in a "bad situation" because they can't afford to have a child. "People make mistakes," she says. "I couldn't deal with adoption. It's my choice. I don't think it should be a method of birth control, but it should be my choice."

"What message would you send to the protestors outside and politicians who are trying to shut down this clinic and overturn *Roe v. Wade*?" I asked.

"Come around and visit and see what's really going on. I understand you're trying to save a life, but it's my life, too. Why bring someone else into a bad situation? Old people are dying every day because they can't afford medication. It's really sad. Why don't you spend more time taking care of people who are suffering? Don't you care about them?"

Lisa, 23, says she's not ready to have a baby because she's a full-time student. "I'm not financially or mentally prepared," she says. "This is America, and we should have the freedom to decide if we have a kid or not. I want three or four kids one day, but I'm just not ready yet."

"What do you think of the protesters outside?"

"I don't put down people for their own opinion. They don't know my situation."

"Their ultimate goal is to shut down this clinic and make abortion illegal. What if they succeed?"

"If you get rid of this clinic, you'll have people killing themselves and their babies."

The woman who counseled Keira and Lisa has been here since 1996 after a long career at an adoption clinic. "That's when I realized the power white men had over women's bodies," she says. "I've also worked in Georgia, and the climate there is also hostile. It's a matter of perception and politics. Judicially speaking, I don't think the government should interfere with a woman's right to make a personal choice. I would like to push forth that point. When it comes to pregnancy, terminations, and stem cell research, it all comes back to personal choices in life. Any external forces should not even be considered. Society or the politics should not at all enter in that choice."

"What don't outsiders understand about what's going on here?"

"Society is setting itself up for major problems. We're already seeing it. We're raising a lot of ill-equipped young women. Society is not effectively educating them. These are real issues. The problems we're setting ourselves up for are health issues, such as venereal diseases and high rates of pregnancy. Often times, the protesters don't realize that our first line of defense is prevention education. We offer alternatives to termination. A lot of those protesters are totally unaware and ignorant. Let me be very candid. What protesters do is merely propaganda. It's not education, nor is it prevention. That's dangerous."

"Are you seeing a change in clientele?"

"We're seeing a lot more young incest victims. Women from their early teens all the way to their 40s. We still try to keep these issues as a taboo. For many years, young children have been victims, but people at the very top were the perpetrators. So here again, I do feel that society has done an injustice to children by not addressing the issues."

"What are your predictions if we continue down this path of abstinence-only and ignoring real issues? What's going to happen?"

"I do strongly see that unplanned pregnancies are not going to go away. We'll see more venereal diseases. What I'd like to see is education. I would love to see it from a religious perspective, but because of shame and blame and southern values, you're not going to see it at that level at all. Quite frankly, education is the key. Overall, America is ill-equipped to deal with this."

"What does this work mean to you personally?"

"It gives me great gratification to be in a position where I can objectively and neutrally inform women and empower them. It's not just termination. I'm pro-choice all the way, obviously, but I recognize there are some who don't support that. I want women to conceptualize that they don't have to be influenced by those external forces. They don't know what their issues are . . . to be able to assist a clinic to help women make informed choices if a woman comes in, and for some reason, I feel she is ill-equipped to make a choice of this nature, as a licensed practitioner, I will recommend she wait."

"Does that happen often?"

"No, not under my counseling. When it does, I advise a woman to pray and seek counseling, but more importantly, to make a sound judgment. Most of the protesters don't have the foggiest idea of what we do. When that client leaves, she's empowered. That's why I love working here. It's all about empowerment."

On our way out, the protesters were still handing out flyers, but they were no longer yelling, so I approached them. Kristin, a 23-year-old who introduced herself as a part-time tutor and seminary wife, said her goal is to give women an alternative. "They can get some free counseling and free help before they make their decision. They can also put their baby up for adoption. I've personally offered to take the baby if they don't want to take it."

"Do you have any kids?"

"No, but without question, I would adopt a baby, regardless of color."

"Why wait to adopt? There are plenty of kids who need a loving home right now," I said.

"The problem is, most Americans are adopting from China and

other countries because there aren't enough babies to adopt here. If women would stop killing their babies, there would be plenty of them to adopt."

"Over 518,000 children are in the foster care system waiting to be adopted here in the U.S."

"I'll have to look into that."

"What would you say to the women inside who believe you have the right to protest, and they have the right to choose?"

"It's also your right to choose not to have sex. Don't punish the baby for your choice. It's not the baby's fault."

"It's easy for you to say, don't have sex, but teenage pregnancy is a huge problem in this country. Do you work on prevention? How do you feel about birth control?"

"I strongly believe that no baby is an accident. Personally I don't take it. I'm opposed to it for myself."

"How do you feel about sex education?"

"That shouldn't be left up to the government. That's a parent's job."

"What if the parent's not available? Not every child has a healthy home life."

"I don't know. This is a difficult situation."

"Right, but if you say, 'Just say no,' where does that leave girls who need information?"

"If they're going to be educated, fine, but don't just tell them about birth control."

The older woman holding the Bible loudly chimed in with a biblical verse.

The next day, I met a 61-year-old male ob-gyn who moved to Jackson in 1984 after practicing in Berkeley, California, for 20 years. He left California because medical insurance was becoming too expensive. An outspoken, long-time pro-choice advocate, he said he wasn't prepared for the culture shock he experienced in Mississippi. "I'm the type of person who speaks his mind, and they don't like that. I had several things against me: I'm black, I was from the North, and I'm pro-choice."

"How did you deal with it?"

"By continuing to speak my mind and using my brain to outsmart them."

"Where does your belief system come from, especially your pro-choice views?"

"My pro-choice views come from my family values. My mother was a single parent. She always told me that a woman has the right to be a woman and have her own beliefs. That stuck with me. Being in San Francisco before *Roe v. Wade*, we saw people come in who had botched abortions. I promised myself then that if I had a chance to do something about it, I would. Seeing a lady come in with a 104-degree temperature made quite an impact."

The doctor ran a clinic on the Gulf Coast in Mississippi, but said antichoice activists did everything in their power to drive him out. They eventually succeeded, and he ended up in Jackson.

"Have you ever been threatened?"

"Back in the early '90s, Dr. John Britton and Dr. David Gunn were killed in Pensacola, Florida. After Dr. Britton got killed, I was under U.S. Marshall protection for 18 months. They picked me up from home, brought me to work, and I couldn't stay in my house. They took me to different places so I wasn't at the same place every time. I had to wear a bulletproof vest and, of course, I wore a helmet. Eighteen months out of my life."

"What impact did that have on you?"

"Of course, there was no social life. I went to work, then they'd take me out to eat and a different hotel every night. The only time I'd go home would be to get a change of clothes. If I wanted something at night, I'd have to call the marshals to come and get me."

"Are you married? Do you have a family?"

"I have a family, but I'm not married. I have a son in San Diego."

"What about your daily life here? Betty said she's always looking over her shoulder. Are you?"

"I'm always alert about my surroundings. I never take the same road to work. I never park in the same place. I don't leave my car out if I don't have to because someone can always slip a bomb under it or something like that. But mainly I don't get into a routine."

"Has anything happened?"

"No, nothing has happened yet. Most people don't know me because I stay pretty low key. I like to spend a lot of time at home. The less I'm in the public eye, the less I'm exposed to anything."

"Your work is your life."

"Yes, my work is my life. The thing that really bothers me is that the pro-choice people here don't stand up for their rights. These women in Mississippi won't say a word. You would think if they really cared, they would say something, but they don't. We don't have a strong pro-choice movement in Mississippi at all. Someone has to speak out and usually it's me or Betty."

"I've met a number of pro-choice women in Jackson, but they're not organized."

"We need more people to speak out. They shouldn't be afraid."

"What would you like to see from national pro-choice groups?"

"I want them to put more pressure on the Democratic Party to have a more unified and more aggressive stance against the restrictions they're putting on abortions. As long as we roll over, they will continue to chip away and before you know it, there won't be any more *Roe v. Wade*. The Democrats are so disorganized, and I've been a Democrat all my life, but they're embarrassing me."

"I don't think people living in pro-choice areas realize what it's really like here. We have occasional protesters in San Francisco, but it's nothing like this. Most people in the Bay Area have no idea how difficult the situation is here. The protesters can be very intimidating."

"They don't have the right to stand out there yelling at women and calling them murderers and baby killers. I've had some teens come in. Unfortunately, some of them have been raped by family members. These protesters don't know about their circumstances, so they have no right to yell at them. They don't know if these women were raped. They don't know if it was incest, especially little teenagers. It's been shown that if teenagers have a baby, a large percentage never finish school and have more than one child. What kind of message does that send? And the men out there. Men should not be on that picket line. They don't know what it's like to go through a birth, what it feels like to be pregnant, to wake up in the morning sick, to go through a C-section. They don't have a right to be out there."

"Do you ever talk to them?"

"I used to be confrontational, but it's like beating your head against the wall. They don't listen."

"Because you've had to face the antichoice movement for so long, how has it changed over the years?"

"They've gotten more aggressive, and the law has gotten much more tolerant of them. They have more rights than we do."

"Why is the situation in Mississippi so dire? The statistics about poverty, illiteracy, domestic violence, and teen pregnancy are so high here."

"That's one reason why politicians should spend time on how to reduce teen pregnancy, how to improve test scores instead of passing restrictive laws on abortion. They pass ridiculous laws, and they know they're unconstitutional. They're not improving education. They're not getting people out to the polls. They're not doing what they should do in this state. There's no leadership. I'm afraid this state will always be backward. It'll always be the good-old-boy system."

"How do you remain so optimistic?"

"Well, eventually the right side always prevails. And you always have to have someone in the wilderness speaking out. Eventually someone will hear you and something will be done."

"What's next for you?"

"When I retire, I'm going to travel, write poetry, and fish."

The next morning, I called all of the ob-gyns listed in the phone book and asked if they performed abortions. A few suggested I visit a "pregnancy center." Most angrily said no. The rest hung up.

Returning Home to Start a Movement

I was looking forward to meeting Donna Ladd, the only person I contacted before we left. She's the editor of the *Jackson Free Press*, the only alternative paper in Mississippi. We met on a Saturday afternoon, so the office was quiet but inviting, filled with loud colorful paintings, art-deco furniture, and political slogans.

Like so many Mississippians with big dreams and a strong desire to forget about the state's racist past, Donna, a self-taught journalist, left Neshoba County thinking she would never return. She started two newspapers and wrote for the *Village Voice* in Manhattan, and she helped launch the *Colorado Springs Independent* in Colorado, but after 18 years away from home, she got tired of preaching to the choir. "It's easy to sit somewhere and be among people who already agree with you and won't challenge you in any way," she says. "That's boring to me. It's not true activism."

Donna knew she'd find challenges in Jackson, but she didn't expect to find so many welcome surprises. "I was very inspired, really, because I started meeting so many progressive Mississippians who stayed here to fight the good fight while I was running like a chicken. I also met many who moved back. They weren't all connected necessarily, but they were here. I was kind of romanced by that. At the same time, they were having the confederate flag election. Two-thirds of the state voted to keep the symbol. All of that was happening at once in 2001, and here I am trying to do this social justice thing everywhere else. I really believe in the power of telling stories, and I realized I needed to go home and tell stories. I thought I would write a book about Neshoba County. 9/11 changed that for me. Long story short: we started this paper."

When Donna sits at her computer, she stares at a wall covered in pins, press passes, and bumper stickers with slogans like, "Doing my part to piss off the radical right." Even though she pisses them off, she says the paper has a strong conservative readership. "We get letters all the time. They really like our paper because it's positive about the community. Jackson gets beaten up on. We're trying to feed this renaissance that's happening here. They like the writing. If there's anything Mississippians can appreciate despite high levels of illiteracy, they like good writing. They like the idea of a thriving young community, even if they don't agree with it. They subscribe because their kids have moved away, and they're trying to get them to move back.

And in one case, it worked, and the young woman is now an intern of mine."

When Donna and her partner, Todd Stauffer, started the paper, their friends thought they were crazy. Who would advertise in an alternative newspaper in Jackson, Mississippi? "Some people signed on right away," she says.

On March 19, 2003, the paper ran a cover story called "13 Myths About War in Iraq." At that time, the *Jackson Free Press* was only a few months old, and with a few notable exceptions, most U.S. newspapers failed to ask critical questions about the Bush administration's justification for the invasion. Donna says the next issue brought in a slew of new advertisers.

"What we have found is a lot of local business owners here are very progressive-minded, but they were afraid of what their customers would think, which ties into the long-term attitude here. 'What will everyone else think if I'm not a Republican or a conservative?' So it's been a gradual process. Part of what our paper is doing is saying, 'You can be something else or you can question your own party.' Not everybody's as conservative as they think they are. I can't tell you how many times I'm out at a bar and a young white person walks up to me and says, 'I didn't know I could be anything but a Republican. I don't consider myself a Democrat, but I certainly don't consider myself conservative.' I respect what I call progressive Republicans."

In addition to hard-hitting journalism about local and state issues, the paper strives to create community and serves as a way to tell the rest of the country that Mississippians are "not all backward hicks." Because Donna has lived in other parts of the country, she's all too familiar with derogatory stereotypes and assumptions. "Progressives do have to watch the elitism, whether it's against red states or rednecks or these assumptions that everybody with a Southern accent is a certain way. I've dealt with this prejudice all my life. I left Mississippi thinking I was running out of here, going somewhere where nobody would be prejudiced. Then you get out there and discover all this bigotry because you're a white girl from Neshoba County and everybody assumes you're a bigot. I ran into that at graduate school at Columbia.

I ran into so much prejudice against Southerners. It was remarkable. Part of what we need to do is to learn to talk to each other."

She was on a roll. As she continued talking, she flung her blonde hair away from her face and raised her voice. Her accent became thicker. "I mean nobody's gonna get anywhere just dumping on the South. Especially since it's really not that different in the big picture. One of our big differences is that we can't keep all our best and brightest. That's really one of the big differences. And then for so many years in Mississippi we had the worst Jim Crow, the worst apartheid, and I believe we have to learn to admit those things."

"Do you feel like you're part of the dialogue the left is constantly having about the future? Do you ever hear from progressives in California or New York?" I ask.

"Not enough. We're sitting here building a progressive movement in Mississippi and in many ways, you're the first person who's asked me about it. I saw something recently on C-SPAN with a lot of representatives of progressive groups and such talking about the young vote. You know, it's in the Northeast, and everybody's from the Northeast, and I know some of these guys, and they're fine. I'm not criticizing that, but it's like, you guys are not talking to our people! Or listening to them, more importantly. They need to feel like they're invited. That's what we talk about with our paper here in Mississippi. Be welcoming. Learn a little hospitality, which we know something about down here. But don't just assume. Don't even get me started about how they run campaigns. It's just assumed that no political money comes in from Mississippi. Run ads here and at least *pretend* that our votes matter."

"You obviously feel like you're making a difference. At the end of the day, how do you feel?"

"Tired," she says laughing. "But good. I can't imagine doing anything else right now. It's mostly about the young people. We talk a lot about the inferiority complex in Mississippi, and it's bad, it's really bad. I often say that inferiority complex benefits the demagogues. So we celebrate our successes. Anything we can do to get young people to think that you're not from a place that you have to be ashamed of.

We're always battling people saying, 'Why do you have to talk about race, that's over and done with?' If our young people don't know how far we've come, they can't even be proud of that, much less understand what there is left to do. There is just nothing more fulfilling than being able to help facilitate that in some way and to help young Mississippians feel good about themselves and where they live. Kids are coming back from college in New York and they can't wait to get back to do something for the *Jackson Free Press*! They want to go deep into West Jackson and do stories, and we let them do that. Personally, there's nothing better than that. And we hear the feedback from it all the time. It's much more positive than negative. Much more. There's really nothing like it."

Conflicted Christians

By this point, we had been on the road for two months, and I desperately needed a mental break, so rather than return to the hotel to transcribe interviews or do research, we decided to spend the evening relaxing at the Cups Café in the Fondren District, one of the most diverse and progressive neighborhood in Jackson. It's full of art galleries, thrift shops, boutiques, a yoga studio ($15 a class), and an old-fashioned barbershop. I've even seen a few signs for "alternative spirituality." The café was packed with young people, mostly young white people. This side of Jackson didn't seem all that diverse. A 50-something man in the corner was reading the paper. A group of college students a few tables over were discussing a class project. A well-dressed 20-something guy was chatting away on his cell phone. Then I overheard two young fresh-faced women talking about Christianity.

I fidgeted with my bag and stared at the girls. "I think I'm going to talk to those girls. They're reading something about rich Christians and hunger."

"I thought you were going to take a night off."

"But I haven't spoken to that many young people yet."

I walked over and introduced myself. Corrie, 23, grew up in

Baldwin, Mississippi, and just graduated from college. She works as an administrative assistant in an architecture firm. Melody, also 23, grew up in northeast Tennessee and moved to Jackson for college in 1999. She works at a neighborhood Christian center that provides after-school tutoring.

I told them about all of my church experiences, both positive and negative. Melody said she can relate, but on a much deeper level because she grew up going to a very strict Southern Baptist church. "We had to wear skirts past our knees. It was so strict. It was all about right and wrong instead of just living your life trying to become closer to what Christ is about."

"What does being a Christian mean to you?" I asked.

"Being a Christian is seeking to reflect that which you believe," said Melody.

"For me, it's being salt and light wherever you are," added Corrie.

Melody and Corrie attend the Journey, a church "for people who don't like church." Several people mentioned this church over the past few days. "I also grew up in a Baptist church," said Corrie. "At the Journey, I feel accepted. You can question. You don't even have to believe in God. We don't do anything unless there's a purpose."

"You can question? It's so rare to hear churchgoers talk about questioning anything. So how does that shape your opinions?" I asked.

"I realized a lot after leaving my household," says Corrie. "I'm much more concerned about social justice and social injustice. I realize that government can't be our savior, but we can't sit back and just watch. Here's how it works. I don't know much, so I'm a Republican. I go to First Baptist, a very conservative church, so I'm a Republican. That makes me so tired and makes me want to go the opposite way. It's prominent in Mississippi because people aren't educated about politics."

"So how does your faith affect your politics?"

"I fall somewhere between conservatism and liberalism," said Corrie. My conservative views come from my faith, but the liberal ideas come from other things. World issues and poverty are being ignored. It's like you have to pick. I don't think you should have to pick."

"On what issues are you conservative?" I asked.

"I guess I'm conservative on gay marriage, but I really think that's because of my faith," said Melody. "I'm trying to base my opinions on the Bible and the teachings of Christ. I can't think of another example, but on the race issue, I'm very liberal even though I grew up on . . . I don't even want to say the conservative side; I would say the racist side. It's really issue by issue, and that's the way politics needs to start moving."

"I vote for both parties," said Corrie. "But we think more than the older generation. We analyze things more. Even if we don't agree with you, we'll respect you more if you raise the issue. We like to think about issues. We want progress and we want change, but most Republicans I know won't do the dirty work and get in there. At least the Democrats are willing to try."

"I agree," added Melody. "I feel like my parents' generation is . . . we're Republican for life. They don't even know who's running, but they'll vote Republican. I'm hoping it's changing."

"What issues are most important to you?"

"Economics," said Melody forcefully. "We talk about international relationships all the time. I want politicians to talk about poverty in third world countries. What does the U.S. do to hold these countries down? When we start talking about what we're going to do to fix a problem, we end up westernizing and hurting the countries. That's very important to me. Things like fair trade are more important than gay marriage."

"So who's dealing with that?" I asked.

"That's one issue where I would not side with Republicans," said Melody. "I'd have to say Democrats or maybe the Green Party. I'm not satisfied with the way any of them are addressing it. We're so concerned with America. Of course, it's the American government, but at the same time, come on, everyone else in the world is sick of hearing about America and so am I. I'm sick and tired of it. There are so many issues that aren't being talked about that young people want to hear about. Just be honest. Young people respect the truth. We are craving honesty and consistency."

Why don't we ever hear voices like these in the national conversation about politics? Here were two young, compassionate women, raised in conservative Baptist families, and they're craving substance and real information. They actually care about what goes on in the rest of the world, and they're sick and tired of celebrity-driven media.

I asked Corrie what issue she cares most about.

"The issue that comes up in my head over and over is that we really are just consumed with ourselves and consumed with consuming," she said. "We really need to have a conversation about our me, me, me society and overconsumption."

It was getting late and I was exhausted, but I had to ask them about abortion before I left.

"I'm anti-abortion, but I'm also against people standing on the street screaming at women," said Melody.

"Do you think abortion should be illegal?"

"I might have to say yes, but I'm kind of undecided. I can't just say yes or no. There are things you really can't dictate. The government should stay out of your business as much as possible. I'm anti-abortion in the sense that I don't believe in killing, but on the other hand, I believe government should stay out of your business. As a Christian, you have to love people regardless of the decisions they make. I went to Christian school before high school, and if you got pregnant, you got kicked out. That was the rule. I don't really think that shows Christian love if you pretty much get hidden and kicked out."

"Did that happen?"

"Yeah, it happened several times while I was there."

"Did the school talk to the students about it?"

"It's a very quiet thing. It's always hush-hush, and that's how it was in church, too."

Corrie was nodding her head. "This is where the churches lose these girls. If the girls get pregnant and have an abortion, they're pushed away, and if they get pregnant and have the baby, they're pushed away. It's a lose-lose situation, but the churches will never admit that."

The café was about to close, so we stood up and said our good-byes. "What's next for you two?" I asked.

"I've been thinking about that a lot," said Melody. "Do I go to these poor countries and try to make a difference or do I volunteer in West Jackson and go across the tracks?"

"I'm not sure," said Corrie. "I want to do my part to help eradicate poverty."

Segregated Sundays

It was our last Sunday in Jackson before heading to the Delta, so I decided to attend three church services. All in one day. Ryan could no longer handle the Southern church experience, so he usually dropped me off and went to a coffee shop or waited in the parking lot "just in case."

Based on the conversations and experiences I'd had so far, Mississippi churches, like most houses of worship in the South, are segregated. Some churches left me feeling like a hopeless sinner trapped in a dark confession box, while others, actually very few, left me feeling inspired and hopeful. When I spoke to people after the services, the question I was constantly asked was not, "Do you go to church?" but rather, "What church do you go to?" After telling a woman at a predominantly black church in Jackson that most people I know don't go to church, she half-jokingly asked, "What do San Franciscans do on Sundays?"

I had a pleasant experience at St. Andrew's Episcopal, a predominantly white church that focuses on the importance of helping the poor and doing outreach. I hadn't heard references to the poor since I attended services at St. Andrew's Presbyterian Church in Austin, Texas.

Across town, at Anderson United Methodist, a black church with between 900 and 1,200 attendees on Sundays, I found a slew of Democrats who oppose abortion and gay marriage, but say they shouldn't be political issues. After the service, Pastor Joe May told me that his congregants are more concerned with social and economic justice. If it weren't for churches, he said, the civil rights movement never would have happened. "Churches were the only things we had. We didn't have social clubs. We didn't have country clubs. Democrats did nothing for black people in Mississippi. It was up to the churches to fight for equal rights and justice. Democrats haven't done us a whole lot of good, but it was the dogs and the hoses being let loose on black kids in Montgomery that really challenged and championed change. It wasn't Democrats who did that; it was folks who said, 'Hey that's wrong.'"

Pastor May said the rise of the megachurches that focus on prosperity and self-help while ignoring the call to serve the poor is a disturbing trend. "Churches should not become country clubs for saints, but hospitals for sinners. These churches are providing for their members."

I unknowingly went to one of those churches next. First Baptist Church had a special evening service in honor of Independence Day called, "Let Freedom Ring." The massive cathedral was filled with hanging chandeliers and flag-waving families wearing red, white, and blue. It was a sea of red, white, and blue. By the time I made it up to the balcony and took one of the few remaining seats, I was feeling dizzy. A 30-piece orchestra and 200-person choir began performing just as I sat down. The female singers were wearing red blazers and black pants, and the males were in black suits. The song list included "America, I Can Still Hear Your Song," "Stars and Stripes," "Salute to the Armed Forces,'" and "I Believe in America." The place was so big and ostentatious, it could pass for an opera house.

A large U.S. flag hung from the ceiling directly behind the choir and another six hung from poles, three on each side of the stage. Two large video screens were on each side of the stage flashing images of the Statue of Liberty and the official seals of the U.S. Navy, Air Force, and Marines. Pastor Stan Buckley then took the stage to recognize navy, air force, and marine veterans, all in uniform. They stayed on stage to watch a reenactment of the famous photo of five soldiers planting an American flag in the sands of Iwo Jima. As if on cue, the man sitting to my left practically jumped out of his chair and the crowd went wild.

Thomas Hamill, author of *Escape in Iraq: The Thomas Hamill Story,* joined Pastor Buckley on stage to talk about his kidnapping

ordeal in Iraq. Hamill was a truck driver working for Halliburton subsidiary Kellogg Brown & Root (KBR) when his convoy was attacked
on April 9, 2004. He was held for three weeks. "This isn't about the
weapons of mass destruction," he said with pride. "It's about the kids.
Hopefully they'll grow up to be free." After he thanked President
Bush for "having the courage to spread freedom to Iraq," the crowd
gave Hamill a standing ovation. I wanted to ask my neighbors if I was
in the right place. Was this a church service or a pro-war military celebration? After the service, I asked the man sitting next to me if this
was a typical service. "It was probably a one-time thing for the Fourth
of July, but I can't say for sure because I'm not a regular. I hop around
from church to church. I come here on occasion 'cause there's lots of
activities goin' on," he said.

"I haven't met anyone who goes to different churches. What are the
main differences?" I asked.

"Attitude. Some churches think it's their way or the highway."

"How does going to church shape your politics?"

"I think we have freedom of religion. I'd be wary of someone who
tells me, 'This is how you have to live.' God loves everyone."

I'm assuming he's a Republican, but that answer makes me think
otherwise. "Do you mind me asking if you're a Democrat or a
Republican?"

"I'm a Democrat, but I'm for our country. I'd vote for a yellow dog
before I'd vote for a Republican."

I was utterly confused. Unfortunately, I didn't have time to ask him
about the statements about Iraq because people were filing out, and
he wanted to get in line for the free ice cream downstairs, but I had to
ask him one more question. "This church is full of people who seem
to be fairly well off. The services probably cost a lot, and the church
itself seems so upscale. Do the big churches around here reach out to
the poor?"

"Well, we're supposed to reach out and help the less fortunate, but
it doesn't seem to be a focus. In two weeks, I'm going to Honduras to
volunteer."

"I also noticed that it's very white. Not very diverse."

"Yeah, I always say, 'It's segregated on Sunday mornings.'"

"Do you always go to church?"

"If I don't go, I feel like I missed something."

He was on a mission for ice cream, so I headed out to the lobby area and found a long line of patriots waiting for Hamill to sign their books. I talked to people about why they attend this church, and the answer I heard over and over again was the same. "It offers something for everyone." Depending on your age and interest, you can attend children's ministry, college ministry, women's Bible study, singles events, international mission trips, and day camps. All you need can be found at church.

Then I spotted Pastor Buckley. A clean-cut man wearing a nicely pressed suit, he was surrounded by admiring congregants. I made my way through the circle, and he agreed to step aside and answer a few questions. Because he was in high demand, I didn't have much time, so I jumped right in.

"Do you bring politics into regular church services?"

"We have two former governors, a Supreme Court justice, and lots of other state and federal officials in our church. But our church itself . . . we don't focus on politics. We would never try to endorse a political candidate. That's not our focus. Our focus is to proclaim the Gospel. We have people of all political persuasions here. As a church, we don't ever try to push any type of political agenda, particularly from the pulpit. I would never do that, but I will speak on social issues certainly."

"Like what?"

"Abortion. Not what I think, but what I believe Scripture says about abortion."

"Was this an unusual event tonight? Or do you often talk about the war, the troops, and supporting President Bush?"

"This was our annual July Fourth presentation. It's a pretty conservative group, obviously, here in the South. We don't talk about that every week. Our main issue is not to support President Bush. I think Tommy Hamill, who was a guest speaker, said something about President Bush. You would never hear anyone from our pulpit say anything about politics or a candidate other than to pray for him, which Scripture tells us to do. The reality is, what we believe Scripture teaches on issues such as abortion would tend to fall in line with the Republican platform, but if it was a Democrat, that'd be fine too."

"Did you vote for Bush?"

"Oh, certainly."

I asked him to explain why so many religious people who call themselves "pro-life" are also pro–death penalty and pro-war.

"I believe Scripture addresses that. Scripture, I believe, allows for the death penalty. In fact, in Romans chapter 13, Paul said it's the government's responsibility to wield the sword against evildoers. Not for me to do it. Not for you to do it. But that's the role of government. I know you get into all those issues of who usually gets the death penalty based on who they killed and race issues, but Sripture allows for it. If Jesus had said, 'No death penalty,' guess what I would be? I would be no death penalty."

"What about the war?"

"If we believe that they are harboring terrorists or doing something that can bring us harm, that's the big debate. Were they really? Everybody agrees on the Afghanistan issue because that's where the Taliban was. This one is a little more difficult. There were no weapons of mass destruction. Was Hussein a great guy? No. Was he destroying people? Yes. Did Bush know there were no weapons of mass destruction? Well, if he didn't, that's highly problematic. Most people around here would probably say we want to support the troops regardless. Because they like him on the social issues, they want to give him the benefit of the doubt on this. Because he's your guy. You want to give him the benefit of the doubt."

Simple enough. "So I assume you've heard of the Downing Street Memo?"

"Sure, sure."

"So you're open to considering that Bush didn't tell us the truth about the war?"

"Certainly. Certainly. I want to be objective about that. Either he did or he didn't. I just haven't been convinced yet. I'm open to being convinced."

"Where do you get your news?"

"I'm a voracious reader."

"Do you have any favorite sources?"

"I'm a fan of *Fox News* obviously, but I read our statewide newspaper. I go from *USA Today* to *Fox News* to more conservative radio such as American Family Radio."

"How many members does this church have?"

"Between 8,000 and 9,000. They don't all show up, obviously, every week."

"How many people does the church seat per service?"

"About 3,000. This is extraordinary. Back in 1989, they did a $22 million renovation and expanded it tremendously. Across the way, there's a $14 million 160,000-square-foot Christian Life Center complete with basketball courts, racquetball, a three-story climbing wall, workout facilities, and 40-something aerobics classes each week. We have a 13-person counseling organization. We have two full-time PhD Christian counselors on staff, plus about 10 or 11 part-timers. They're all certified by the state."

"Counseling for individuals?"

"Drug, alcohol, marital. Any subject that you can imagine. Any need you would have, this church would hope to meet it regardless. We just finished a brand-new multipurpose building complete with a gymnasium and a full-time kitchen. We have six people who work full time down there, so we're committed to being down there. This church elected to stay downtown and be a downtown church whereas most leave and go out to the suburbs. We have a half-a-million-dollar budget every year, just for that alone. When we decided to build this $14 million facility over here for our Christian Life Center, the pastor before me had the wisdom to say, 'If we're going to do that, we're going to dump a million downtown.' We go all over the world. We hit every continent. We hit Antarctica this past year on mission trips. We send 400 to 500 of our own people out. I led a team of 29 down to

Trinidad. We took two dentists and dental students and did all kinds of dental work and worship services. We go to Africa, Asia, you name it. We go all over the world doing mission work with people of all political persuasions."

"Where does your funding come from?"

"Our people give. We don't do fundraising. This just happens to be, for whatever reason, an affluent church. But these are people who use what they've been given for kingdom purposes, which is exciting. The offering today was probably $120,000. We teach to give 10 percent of your income. Some give a lot more than that."

Did I hear him correctly? "$120,000? For one Sunday?"

"Yes, that's about average."

"Because we're so focused on the war, we rarely address the issue of poverty, which is a huge problem. Do you think it's the church's responsibility to address that problem rather than the government's?"

"The church has a responsibility and we have neglected that. The church is focused on evangelism and not those social issues of feeding the poor. We've been commanded to look after the poor, but we've dropped the ball. I don't think it has anything to do with the war. This country has enough resources and our churches have enough resources. We're just not doing it."

At that point, Ryan ran in, sweaty and disheveled. His hair was a mess. "We need to leave."

"Excuse me," I said to the pastor.

Ryan grabbed my hand and pulled me toward the door. "What happened to you?"

"I was putting articles about veterans on cars and the security guards started chasing me. We need to leave now."

"I was interviewing the pastor about poverty!"

"Sorry, I got bored."

The pastor was mobbed by fans, so we took off. On our way to the van, I saw white sheets of paper on car windshields. It was probably the first time First Baptist churchgoers had ever been flyered.

Exploring the Mississippi Delta

Just when we would start to feel comfortable in a new city and become friendly with the locals, it was time to say good-bye. We stayed
in Jackson longer than expected because we found such a diverse,
friendly, and warm group of people to interview, including an older
couple (he's a conservative, she's a liberal) who had us over for dinner
a few times, and a number of pro-choice Republican and Democratic
women who invited us into their homes with lemonade and cookies
on the table. I can finally say I've experienced Southern hospitality.

On our way to the Delta, I realized that I was spending too much
time with my head down transcribing interviews onto my laptop
while Ryan drove, so I decided to put the computer in its case and
take in the landscape. By that time, we were in Yazoo City (population 14,500), "Gateway to the Delta!"

The poverty in the Delta, the poorest region in the poorest state
in the country, was overwhelming. We drove slowly by demolished
buildings on the verge of crumbling, piles of garbage and old tires in
the front yards of abandoned shacks, and a downtown that looked
like it could transform into a ghost town at any second. Store after
store was empty and boarded up. We parked downtown on S. Main
Street, and I decided to go into the Black & White Store. On display in the store window were pastel-colored bras and underwear,
"God Bless America" flag T-shirts, a variety of silver and pearly white
high-heeled shoes, and a mannequin wearing a bright pink blazer
and matching floral skirt. Her left arm looked like it had been sliced
off, just below the elbow. Inside, I found a random mix of children's,
men's, and women's clothing.

Sixty-four-year-old James Chisolm is the proud owner of the Black
& White Store. A soft-spoken man wearing round eyeglasses and a
blue polo shirt with two bass fish jumping out of his left breast pocket,
he says he's barely getting by because the economy is in such bad shape
and people aren't shopping. "I live paycheck to paycheck. This town
used to be an oil field. Big families back in them days, so you'll see
a lot of big homes. Then Mississippi Chemical came along. That's a

fertilizer plant. That held the town together with good jobs. Then it started going down about 10 years ago. We can't seem to get any industry here now. It's just like all the other small towns. The jobs went overseas."

"What message would you send to politicians about the realities you're facing?"

"We need more jobs. Put more people to work. Get the war finished up and get our soldiers back home. That would help some. We had garment factories around here making uniforms. All of them are gone. If it wasn't for the health industry and nursing, there wouldn't be any jobs for the ladies. Now we need something for the men. A lot of young men don't have jobs. NAFTA (North America Free Trade Agreement) has hurt us real bad."

James says the whites in Yazoo tend to vote Republican, and the blacks tend to vote Democratic. James is a white Republican.

"Do you think the Republican Party is doing enough to address these issues?"

"My first boss always told me, 'Jimmy, we always do better when a Democrat is in office.' He never did explain it to me. It seems that way. I don't know if people are more relaxed and spend more money or what, but it's always been that way. When a Democrat is in office, our sales are always better."

"But you still vote Republican?"

"Well, yeah. I've asked myself that, too," he says laughing. "They need to do more. When I started working here, we had a shoe plant. We need jobs. We're not goin' to be trained to do anything. I look at my son and my grandkids and think about health insurance. They can't make it. People out here are workin' at McDonald's for minimum wage. How they goin' to make it on that?"

"How do you feel about minimum wage as a business owner? The Republican Party says we can't raise wages because people like you will be driven out of business."

"I disagree. Every time minimum wage goes up, our sales go up. They got a little more money to spend. I know what you're talking about. I don't know why they keep sayin' that. I remember when it first went up from $1 to $1.25 in 1963. I made $5. The women made $4. My boss was frightened. When it went up, he was so surprised. His sales went up the first year. Three years later, it went up and his sales went up. It caused some inflation. Our blue jeans went up from $4.99 to $6.99, but still, it gave more people more money."

A few customers had questions, so I thanked James for his time. He recommended we drive around the neighborhood before we took off. "You'll see people just hangin' around and sittin' on porches. There are no jobs. People around here want to work."

After we walked out, I felt guilty for not buying anything.

As I was about to hop in the van, I noticed a hip-looking store-front called Corner Boy Records. "One more interview! I promise, this will be quick." I walked in and gave the young African American guy behind the desk my usual spiel. Before I could finish, he asked me to take a seat. The majority of the people I was meeting had never been interviewed before, and it can take a while before they feel comfortable. I didn't have that problem with 24-year-old Danieal Powell. He's the director of operations at Corner Boy, which he describes as a hip-hop label working to get young kids off the streets by giving them something to believe in. The label works with four artists and 22 interns. "One of our interns was smoking pot," he says. "He came to us and said, 'I need something do.' So we hired him to be an intern."

Danieal is also a Gospel artist and head of the local youth community choir. He's the kind of guy a town like Yazoo City can't afford to lose. He says he's trying to do what he can to modernize the city and give kids a reason to get involved and stay out of trouble, but it's an uphill battle. "I work with some of these children and see dysfunctional problems. There's problems with domestic violence. Just about anything you think of, and we don't have any funds for that. Some of these interns have problems. Interns bring their lunches with them, but some of them can't afford food, so we have to feed them and pay for it out of our pockets. They need something to do, so we open our doors for them so they won't go out there and do something crazy."

Danieal says there are very few extracurricular activities in the area and to make things worse, the town is still segregated. "You have some of the white kids in the Manchester area going to private school with a lot of activities. The public school system, which is predominantly black, doesn't have much. We have parades and marching bands, but it's still segregated. When there's a carnival, you might see white people. When there's a parade at Christmas, there's a nice turnout."

"Schools are pretty segregated?"

"Yes. As I grew older, I always wondered why there weren't any white kids in my schools. Now that I've graduated from high school and college, working on my master's degree, I understand."

"What about neighborhoods?"

"Oh, god. For us, we're trying to get rid of that. Some of these white kids come to our door and say, 'Help me, please.' Our web designer is a white guy. We have on the street team a guy who's Filipino and Mexican. We are leaders with a big vision. This place will never be segregated."

"What about the economy? I just spoke with the man who owns the department store across the street, and he said there are no jobs. Other than moving to a bigger town, what options do you have?"

"This is so sad to say, but the chemical plant provided jobs, but they went bankrupt. We may not have a chance. We might have to work two dead-end jobs and that's not fair. My grandma shouldn't still be driving and working. That's dangerous! I'm scared of going into the world. We want to know, what's really going on? But we don't say anything."

"Why don't you say anything? Do you ever organize to demand better education or after-school programs?"

"I guess I need to do more and know more. Before I start going out, I need to do research."

"Sounds like you know a lot."

"I vote, but my guy never wins."

"So you're a Democrat?"

"Yeah," he said, laughing.

"What makes you a Democrat?"

"I'm for the people. Whatever it is that I need to do to help someone along the way, I do that. But it's hard when so many people are apathetic. My mom is apathetic. She don't vote. My sister don't vote. She's 29. She started voting, but things are so screwed up, so she don't vote. And that's sad."

"What would it take to get your sister to vote again?"

"My sister has two children. She's looking for a job, but she can't find one. A lot of people are looking for jobs, but the doors are always slammed. We're judged based on how we look. I've never committed a crime, but I'm treated like a criminal. My sister doesn't have a voice. People don't feel like they have a voice. But I'll keep doin' what I can."

Later that night, I was reading statistics about poverty, and I couldn't stop thinking about the church that brings in $120,000 every Sunday. And what about Danieal and the passion he has for the people struggling to survive in this impoverished community? As we searched for a hotel, we passed abandoned homes and decrepit buildings, a broken-down Ford with cobwebs on the rearview mirrors, and a faded American flag hanging above a rocking chair on the porch of what looked like an abandoned home. How does Danieal find hope surrounded by so much poverty and despair? According to the latest U.S. Census data, 37 million Americans (12.7 percent) live in poverty, but for most of us, it's hidden and easy to avoid. Since 2001, that number has increased by 5.4 million. On any given night in the United States, anywhere from 700,000 to 2 million people are homeless, according to the National Law Center on Homelessness and Poverty.

The next day, we hopped on Highway 149, and Ryan asked for the map. He loves maps. I prefer asking for directions. It's a good way to meet people and learn about hidden treasures or restaurants with vegetarian options. We were heading toward Greenville, so we had a destination in mind, but we were in no hurry to get there. I wanted to drive and get lost. And that's exactly what happened. On Highway 16, there are no convenience stores or warning signs like, "No Gas for 30 Miles." You're pretty much on your own.

After 40 minutes of driving through vast expanses of lush green farmland, we stumbled upon Lake George Grocery, a store and small restaurant in Holly Bluff (population 142), the smallest town we'd found so far, so we stopped in to escape the heat and get a drink. Gale and Chuck Perry run the restaurant and a hunting business to supplement their income. That explains all the animals nailed to the wall. I couldn't quite figure out how they got the bobcat up there, but I was afraid to ask. "A duck hunt is $350 per person per morning," says Chuck, a heavyset man wearing a bright green T-shirt, eyeglasses, and a brimmed wicker hat. "Duck huntin' is a rich man's sport. They'd rather pay a poor man like me to take them out there and clean their shoes when they come back. If the price is right, I'll do it. I've done real well, but lately the business isn't so good. Poor people hunt for food and for the family. We eat a lot of deer meat. That's not a rich man's sport."

Chuck and Gale, both in their late 40s, were born and raised in Holly Bluff, also known as their village. They don't have a mayor, school system, fire department, or police force. It's all 30 miles away. "It's been like that all my life. Same little town. One street. No stop light. Don't blink your eyes or you'll miss it," says Chuck, laughing softly. "Everybody's close," adds Gale. "There's not much crime, it's away from city life. If anything happens, everybody's there and ready to support you."

"What's changed over the years?" I ask.

Chuck removes his wicker hat and rubs the sweat off his head. "You don't have nothin' but big farmers, you know, corporate farmers. I call myself a gardener, you know. Used to be 70, 80 farmers here; now it's seven or eight. The average farm now has 15,000 to 20,000 acres, so it's work. I used to do all my huntin' with my son. I have to do it as a business now."

"I mostly work," says Gale, bringing over a basket of piping hot French fries. "I'm married to the store."

Chuck and Gale seem to take pride in the cotton, corn, soybeans, peanuts, and sweet potatoes their tiny town produces, but they've clearly been hit hard by the corporate takeover of farming and agriculture. I still can't tell where they stand politically. They farm. They hunt. And their restaurant is filled with dead animals on the walls. Conventional wisdom would say they're Republicans. Conventional wisdom would be wrong.

"I vote for Democrats," says Chuck.

"I was raised Democrat, so I vote Democrat," adds Gale.

I ask Chuck why he's a Democrat.

"I just think there's too much corporate stuff goin' on."

"Have things changed much since 2000?" I ask.

"For the big man, yeah. They're gettin' bigger. They're takin' over," says Chuck matter-of-factly. "The small man don't have a place no more. I've seen it in my lifetime. It's not what you know, it's who you know, and they'll buy up all the land they can."

As a member of the National Rifle Association (NRA), Chuck says the right to bear arms is an important issue, but he doesn't believe the talk he constantly hears in the news and from friends about Democrats wanting to take away his guns. He's more interested in farm subsidies and the unequal power structure between corporate farmers and small farmers. "A man like me can't afford to buy equipment, and all these corporate farmers get all the subsidies. They're taking a government handout more than anybody. It used to be all of ours. But it's a corporate world, and the little man don't have a place."

"There's not much demand for workers anymore because they have the bigger tractors and machines to do the work," says Gale.

"I have a fairly decent yield, but I don't have enough acres to reap the benefit if something goes wrong, like a drought. The government should look out for the little man instead of the big man," says Chuck. "This country was built on small farmers. Small farmers used to support a family of five. These days, you don't see kids around here getting married. You know why? They're makin' minimum wage. They can't afford to get married. They either move to a big town or they make no money. Politicians need to look at rural areas. They [the government] need to get the corporations out of the farming business. But I think it's too late. What they're [corporate farmers] not rentin', they're buyin'."

With that, Chuck got up and said he had to get back to work. "You're welcome to stay for dinner and try some freshly caught deer meat," he said. Ryan smiled and licked his lips. I thought of Bambi. Chuck said if we needed more interviews, he would be happy to introduce us to the regulars who come in for dinner. I was tempted to stay, but we were a few hours from the next major town on the map. I wanted to spend some more time getting lost; but with no signs on the road, I didn't want to drive in the dark. We politely declined. Then Chuck noticed my "Veggie Heaven" T-shirt. "Oh, you don't eat meat! We could throw on another order of fries," he said with a chuckle. On our way out, a number of older couples who arrived for an early dinner told us to avoid Greenville. We've heard this a few times already. "It's dangerous."

We drove with the windows down for more than an hour on open flat roads that went on for as far as the eye could see. There was hardly anyone on the road, the sun was shining, and Ryan was blaring tunes from the famous Delta bluesman Robert Johnson. I got to thinking about all the people we met in Jackson who've never driven through the Delta. I immediately fell in love with the place.

As we slowly drove through small towns along Highway 61, people sitting on their front porches waved and smiled. We decided to pass through Greenville (population 41,633), the "Heart and Soul of the Delta," and then head to Rosedale, the city Robert Johnson sang about in "Traveling Riverside Blues": "Lord, I'm goin' to Rosedale, gon' take my rider by my side. We can still barrelhouse baby, on the riverside."

A little over an hour later, we arrived in Rosedale, "The Delta City of Brotherly Love." The median income of families living in this small town is $17,955. On the way, we passed a few small churches, American flags lining various sections of the empty highway, and even more friendly, waving townspeople. After passing another set of boarded-up shops and abandoned homes, we decided to stop and take a photo of the White Front Cafe: Joe's Hot Tamale Place, a white wood-framed restaurant that looked like it used to be a house with three small, round, concrete steps leading to the front door.

A man walking in said, "Come on in. It's open." I was hungry and Ryan always has an appetite, so we turned off the van, grabbed our stuff, and followed him in. A woman was busy preparing hot tamales steamed in cornhusks on the stove behind the counter, the only item on the menu. I was disappointed to learn that all of the tamales were filled with beef. Ryan excitedly ordered three, and I searched my bag for granola. I found crumbs. I wanted to leave and search for something to eat, but 60-year-old Johnny Todd, the man who invited us in, asked us to join him and his friend, 50-year-old James Boban. We took them up on their offer and asked about all the empty storefronts.

"It's been that way for 10 years or more," said James. "A lot of major industries have left. When they close doors, no one else is coming to replace them. The biggest economic boost for the state was the Nissan plant that opened. It created numerous jobs in Madison County and the surrounding areas, but gaming replaced employment. When gaming came in, it was king for a long time, but plants are closing on a monthly basis."

"We are in need of something to replace farming," added Johnny. "We haven't found anything yet that has made a difference. We need jobs. Job training. Housing is OK. Young people leave because they can't find jobs. People want to work."

"What jobs are available?"

"A lot of people work out of town," said Johnny. "Most of the income in this community is transfer payments from the government. That's been that way for the last 25 or 30 years. We don't have any large employers. The largest employer we had closed down a few years ago. We have teachers and people working at the casino, but a lot of people are unemployed. The government will have to become more involved in the lives of the poor. You can't have a country with 285 million and expect people to take care of their needs without jobs."

"Jobs bring money, economic growth, and people feel a lot better about themselves with a little money in their pockets. It's bad here," added James. "During the Clinton administration, I must say, there was more money in circulation. Over the past eight years, there hasn't been much money circulating. The price of gas skyrocketed, and the price of other things has skyrocketed, but wages haven't gone up."

"What was Rosedale like before jobs started disappearing?"

"I'm told by older people that Rosedale was open 24 hours a day. Rosedale was a hub," said Johnny. "People would spend their weekends here going to eat, listening to music. It was told to me a long time ago during the Ronald Reagan era, each town was receiving revenue sharing to survive. Those programs were cut and those towns never recovered. On top of that, plants started laying people off and closing. When that happened, people moved. Then you lose your tax base. And when you lose your tax base, the city virtually dries up. Once upon a time, every boarded-up building that you see was thriving. The town turned into a ghost town. But it don't bother me. Crime is low. But not every town is as lucky. Greenville is full of crime. I'm afraid to go in a convenience store after dark. If I pull up and no one is around, I leave."

"That's what we've been told. 'Don't go to Greenville. It's dangerous,'" said Ryan.

"You should fill your tank and have everything you need before nine p.m. Greenville is a large city. In Rosedale, everybody knows everybody."

"And everybody waves," I said.

"That's Rosedale."

Questioning My Pastor

The next morning, I went down to our hotel's front desk and got to talking about segregated churches with the young African American clerk. "That's what we're used to ma'am," he said. "After a while, you forget about it." It was Sunday, so I asked him for a church recommendation. He grabbed a binder filled with church schedules and suggested we go to an early afternoon service at a nearby Baptist church. I assumed he was sending me to a black church, so Ryan decided to join me because he hadn't been to one yet.

We arrived a few minutes late and were surprised to walk into a white church of mostly senior citizens in their Sunday best. Their outfits were impeccable, not a hair was out of place, and their makeup was heavily applied, especially on the older women. The kids were waving small American flags. Several people smiled and nodded as we found just enough space for two in a pew near the back of the traditional church.

We were trying to squeeze our huge backpacks near our feet without making too much noise, and all of a sudden the pastor raised his voice and began making vitriolic statements about Muslims. "When any type of nation would say, 'Kill all the men and kill all the women and kill all the children,' that don't seem very fair to me to kill the little children. It don't seem very fair to me to kill all the women, but you know something, from the day these children were born, they were told to hate the Jews."

This was not what I had in mind. "The Jews were nothing but dogs. If you had a chance, kill a Jew. It's the best thing you can do. The only good Jew is a dead Jew. So that child, if he raises up, what do you think's gonna happen if he gets to a position of power and influence. What's gonna happen?"

I looked around at the expressionless faces in the room, wondering what they were thinking. Ryan looked horrified and took a deep breath. I was afraid he was either going to stand up and tell the guy off or walk out in a fury, so I squeezed his arm.

The preacher went on to slam the Supreme Court and judges across the country for ruling against school prayer and the public display of the Ten Commandments on government property.

"What happens when God's presence is removed? Every kind of evil can come in. When prayer in school was removed, *Roe v. Wade* took its place. You had homosexuality, which nobody in this room would imagine would reach the magnitude it has in this nation, but folks, it has, hasn't it?" Silence. I wondered if people were even allowed to move their heads or nod. Other than a few coughs, there was no smiling, no nodding, no facial expressions showing solidarity, nothing.

I couldn't believe what came next. "Your children will be given over to murderers. Twenty percent of U.S. children live in poverty. The U.S. ranks last in child welfare, according to Annie E. Casey. Gannett reports three children a day die from child abuse. We see mothers killing their children. In our land, children are being turned over to the slayer. Nearly 5 percent of all murders are children. The worst sin is child molestation. Abusing a child sexually and damaging them. To me, that's the worst one. I don't understand that."

The kids I could see looked frightened, and they were no longer waving their flags. I looked at the woman to my right with a shocked and confused look on my face. She nervously smiled and looked away.

Separation of church and state was next. "Whatever separation between church and state there may be, we must pray that a separation will not extend to a separation between state and God. Both the church and the state must be subject to Him and His law or we will perish as a nation." And on a positive closing note, he said, "I love the Lord and I love this land. I really am glad that I'm American. I wouldn't want to be anything else. And to be a Christian American— I can't think of a better combination."

Amen.

And with that, the service was over. Ryan quickly stood up and said, "Unbelievable. I'll be right back." Before I could ask him where he was going, he took off. The woman to my right grabbed my hand and said, "Very nice of you to come." A petite woman with rosy cheeks, who looked to be in her 70s, she was wearing short white gloves, a beautifully tailored yellow skirt and matching blazer, and pearls. She must have spent all morning on her perfectly coiffed shiny white-gray hair and makeup. "Thank you," I said nervously. "I must admit. This service wasn't very uplifting. Is it always this negative?"

She looked over her shoulder, turned back, and whispered, "I know what you mean. I'm fed up with it. I'm real sorry if it made you uncomfortable."

What?

"Can I ask you a few questions? I'm from San Francisco and I'm traveling around the country talking to people about—"

"I have my ladies lunch right now, but y'all . . . are you with that man who just got up?" She was still holding my hand.

"Yes."

"Well, y'all are welcome to come by the house later this afternoon. Say three o'clock or so?"

"Um, OK." I couldn't find a pen, so she said her phone number into my microphone. "See you then." She squeezed my hand, smiled, turned around, and walked away.

I couldn't find Ryan, so I approached a man who happened to be the chair of the deacons. I asked him if this was a typical service.

"This is because of the Fourth of July and patriotism. This was an unusual sermon for our pastor."

"It wasn't very uplifting."

"It wasn't supposed to be. I think it was more of a wake-up call and why we as conservative Christians aren't taking the role we should in politics and how God will, we feel, judge our nation and is judging our nation because of the sin of the nation. We're so far to the left compared to where we believe."

"A lot of people would say conservative Christians have a lot of power today."

"Hardly. Compared to where we were when Clinton was in office and so many things were swinging so far to the left, the Ten Commandments aren't on display and kids aren't allowed to pray in public schools."

"Swing so far to the left? What do you mean by that?"

"Legalizing homosexuality. Rights for gay partners. Required health care. I think there's reasons for improvement. The government is trying to control our freedom of speech."

"What do you mean by legalizing homosexuality? You want to make it illegal to be gay? Sorry, but I live in San Francisco. One of the nicest neighborhoods in San Francisco is predominantly gay. We just had a gay pride parade in San Francisco and our police force marched. I don't understand this obsession with gays."

"I have nothing against gay people. I have friends that are gay, but it's the pressure and promoting the gay lifestyle. You turn the TV on now and everything's gay."

"Everything's gay? What are you watching?"

"It boils down to this. I don't want my children watching that and thinking that it's normal because it's not. We're teaching this in our public schools."

I became irritated and knew it was time to move on before I said something I would regret. I also spotted Ryan speaking to a group of people. "What if we spent as much time focusing on our broken education system as we focus on gays? Don't you think we'd be better off as a country?" I asked.

"Well, it depends on what you're trying to teach them. Our public schools, at least in this part of the country, are so poorly performing. If you want your kids to get a quality education in this part of the country, you have to send them to private schools."

"If you're lucky enough to afford it."

"My wife is waiting for me. If you want to continue the conversation, you're welcome to join me and my family for lunch."

"Thanks, but we just made other plans."

I darted over to a conversation Ryan was having with two women and a man. "I was deeply disturbed by the comments he made about Arabs killing Jews," he said. "I'm Jewish and I have plenty of Arab friends who don't want to kill me. Do you believe these kind of racist remarks?"

A woman wearing a long jean skirt and button-up white top said, "I can do my own thinking. A lot of points I agree with, but I don't agree with everything he says. This was pretty political. This is not normal."

"We were surprised by the politics and anger," I said.

"So y'all are not from the Mississippi Delta?"

"No."

"This is not that unusual for the Mississippi Delta."

The others said they were late for lunch. "Nice meeting you." The man shook Ryan's hand, nodded to me, and took off.

I asked the woman what she thought of the service overall.

"I can think and judge what he says. If there's an election, there will be political statements made."

"What did you think about the Arabs wanting to kill Jews statement?" asked Ryan.

"You realize that in the Mississippi Delta, we do not have a number of Arabs. We had an evangelist who came here once who was an Arab. We just don't come in contact with Arabs. I know the conflict in the Bible, but I don't have any personal experience with any Arab people. We do have Jews because this area did pull in a number of Jews. But there aren't many opportunities here, so they leave. I have seen people in town dressed as I assume Muslims would dress. I can read the Bible and I can read the newspapers. We are limited in our experience of dealing with other people."

"Do you think the others feel the same way?" asked Ryan.

"I would think so."

"The comments he made about molesting children were also disturbing, especially with so many children listening," I said.

"They hear it on TV. We had a case here in our church. Look, he's my pastor and I support him. He's my boss."

We thanked her for her time and asked if we could meet the pastor. She said he had already left for the day.

A few hours later, I called our lady friend wearing the yellow suit, and she told us to come on over. She answered the door wearing a more casual outfit: baby-blue jeans and a multicolored pastel top. Cookies and lemonade were on the table. She never once asked for my last name or a business card.

"I really appreciate your inviting us over," I said. "If you hadn't grabbed my hand, I probably would have assumed you agreed with everything your preacher said."

"I was fidgeting and I didn't want to bother you. I'm so sorry. I didn't like that service today. I really didn't. He is not what I call a typical Baptist preacher. I have complained. I guess I'm too outspoken. If you go to a service, once the speaker gets through, I want to take that thought home with me and think about it. He's got a good sense of humor. He's just a little bit different."

"Is he always like that?"

"I got so upset one night, I quit going at night. He was talking about the crucifixion of Christ. I don't know what faith you are, so I hope you're not offended. He had graphic details about how Christ was beaten. I looked around and there were little children. I started to get a little sick. Are we in the end time now? I don't know. I do not know. As far as religion, I have my own beliefs. I'm not gonna push my faith on you or my politics on you. But people say we are in the end time. The world is in such a mess, but the Lord only knows." She took a deep breath and shook her head.

"Is it safe to assume that race is one of the most important issues around here?"

"Race is *the* most important issue. Our politicians are black and we've got some good ones."

"What political party are they?"

"A lot of Democrats. When you go to the polls, most of them are Democrats."

"How does the church lean politically?" I asked.

"I'd say it's half and half. They won't tell me how they vote. We don't talk about it at church. We can get in some heated discussions outside of church."

"You talk about politics outside of church?"

"Oh, yeah. I try to talk about politics except with my husband when he was alive. He would tell me to vote for so-and-so, and I might not want to vote for so-and-so, so I didn't vote for so-and-so! I came home one day and I told him who I voted for and he said, 'You canceled my vote,' and I said, 'Sorry about that.'"

"Can we ask what vote that was?"

"No," she said, laughing.

"Off the record?"

"No. I will say it can be very heated."

"Do you tend to vote for one party?"

"I change. I go with what I think is right. I'm liberal on some things and conservative on other things."

She changed the subject and asked us if we've ever traveled outside the country.

"I studied in India and lived in Australia for a while," said Ryan. "I've been to Muslim countries and that's another reason why that service made me feel so awful."

"I'm so sorry," she said.

"No, I don't want you to apologize for him."

"I don't understand that. I was about to lose it. But I'm that way every Sunday."

"I'm a guest and I'll show respect," said Ryan, "but this was the only time I wanted to really express my feelings. It was very disturbing."

"I've heard one good sermon from him."

"Why do you keep going?" I asked.

"Church can be a habit. I come away from there sometimes so up-set and today was one of those times. I want to be uplifted. I want to be helped. Sometimes I come home, stare out the window, and wonder why I still go."

"Do other people have similar concerns?"

"Oh, yes. The older crowd does. The man I was sitting by. Let me tell you that tale. He has been a member of that church for I don't know how long. He had the nicest wife. She was so much fun! She died, but he kept coming to church. I sit by him and someone else takes him home. So I love the people, I'm just hoping the pastor will leave. Very few pastors in the Baptist churches are asked to leave. I don't know how much longer we can handle this. We're losing membership. We're losing money. I am very concerned. I really am. You don't know what he's gonna say. He was pretty mild today. I'm gonna tell you. We call each other now. Are you going to church? Are you going? Yes, but I don't want to. My goodness, alive! I can raise my voice. Y'all better leave before I give you too much information," she said, laughing.

She gave us a hug and said we're welcome to stay in her extra bed-room if we ever return.

Back at the hotel, the clerk who gave us the church recommenda-tions was still behind the desk. "You're still here?" I asked.

"Yeah, someone called in sick, so I'm doing a double shift."

After telling him about our church experience, he apologized, say-ing he randomly chose it from the hotel's church directory.

Advocating for the Poor

On our way out of town, I spotted a sign for the Delta Housing Development Corp. I was curious to learn more about housing and poverty in the Delta, so I decided to stop in. Clanton Beamon, the organization's 61-year-old executive director, was more than happy to talk about the lack of housing in the Delta and all the crumbling, abandoned homes we'd seen.

"They were provided by the farm owners for their workers. But now, as machinery and mechanization have replaced the hands, farmers have reduced the labor force. People have either moved into towns or into apartments. In some cases, they've bought homes. I remember growing up in Sunflower County. There were houses all over the place. Now you can drive around and see no houses, because people have left. Take me, for example. My siblings all left. But Mississippi was changing in the early 1960s, and I liked the changes I saw, and I wanted to stay here and be part of it. I guess I always liked small-town living."

"Are you still seeing changes?"

"Yeah, everybody gets along better. Somehow people have found that we gotta figure a way to coexist. Regardless of your race, we have the same needs, the same wants and desires. We don't put a lot of emphasis on race as much as we used to. We have room for improvement. Our schools are still segregated. Economic development is dependent on adequate schools and adequate education. Another place we're still segregated is our churches. Sometimes you wonder, if we can't worship the same God together, what does it mean? I don't think heaven will be segregated. It's really puzzling and troubling."

"Have you ever gone to a white church?"

"Yeah, for funerals, but not just to go and worship on Sundays."

"Have you ever thought about it?" I asked.

"No, I never really thought about it. The big difference is, black churches welcome anybody."

"Yeah, I've been the only white person in black churches on many occasions and other than smiles, no one looks twice."

"We don't turn people away because you're white."

This got me thinking about what my experience in Mississippi would have been like if I were a few shades darker or black. I asked Clanton, a Baptist, if he thinks he'd be accepted into a white church.

"I think there would be resistance from somebody. We have some work to do."

"Most of the people I've met so far say race and the economy are the most important issues here."

"Well, you have the very rich and the very poor. Our economy is starting to look like an hourglass. There's nothing in the middle."

"Is the situation here any better when Democrats or Republicans are in office?" I asked.

"It's really interesting to listen to the conservative versus liberal argument. The average person, if they would tell you truth, does better with liberals running the country than we do with so-called conservatives. The Reagan administration started this. When he left, he had a record deficit. Bush is leaving an even bigger deficit. And this is conservative. For them, it's all about money and who gets it. It's really bad when you look at it. The war in Iraq is a great example. Now you tell me what's conservative about that. People have been tricked, and they don't want to admit that they've been hoodwinked. To go into a country, killing innocent people and say that's OK, we'll fix it. You can't give back a life. What makes you think these people are gonna think it's OK to see you riding around in tanks? Americans are sitting ducks in Baghdad."

"Do you know anyone over there?"

"My son just got back. He's a good soldier. He's been trained to do what he's supposed to do."

"Where was he stationed?"

"Mosul. It got tough there. He just happened to be out on patrol when they bombed the mess hall. My biggest problem with the Bush administration is no facts, all lies. They haven't done anything for human rights in their own country. What makes anyone think they're gonna do anything in another country? People coming back with no legs, no arms, one arm, one leg, brain damage. And for what? Because you have somebody that decided the war in Iraq would solve a lot of economic problems. Tax-free money. People are not stupid. We're finding out. We found out too late. We are not trained for guerilla warfare. It's crazy. It's time for this political blunder that we've made to come to a halt. It's not getting any better. Think about the toll it's putting on the Iraqi people. Look at the infrastructure that's torn up. No electricity. No sewer system. It's frightening to think the conservatives think it's OK to do something like that."

"What about the Democrats? What do you think of the Democratic Party?"

"The Democratic Party has to stop dodgin' and duckin' every time somebody calls them a liberal. Liberals have been the best thing that ever happened to this country."

"What would you say to them?"

"It's time for Democrats to be Democrats. Tell the truth. You can't be weak. When the first troops came back, the barracks didn't have air conditioning. The toilets were exposed. It was squalor conditions. I had to buy my son equipment. What's religious about dropping bombs on people who haven't done a thing to you? At the end of the day, when you think about it, something is going to come of this because God is paying attention."

Overworked and Underpaid

After two months of staying in motels and hotels, I'd met approximately 20 housekeepers struggling to survive on minimum wage. And contrary to the widely held belief that only teenagers make minimum wage, the women I met were all over the age of 30. In Texas, they were mostly white and Hispanic, and in Mississippi, they were all black. They have no idea the government has the power to raise their wages, and none of them vote. "Why should we vote? Politicians don't care about poor people like us," said a woman making beds at a Red Roof Inn in Texas. "It's not an easy job. I spend most of my time cleaning up rooms and picking up people's messes. I'd rather work in the medical field, but I can't save enough for school."

Most housekeepers have been hesitant to talk while on the job, but an African American clerk and a housekeeper I met while checking out of a $65 a night room at a well-known hotel chain in Clarksdale were willing to share their opinions about the realities and challenges of living in the Delta, as long as they remained anonymous.

"Clarksdale is a sad town," said the 31-year-old male clerk. "You have high crime because there's no jobs. There's nothin' for youth to do. That's the reason why crime is high. How could you tell any young black man out there that has two or three kids that's trying to get work or has been in the system before and is trying to get a better life and everywhere he goes, they're slammin' doors or judgin' you based on your past. There's nothin' for them to do. I got a lot of friends who had a troubled life. And nobody's tryin' to change it."

"Do you have a lot of friends like that?"

"Yeah, most of my friends. Most of them. You have people that want to do better, but there's only so much you're allowed to do. I give anybody a second chance in life. But nobody cares. The politicians lie. You don't know them until election time. They come in the churches. They politikin' [*sic*] in the neighborhoods just to get a vote. But they don't do what they promise. That's Mississippi right there."

"What about you? Do you like your job?"

"I like the job, but it's not enough money to survive. You're barely makin' it. It's paycheck to paycheck. You know, it's tough. I'm not doin' all that well, but I'm livin'. I'm breathin'. I get up every day, and I can come to work. I know people who've left to go to college. They come back to Clarksdale and the only option they have is workin' at McDonald's. 'How can I help you?'"

"So, people who go to college tend to leave?"

"They have to. It's a must. It's a must because there's nothin' here. Nothin'."

"What kinds of changes would you like to see?"

"I would like to see job development. I would like to give the youth something to do. I would like politicians to get out and go talk to that one gangbanger, that one person who's thinkin' about takin' a life. You'll never know their situation. If you just sit back, nothin's gonna change. If you get out and talk to people, you never know. You can't reach everyone, but you can reach one."

"What message would you send to politicians?"

"Stop politikin' in church and stop lyin'."

"And they visit your church?"

"Yeah, they come, but I don't listen. They're not gonna to trick me. They'll give a barbeque, fry a little fish. They need to tell the real reason why they're runnin'. We need some new people in office. Nothin's changed. Things are so tight. What's important is that I feed my family. This job don't pay that much, but it's a job."

"You have a family?"

"Yeah."

"How many kids do you have?"

"I have two. Actually, I have four."

"Why'd you have so many kids if you can't make ends meet?"

He raised his eyebrows and paused. "I can see why you'd ask that question. It just happened."

Other than a few incoming phone calls, the lobby was quiet. I continually looked over my shoulder because I didn't want to get him in trouble, but he didn't seem to care. He obviously had a lot to say. His tone switched back and forth between anger and frustration, but his somber facial expression never changed.

"I come from the roughest part of the city. There's probably nothin' I haven't seen. Probably nothin' I haven't done. It's one thing dealin' with the situation you're in and the people you're around and then you're tryin' to focus on the positive side of everything."

At this point, a black female housekeeper walked in the lobby area to do some dusting and stopped to listen.

"It's easy for me to say you should get your friends together and organize," I said, "but I'm assuming that because you barely make ends meet, you probably don't have time."

"It's that hard. It's that hard. I'm a little more fortunate now, but I know a lot others that aren't. I chopped cotton. I did that. A lot of people still do. More people are focused on making sure their lights stay on and their gas stay on. They really don't have politics on their mind. They don't really care. I feel for young black men because there's nothin' here for them. It's not really their fault. You don't have a YMCA. You don't even have a place to gather. You gotta catch them when they're young."

"There's nothing to do after school? No after-school programs?"

"No."

"What do kids do at night?"

"They roam the streets. It's rough on a lot of people. It's not just

Clarksdale. It's the Delta. It's modern-day slavery. Take this lady here. You see how hard they work. How long do you work?"

"Thirty hours maximum, maybe," she said with a straight face.

"So you don't have benefits?" I asked.

"No. You don't even have a sick day. If you're sick three times in six months, you're terminated."

"So you come to work sick?"

"You have to. Flu, whatever it is, you bring it here."

"And you start off making minimum wage?"

"Yeah."

"I don't work as hard as her and I make more," said the clerk. "She's been here 17 years."

"Seventeen years? Do you mind me asking what you make now?"

"Seven-sixty," she said.

"Seven-sixty? What did you start at?"

"Three-fifteen in 1988. It's rough."

"Do you ask for raises?"

"I ask for raises. They don't give 'em." She seemed to be ashamed to admit that she makes so little after 17 years of hard labor with the same company. She's 46, but looks well beyond her years. She's frail, her hair is short and brittle, and her face is worn and wrinkly. Even when the clerk spoke, she stared at me with a straight face. I wondered what she was thinking.

"I've been here for four years," he said. "She's been here for 17. My raise was one nickel. Hers was two cents."

"Two cents? For a year?"

"Yeah. We work for a large corporation," he said. "No insurance. No health care. No nothing. What you make is what you get."

They said their requests for additional hours are never granted and if business was slow, they might get 20 hours a week or less. I asked them if they've looked for better jobs.

"We got a Wal-Mart. They hired 300 people and then laid them off. They said they weren't makin' enough money. Some people left their jobs to work for Wal-Mart, then they got laid off," he said.

"After 17 years, I'm afraid to leave," she added.

"See, people in San Francisco, New York, L.A., Houston, they don't know. They'd probably blow their head off if they had to live here," said the clerk.

"They wouldn't come here to live," she said, raising her voice. "They'd probably live in their cars before they'd come here to live."

"I've met so many people on my trip who say, 'This is America. You have so many opportunities. You can pull yourself up.' How would you respond?" I asked.

"If you come from nothin'," said the clerk, "you're not gonna let nothin' stop you from achieving a goal, but to achieve that goal, it's gonna take a lot. I mean a lot. You're gonna take a lot of risks, a lot of chances. Nothin' about the American dream here is true. If I was a rap star, a movie star, all these people with millions. Why should there be any starving, hunger, you know? Why should this kid be without shoes? Why? That should tell you something. Somebody don't care. Either they don't know or they don't care. Morgan Freeman has a restaurant here. You'll never see a black in there 'cause they can't afford it. He has a nightclub and a fine dining restaurant. If you see blacks in there, they're not from here. They'll have black people workin' in the kitchen. This is my question. I would like for this to run across CNN. For all the money and millionaires we have in this country, have you all ever heard of the Delta flatlands of Mississippi? I'm not talking about Jackson. Have you ever heard of a place called Clarksdale? Greenville? Cleveland? Greenwood? Have you ever seen how people live in that area? I don't believe so. I don't believe so. The Delta area. I know it's the worst part of the country. It's a hard day almost every day. Nothin's gonna be easy. Nothin'. Nothin' comes easy. Nobody's gonna help you."

"Where do you find hope?"

"You better find hope in God. That's your only way out. That's your only way out."

Before leaving the Delta, I spent a few hours in the parking lots of two military recruiting centers (they wouldn't let me in) interviewing a number of young black men who were thinking about joining.

I asked them why they would join knowing they might be sent to Iraq.

"Because there are no opportunities here," said a nineteen-year-old who just finished high school. "It's either the military or McDonald's. What would you do?"

III

OKLAHOMA

The Unplanned Adventure

WE HAD NO IDEA what we'd find in Oklahoma. On our way there, I spent a lot of time thinking about the power of storytelling and listening. As much as I love telling other people's stories, I was beginning to wonder if I really knew my own. I'm lucky enough to still have three living grandparents, and I've interviewed them all at different stages of their lives, but I wondered what else there was to uncover. What don't I know about them? My grandmother on my mom's side was born in a caravan in Canada. When her family traveled from the eastern United States to the West, local authorities would meet them at the border and tell them they could spend the night, but that they had to be gone by morning or face arrest. She had an arranged married at a young age and raised eight children.

During World War II, when women workers were in high demand, my grandmother on my father's side worked for the government as a welder making almost as much as my grandfather, who was a trained journeyman sheet metal worker. When my grandmother was a child growing up in Ukiah, California, she faced harsh discrimination and racism and was often turned away by local businesses. Signs saying, "No dogs or Indians allowed" were common. Her mother, my great-grandmother, was captured by authorities at age 11 and forced to attend a boarding school for Indians. She eventually became a well-known basket-maker, who believed in sharing her skills with non-Indians at a time when that was frowned upon. Several of her baskets are on display at the Santa Rosa Junior College Museum.

From then on, I made a point of calling my grandparents a few times a week to check in and tell them about our adventures. My grandfather could not understand why we would drive all the way to Oklahoma to interview people about politics.

When we arrived in Oklahoma City, we were struck by two things: the bottom of the state's license plates say NATIVE AMERICA in red letters, and we rarely saw any sidewalks. According to *Prevention Magazine*, Oklahoma City is the worst city for pedestrians in the country. We decided to visit Oklahoma because John Kerry failed to win one county in the entire state in the 2004 election. Other than that, I knew absolutely nothing about Oklahoma and had no idea what I'd find.

We assumed we'd be in Oklahoma City for a week, so we decided to stay in an extended-stay hotel. They're cheaper by the week, they're clean, and they come with a full kitchen and a fairly large workspace. In order to get my bearings, I decided to stay in the hotel for the first day to do research and set up a few interviews. It was the middle of July and the heat was still unbearable, so the only place to do random interviews was in air-conditioned malls.

For some reason, I kept stumbling upon several articles and websites about Jim Roth, Oklahoma's first openly gay politician. As luck would have it, the local chapter of the Victory Fund, an organization dedicated to increasing the number of openly LGBT (lesbian, gay, bisexual, and transgendered) elected officials at all levels of government, was having house parties for Roth and a few other gay politicians running for office.

Later that night, we learned how *not* to plan our day in Oklahoma City. After finally deciding to grab a bite to eat at 9:30 p.m., we found ourselves on a harrowing search for a restaurant with some sort of vegetarian option. We passed an endless array of restaurants, including Cattleman's, Earl's Rib Place, and the Deep Fork Grill, but they weren't exactly veggie friendly. After becoming extremely restless, we settled for Taco Del Mar and went to Borders to try to get a change of scenery. It was closed. We didn't want to go back to the hotel just yet, so we turned on some music and ate in the parking lot. Much to my dismay, my supposed vegetarian taco turned out to be a beef taco. Ryan tried not to laugh. He happily ate the beef taco, and I had a bowl of cereal back at the hotel.

A few days later, we met Jim Roth at a Victory Fund party in a private home. Jim was elected on November 5, 2002, to represent the citizens of Oklahoma County District One for a four-year term. He was reelected with 65 percent of the vote. Three parties were happening that night, so people were bouncing from one to the other. When we showed up, two women and nine men, including Jim, were mingling and talking politics. In 2002, Jim's Republican mom moved to Oklahoma City from Kansas City for eight months to help him with what turned out to be a long and nasty campaign. She had no idea what she was in for. "At one of our debates, a Baptist deacon physically assaulted my mother. He was passing out antigay literature, and my mom was going around picking it up. He grabbed her by the arm and started twisting her arm. The sheriff had to break it up and kick him out. My parents went through a lot," says Jim. "She went home and changed her registration because she was so turned off by Republicans."

And his dad? "It's amazing," he says, smiling. "My dad is a donor to the Republican National Committee and a Rush Limbaugh radio listener, and he and my partner trade Bill Clinton dolls and gifts and everything at Christmas. They have a great relationship. My dad is always asking about him."

"Is your dad still Republican?"

"Oh, yeah. Then there's my brother, who I describe as a hunter-gatherer type. He's like a fisherman on the weekend kinda guy and just real macho. He came to help campaign and do what we call 'honk and wave.' We hold up the big campaign sign, and we wave at people as they drive by. There was a polling place at a school. My brother was on one end of a hill, and I was on the other end, so we couldn't see each other. This guy pulls up in his minivan, and he's like, 'You know that Roth is a homosexual?' I'm holding the sign. I'm like, 'Really? Are you sure?' He goes, 'Oh yeah.' When people call our campaign and ask that question, I would always take every call and I would say, 'Yes, I am, but you know I'm running because of these things.' I was always real honest about it. So he tells me this from his minivan. 'Yeah, he is. Call him, he'll tell ya,' he says, laughing. So I'm like, 'Well sir, why does that bother you?' He still doesn't know it's me. He says, 'Well, 'cause it's against the Bible.' I said, 'Well, sir, being judgmental doesn't seem very Christian.' He kinda seemed flustered and I said, 'Well I'll tell him you said so. What name can I give him?' He's like, 'Uh, John Smith.' I couldn't believe it. I said, 'Sir, that doesn't sound very honest. That doesn't sound very Christian of you,' and he squealed off. We walked back to the car with my brother. We got in the car and drove to the next polling place. My brother was looking ahead and said, 'Did you meet the guy in the red minivan?'"

Jim says being the first openly gay member of Oklahoma's government is an honor, but it's a hell of a lot of work. "I think we have to run twice as fast and think twice as fast and be twice as smart because we have that disadvantage in other people's minds, so I carry that as an extra responsibility not to make a mistake."

"I heard that when you were campaigning, various communities came together that traditionally don't work together."

"We had a wonderful outpouring from the African American community. America is at its worst on Sunday mornings because it's at its most segregated. You go to a black church and they see me. There I am. They are so wonderfully welcoming and affirming. I call it genuine faith."

"We've met a lot of African Americans who say homosexuality is wrong according to the Bible, but they say a person's sexual orientation shouldn't be a political issue. Same with abortion."

"I think that's right. I say genuine faith because the Bible has 1200 passages about helping the poor and seven about homosexuality or whatever it is, so I think they have a true faith-based mission. When

I talk to pastors, we're talking about their parishioners' needs, we're talking about seniors, we're talking about health care, grandparents raising grandchildren. There's a whole lot going on. We as a state incarcerate more women than any other in the country per capita."

According to the Bureau of Justice Statistics, 129 of 100,000 Oklahoma women are in prison, and nearly 80 percent have children. That's more than double the national average of 60 women per 100,000.

"It's amazing. It's shocking."

"What are they in for?"

"Mostly drugs. In our county jail, 22 percent are mentally ill. Now that I'm a county commissioner, I try to expose some of these issues. When feds got out of the mental health care business in the '80s with Reagan and the states got out of it in the '90s, well guess what? They ended up in our parks and our prisons. We don't have officials that say, 'We have to be pragmatic,' because they don't want to be soft on crime."

Because over 70 percent of Oklahomans are regular churchgoers and identify their faith as their top priority, Jim says his religion almost always takes precedence over his policy ideas.

"I belong to a Kiwanis Club in a rural community that's in my district, and every time we meet, they ask, 'We need a church count. Raise your hand if you went to church this week.' Kiwanis. This is an environment where there's peer pressure to go to church."

"Did people ask you about your faith when you ran?"

"A lot. I would introduce myself and say, 'Here's why I'm running. If you would, please take a look at some of this literature.' Some would say, 'Are you a Christian?' 'Well, as a matter of fact, I am, but I'm running to repair your roads and bridges,'" he says, laughing. "You just try to be polite. You never lie and you just be yourself."

"How did you deal with the antigay stuff?"

"Tonight is a gathering focused on the Victory Fund and the work they're doing. They insist that you be the person you are. There was never any hesitation that I was going to be openly gay in my campaign, but it gave me extra armor to stand there and take it. If I would have bought into it, I would have let the world see it as an appropriate debate, so I just stayed focused on my predecessor's overspending of the budget and what I thought we ought to be doing about the jail population and the issues I thought were germane to the job. I approached it as a job interview. To make that point, I distributed resumes. I'm asking to be hired for a job. In a job interview, would it be appropriate for someone to be inquiring about your family life or your spouse or your faith? It's not going to stop them, but you try to raise your own professionalism and hope they get with you."

"And they did."

"They did. The majority of them did. We beat an incumbent Republican who was a known homophobe. We beat him by 11 points."

I asked Jim to share a memorable story from the election.

"There was a small town in the northeastern part of the district, where the mayor had been there since 1969. He had helped my opponent. After I won, he refused to run again because he didn't want to work with the gay guy. He had served his citizens of that town for 30-plus years, and we've done such a good job with our district and the road and bridge work in and around that area and other areas, he's like my new best friend now. I was in their town parade on July Fourth and he was in the car behind me and we talked for 30 minutes, just kinda hanging out."

Jim says he's often on the receiving end of his colleagues' homophobic slurs, but in the long run, he believes the vitriol might help because "moderate-minded people get to see the ugliness and bigotry." And when a commissioner is on an antigay tirade, Jim listens and waits his turn to speak. "I have the mike next. I'm his equal, and I get to vote. It's all about equality."

"How do you do it?"

"I can handle the nastiness. A lot of us have these experiences with our families, so we come conditioned. I was emotionally ready to spend my life without my biological family because you don't know how they'll react, right, so you prepare yourself. So when you've done that you don't mind what strangers think."

And what about that gay agenda I've been hearing about since arriving in Texas?

"Oh, yes, the gay agenda. My former partner died in 1996, and I went through the experience where I had no legal rights to be in the hospital at all. If the gay agenda means that partners should have hospital visitation rights, then that's worth fighting for. I think it's just a matter of describing to people what it really means. This is such a 30-second sound-bite world. The rhetoric wins. How do you pierce through with reality? The conversation that America is having, as painful as it feels, is a good thing."

Once Jim took office, gay issues became a priority in the Oklahoma legislature. "I'm on our county board, and Republicans spent so much time trying to get gay-themed books moved to the adult section. Go cure illiteracy. Do the job you're being paid to do to cure the lives of Oklahomans. It's crazy." According to the National Adult Literacy Survey, Oklahoma has the fourth-highest illiteracy rate in the nation, with as many as one in five Oklahomans unable to read.

Almost every person at the party was a Republican turned Democrat, including Jim. "I was a Republican through law school. I voted for George H. W. Bush over Bill Clinton in '92. I moved here and didn't know who I really was. As soon as I realized how mean-spirited Republicans were and are, I became a Democrat. The Democrats are a little less mean, but I have been disappointed by their intolerance. I'm waiting for someone to emerge on the national scene that says, 'America, get over it.' As a state, we're second in the nation for divorce. And remember, these are all the people going to church on Sunday. Second for divorce. We have the highest per capita number of grandparents raising grandchildren. I already talked about incarceration rates and these are people who profess faith. It's really amazing. I call it diversion by rhetoric."

"What advice would you give to the national Democrats?"

"National Democrats never come here because we're considered flyover, but I would say be a party that's willing to represent all of America, as Robert Kennedy described, even the people in the shadows."

Off the Front Lines and Forgotten

We took our time driving east from Oklahoma City to McAlester. The church billboards along the way were all worthy of being photographed. They said, "Best Vitamin for a Christian Is B1," "Gambling Is Robbery Without a Gun," "Free Trip to Heaven! Details Inside," "Sorrow Looks Back, Worry Looks Around, Faith Looks Up," "Is Life a Puzzle? We Have the Missing Peace," and "I Am a Jealous God." A wooden sign that said, "Abortion Stops a Beating Heart" stood behind a "Faith Assembly" sign. I needed to escape the heat, so we stopped in a church, but the fire and brimstone preacher was too depressing, so we left.

Then we had our first breakdown. Luckily, it happened in the parking lot of a motel, and the damage wasn't too bad. A loose connection to the battery set us back $50. I ran to the store to grab water and a few snacks, and when I returned Ryan surprised me by adding a few more animals to my side of the dashboard. He added a kissing zebra and horse in honor of the animals we had seen in Kerrville, Texas. He completed the scene by painting grass under the animals, blood on his fighters, and a dark blue river dividing his war and my version of utopia.

From McAlester, we drove to Muskogee, home of Oklahoma's largest Veterans Affairs (VA) hospital. Along the way, we saw a truck with a U.S. Air Force sticker above a bumper sticker that said, "I'm Tired of All the BUSHIT."

It didn't take long to find Iraq veterans who had returned home with excruciating mental and physical ailments—and the treatment they've received is shoddy at best.

Michael Thomas, in the navy since December 2002, was on the ship that fired the first tomahawks on Baghdad in March 2003. He served as a supervisor for a five-inch 54-gun mount. "They fired from the front launcher so I knew right then that something was going on," he said. "I sat right next to the launcher. The missiles were shooting all over the place." Michael was discharged for psychological problems three months later. He was still visibly shaken by the experience and shivered when he spoke. On his "bad days," he locks himself in his room. "I usually don't talk to anyone. I usually cry and get depressed. No one sees it because I isolate myself."

Michael was 25, but he could have passed for a demure 15-year-old. His blond spiky hair was gelled in place and he was wearing a cream-colored button-up shirt over a white T-shirt, jeans, and eyeglasses. He was seeing two psychologists and taking three different medications.

Like tens of thousands of veterans, when Michael returned to the States, he attended a class about federal benefits but said it didn't help. "They send you to a three-hour course and give you a book. If you don't ask questions, you won't get the answers. I'm still trying to get my claim. If it wasn't for my cousin, I wouldn't know what to do."

Michael's 30-year-old cousin, Dennis Hammons, was a Marine from June 1993 to August 1997. Dennis was discharged in 1996 after he experienced a parachute malfunction and fell 500 feet at Camp Lejeune, North Carolina. He suffers from post-traumatic stress syndrome (PTSS) and has knee, back, and neck injuries. "I'm one of the people that falls through the cracks. I was in during Clinton's police actions," he said. "I was all over Liberia and Rwanda. I got stabbed and there's no record of it. I'm not eligible for benefits because it didn't happen during a conflict. As soon as I got hurt, I was treated like a piece of crap."

Hammons, a serious guy wearing a black T-shirt, jeans, and a DAV (Disabled American Veteran) Oklahoma baseball cap, said the claim he filed with the VA took 14 months to process; it took another four months to get into the VA medical system. "My experience with the VA has been horrible. I go to a private doctor for pain meds. If I need to see a doctor here [at the VA], it takes three to four months to get an appointment," he said. "I took my son down a slide, which wasn't real smart, and I couldn't walk. I had pain shooting down my arm and leg. That happened in April. I got in the second week of July. That's how it is here."

I met Michael and Dennis in Bill Huber's office. Bill was coordinator for the DAV Hospital. Each year, the DAV transports 24,000 disabled veterans to and from their doctor's appointments; many live three hours away. Volunteers do the driving, but the DAV relies on private donations to pay for the 16 vans and the gas, which is rising by the day. The program costs $175,000 per year to operate.

"I'm seeing those yellow 'support our troops' ribbons almost everywhere I go. Does the community go any further than slapping ribbons on their cars? Do they support you financially?" I asked.

"They don't support veterans in this town. The biggest employing agency in this town is the VA. They have over 500 employees here, and you'd think that they would support veterans. We have a breakfast fundraiser once every three months, and the only ones that will come are our members. We have that fundraiser so we can go on with our projects, but we don't get support [from the locals]. That's disheartening," said Bill.

The transportation service was recently asked to cut back its operations by 45 percent because of budget cuts, but the director refused to comply. "What kind of people do we have running our government? So many are nonveterans. The ones that are veterans aren't supporting the veterans."

In August 2001, Oklahoma Senator James Inhofe and then-Senator Don Nickles both voted against an amendment to increase medical care for veterans by $650 million. In October 2003, they voted to table an amendment that called for an additional $322 million for safety equipment for U.S. forces in Iraq. In March 2004, they voted against an amendment to increase medical care for vets by $1.8 million by eliminating abusive tax loopholes. The bill was defeated 51 to 49. Not one Republican voted for it.

"I've noticed that health care for troops is a partisan issue. Why is that?" I asked. "Republicans say they support the troops, but their voting records don't."

"You find that all the time," said Bill. "Democrats are the ones supporting the troops. Republicans aren't supporting us. I'm 71 years old, and I've been around a while. The problem is, veterans don't protest. We take what we get. I tell my people to write to their congressmen. They just sit back and let our lobbyists do it. They can't do it by themselves; we have to help them."

"Can you name any politicians that consistently stand up for the troops and try to increase health care?" I asked.

"Our senators consistently vote against veterans' issues and one of them is a veteran. He'll tell you he supports veterans, but he never does."

"Which senator is that?"

"Senator Inhofe."

"[Senator] Coburn is the same way," added Jennifer Hammons, Dennis's wife. "My husband has had numerous interactions with Coburn. He's actually a local doctor. He doesn't care about veterans. He would rather label condoms and get it to where minors have to tell their parents they want birth control. He would rather make the veterans pay a co-pay when most of these veterans barely get by."

"He [Senator Coburn] wants to do away with the VA Medical Centers to where we have to go to private doctors," added Bill. "What's gonna happen there is they'll give us a medical card and the only thing that we can be treated for would be for a service-connected condition. If we had any other condition, we'd have to pay for it. Here we don't. I'm opposed to issuing the card because a lot of doctors don't know how to deal with a lot of the problems we have. I'm in full support of keeping the VA hospitals, but they need to provide better care."

"This issue gets very little attention. Do you think it's because we're shielded from the realities of war? Bush hasn't gone to any funerals and we never see coffins on the news," I said.

"People are afraid to know what's going on," said Jennifer. "They keep saying they'll send our boys back but never give us a timeframe. That's why I'm glad my cousin got a medical discharge. We're still trying to get him the care he needs. I'm married to a disabled vet, and I know what these guys are going through. I'm hanging in there. All we can do is try our best. There's only so much we can do as an organization. We try to help vets with the VA system, but the VA gives us the same runaround that they're giving the veterans."

Dennis Hammons said he was glad the media and politicians were finally paying attention to veterans' issues, but he didn't believe it would improve the situation. "They need to put their money where their mouth is. They're liars. Look at their voting records. If they supported our troops, Iraqi war veterans that come back with missing legs wouldn't have to wait six months to get an appointment. Until that's taken care of, they're lying," he said with an angry and irritated tone. "You don't send people to war without taking care of their injuries. These politicians don't think about it like that. If it was their sons, what would they think? Also, here's something else that gets no attention. If you're a disabled veteran, you're not getting a job. I put disabled veteran on my job applications and couldn't get a job. As soon as I put veteran and left off disabled, I got a job. I know personally, I'm not letting my kids join the military and have their lives destroyed."

Keeping Tabs on the Right

I could have spent the entire day listening to 69-year-old Fred Gibson talk about Iraq, education, health care, and his conservative neighbors. "Try as I may, I do everything I can to get people in Oklahoma to read and study and try to understand these things. I love every one of 'em, but they have old-time sayings, and they go through life with that. It's very difficult. They're always surprised when they sit down with me and discuss things."

Fred was born and raised in Tahlequah, Oklahoma, a former Democratic stronghold and capital of the Cherokee Nation. Fred spent three years in the army, taught for 32 years in Southern California, and returned to Tahlequah with his wife in 1995 to retire.

We met Fred, a sweet, passionate man, at a luncheon for Tahlequah Democrats on a sunny Friday afternoon. "I'm primarily interested in making the Democratic Party see things my way," he said, laughing. "I'm essentially the glue that holds the party together."

"Why are you a Democrat?"

"The whole purpose of the Democratic Party is to be progressive and step out ahead of the group, sort of like leading a wagon train. They have to go out and see what mountains can be passed. The Republicans are the ones who say, 'I'm getting tired. We need to rest a while and rein in our adventurous spirits.' Republicans have no respect for government. They have no desire to make government work. They realize by now that a certain amount of government is necessary. They always talk about reducing government, except for their own benefits," he said.

"Just about every Republican we've met has said they're for small government, yet George W. Bush was the biggest spending president in 30 years," I said.

"Exactly, but they won't admit it. Newt Gingrich said early on, 'If you want to win, you're being too nice.' That's why every right-wing radio host is always mad about something. Or if not mad, then insulting."

"Do you listen to a lot of right-wing radio?"

"Oh, I listen all the time. I've probably read more right-wing books than the entire Republican Party in Cherokee County," he said, laughing. "I enjoy Rush Limbaugh and his brother Hannity. I could go down the list. The talk show hosts do our thinking for us. They say, 'Up is down' and everyone starts saying, you know, 'Up is down.' They start saying 'Down is up.' They say, 'Well. I don't know. Down might be up.' This is all an outgrowth of the neoconservative movement. Irving Kristol and his neoconservative ideas, which no one understands until you read their books. It's Greek to everybody. Bless their hearts."

"It's interesting you listen to Rush. I've heard so many Democrats say they closely follow right-wing media, but I never hear Republicans express any interest in reading progressive media or listening to liberal talk show hosts, not that there are many of them."

"There is an awful lot wrong with the left wing. Very often people are much more effective at doing things than they are talking about them. It's Republicans acting so mean that will stimulate the Democrats," he said. "When Reagan got into office, he scrapped the Fairness Doctrine. Thousands of radio hosts, day after day, hour after hour, hammerin' away the right-wing philosophy. We didn't have anything to counteract it. Every day, they'd hammer away the same old insults, same abuse. People being such sheep were willing to buy into that. They tap into people who are angry."

"Like people who've lost their jobs because the factory moved to China. They're mad and rightly so, but the talk show hosts steer their anger toward liberals and social issues instead of our corporate power structure."

"Even if the anger has nothing to do with what they're saying."

"How do you reach those people?" I asked.

"They won't discuss it. Once they make up their mind, they don't want to hear anything else."

"So there's no discussion?"

"No discussion. It's a one-way street. Sometimes I corner 'em in the Chamber of Commerce meetings, in the Kiwanis meetings, even the Democratic meetings. You want to discuss those things with 'em and it's very difficult. They have no ammunition. I get responses from the things I write. And I number each paragraph and go back and answer each paragraph. Well, it doesn't take but two or three of those letters and they give up. Usually, it just takes one response."

"The reason we have this big file of articles is to give people information about various issues. We'd mention specific stories or facts, but they wouldn't believe it, so we decided to print articles and reports to hand out, and even then, they'll say, 'That's liberal. I'm not reading it,'" I said.

"That's it. If you catch 'em on one thing, they immediately switch to something else. Or it's the liberal trap!" he said.

"What issues are most important to you?"

"I study all the issues. They're all important. I try to encourage our people to think about poverty, health care, and education and come up with ideas."

"Besides right-wing radio, where do you get your news?"

"I subscribe to all kinds of magazines. *Wired, Atlantic Monthly, Business Week, Harper's, The Nation, Jim Hightower's Lowdown, U.S. News & World Report.*"

"That's a lot!"

"TV, NPR, newspapers, of course, any number of things like that. Almost every newspaper is grist for a response. It drives me crazy sometimes. I've had three heart attacks, so you can see I take it seriously, but that's the way it is," he said, shaking his head.

"It's not always easy to be informed."

"It's not, as you well know. Fortunately, I retired when I was 57, my wife retired when she was 55, so we can indulge."

"Is your wife political?"

"She's more liberal than I am! I give her papers and things of mine and ask her for her comments and opinions and so forth, and she really gives 'em! She's interested in music and they have a string band. Violin. Guitar. Auto harp and things like that. They play all over this part of the country. They do Civil War reenactments. She stays busy. Then we have our church work and political work. I didn't retire to work this hard. Believe me! I came home and found that Oklahoma changed so drastically. I couldn't stand it. The church had been completely overrun by people who didn't see religion as the religion I read about in the Bible. I'm a Christian. Fundamentalist, for that matter, but I have a different point of view about God. God put us here to be stewards of the earth and to manage our affairs intelligently. That's how liberalism got involved in all this. They objected to being under the king's thumb and the church's power."

We wanted to meet Fred's wife, but we had to drive back to Oklahoma City to go to a gun show. Before we said our good-byes, Ryan and Fred exchanged book titles and articles.

"I've enjoyed the interview," Fred said, laughing. "Anyone does when they're asked their opinion."

Oklahoma City Gun Show

The heat was starting to bother me again, so we decided to drive back to Oklahoma City to spend the day indoors at a gun show. As we pulled into the fairgrounds parking lot, we passed monster trucks with confederate flag license plates and large yellow stickers on back windows that said: FEDERAL PERMIT NO. 91 101 TERRORIST HUNTING PERMIT. American flags were on almost every bumper. We also saw a few POW-MIA black ribbons and SPECIAL FORCES stickers. The sign on the entrance door said:

NO LOADED FIREARMS ALLOWED

NO LOOSE AMMO

NO LOADED CLIPS OR MAGAZINES

The security guard casually checked our backpacks and said, "Have a good time." We hadn't walked 30 feet when two portly men approached us. "Take a look at these two here," said the tall, bearded man wearing jean overalls and a red T-shirt. "They got backpacks on. They're probably terrorists comin' here to blow us up."

By this time, we were used to receiving paranoid stares when we both wore our large backpacks, but being called terrorists was a first. Ryan said, "I appreciate you telling me to my face rather than give me an ugly stare 'cause that's all we get."

"An ugly stare's all I can give. I used to have a great smile until this." He flashed a big smile and proudly showed off his missing teeth. We weren't sure if it was OK to laugh, so we both smiled nervously and lightly chuckled. "What brings y'all here?" I gave him a shortened version of my usual spiel, and he offered to introduce us to his friend Dave. "Follow me."

The first thing I noticed as we entered the hall was the booth displaying huge Confederate, American, and Oklahoma flags. Then I noticed the guns. Every type of gun you can imagine—pistols, shotguns, semiautomatics—was for sale. They were displayed like a breakfast buffet on tables draped in American flags and red, white, and blue tablecloths. We passed a few families pushing babies in strollers, but most of the gun enthusiasts in the hall were men, and almost all of them had rifles slung over their shoulders. Then we reached our destination: one of the largest booths in the hall. Four long tables set up in a square shape were filled with automatic and semiautomatic machine guns. Four men, including one in a wheelchair, were in the center of the square answering questions and helping customers. "Hey Dave," said the man who had called us terrorists. Dave turned his wheelchair around and wheeled toward us. "These people are from San Francisco. They're travelin' around the country talkin' to folks." Dave raised his eyebrows when he heard we were from San Francisco. We introduced ourselves and shook hands.

Dave stared straight ahead at Ryan's chest. He had a menacing look on his face, but didn't say anything. After a few seconds of uncomfortable silence, Ryan asked if there was a problem. "Your T-shirt. We don't see many of them shirts around here." His shirt? Ryan's flannel shirt was unbuttoned and his "Free Palestine" T-shirt was showing. Of all the T-shirts he had, he had to wear that one. Without thinking, I grabbed one of the guns and pointed it at the ceiling. I tried to change the subject by asking Dave to tell me about the gun. He didn't fall for it. Instead, he asked Ryan why he was wearing that shirt. Fearing Ryan would go into lecture mode, I walked away. I couldn't handle another debate, and I was angry with Ryan for wearing a political T-shirt to a gun show of all places.

I walked over to the booth selling the confederate flags and found knives and wallets next to shotguns and pistols. Every few minutes, I looked over at Ryan and Dave. They weren't yelling, so I took that as a positive sign. I returned ten minutes later to find them discussing immigration.

"It's not a republic anymore," said Dave. "We have so many people who come into our country that have no morals. Look at all the Mexican and Chinese coming in. The American symbol no longer exists in California because you have so many ethnic groups."

"The only people I consider to be true Americans are Native Americans and that includes her dad's family," said Ryan. "Aside from that, we're all immigrants."

"Absolutely."

"Based on your logic, you can make an argument that the people who stole her ancestor's land have no morals," said Ryan.

"That don't mean that her morals are better than ours."

"Or that ours are better than Mexicans or Chinese."

"All I'm sayin' is, you gotta close the borders. In California, you couldn't use most of these guns. How you gonna defend yourself?"

"Defend myself from what?"

A man who was waiting to ask Dave a question was listening to their conversation and didn't look very happy. I was afraid Ryan was going to get us kicked out, so I thanked Dave and said he should get back to his customers. Ryan buttoned his shirt, walked to the snack food booth at the back of the hall, and promised to stay put until I got a few interviews.

I continued walking around and passed a random assortment of items for sale, including beanie babies, camouflage baby jackets, coloring books, cookbooks, and gold jewelry. There was something for every member of the family at the gun show. I then found a table filled with newspapers carefully wrapped in plastic. There was the December 14, 2000, edition of the *Baltimore Sun*. The lead story was, "Bush Wins, Vows Unity as Gore Concedes Race." Remember that? Unity? And, of course, the September 12, 2001, edition of the *New York Times*: U.S. ATTACKED: HIJACKED JETS DESTROY TWIN TOWERS AND HIT PENTAGON IN DAY OF TERROR.

The man selling the papers was wearing dark blue pants, a light blue button-up short-sleeved shirt, and a U.S. Army cap. He looked to be in his 50s and had a serious expression on his face. "I have newspapers from Y2K, when we didn't have a president for a while, 9/11. I have papers from cities where a lot of this happened. All new, crisp papers. They've never been opened or read."

"Where do you get the papers?"

"I do a lot of traveling, so when I'm in different areas, I collect them."

"Is this a hobby of yours? Or are you a news junky?" I asked.

"No, it's to make a buck."

"How's business?"

"A lot of people came by to see them today. They'll buy them tomorrow. More importantly, when school is getting ready to start, teachers will come and pick them up."

"Are you trying to make any sort of political statement with the papers?"

"I have everything from conservative to liberal, so I stay out of it. There's the history."

After some prodding, he told me he's a proud Republican. "First president I ever voted for was Nixon. I've never voted Democratic."

"Why not?"

"Democrats are just too liberal. I like conservative values. I'm a Christian myself. Republicans are more in line with what I'm thinking. In the '80s and '90s when the liberals took over, that was way too far out."

"Can you give me an example?"

"The homosexuality. There is nothing right about homosexuality. Where do you draw the line? In a conservative society, there's punishment. Where's the line? I think we oughta bring spanking back. Get rid of abortion. Get rid of gays. Get us back to our religious beginnings."

"Get rid of gays?"

"Gay marriage."

"Do you care about things like health care and the economy? Or just gay marriage and abortion?"

"Only the rich can afford to be sick."

"Do you have health care?"

"Not at this time, ma'am."

"You travel a lot. You must be affected by high gas prices."

"Gas prices are out of control. Those speculators up on Wall Street take workin' people like me for a ride."

"Yet you vote Republican because of gay marriage and abortion?"

"Yes, ma'am."

"Thanks for your time." I walked away shaking my head. I would have asked a few more questions, but a man was waiting to buy a 9/11 paper.

I quickly checked on Ryan. He seemed content reading and people-watching, so I decided to do a few more interviews. I've read that gun sellers don't like talking to reporters, so I wasn't surprised by the reactions I received. After introducing myself to a man selling pistols, he said, "You wouldn't catch me dead in California." Another man selling a random mix of children's toys and switchblades simply said, "Those damn liberals."

A man wearing a black muscle shirt, jeans, and a Harley David-
son baseball cap was more than happy to talk about his selection of
knives, compasses, sporting equipment, and gun holsters. "I don't
hunt. I don't even own a gun, but I've been settin' up at gun shows for
22 years. I make decent money. I enjoy meeting people. I'm probably
one of the nicest people here," he said, smiling. He was a friendly man,
selling some of the scariest looking knives I've ever seen.

"The name's Richard. Have a seat."

"What's the deal with the knives?" I asked.

"Only two reasons to have a knife. Collectors buy 'em. Or you can
use 'em for things like deer huntin'."

"Are there any rules here?"

"They make you tie all of the guns. If they catch one on the table,
they'll warn you once, and then you're out. It depends where you're at.
At other shows, you have to put them under glass."

"So you don't own a gun, but you've been coming to gun shows
for 22 years?"

"Yeah, I'm a member of the NRA, but some of the things they do
I don't agree with."

"Like what?"

"Some of them have attitudes. It's not that I want people to lose
their guns rights. It's not that I want everyone to have a gun. I'd be
scared to death to see some of 'em have guns."

"What do you think of gun control?"

"There's loopholes in everything."

Richard was in the process of moving back to Oklahoma from
Wichita, Kansas. "Some of the most unfriendly people I ever met live
in Wichita." Without thinking, I asked him if he'd heard of Thomas
Franks's *What's the Matter with Kansas?*

"No. What's it about?"

"It's about why people vote against their economic interests by voting Republican."

"Sounds interesting."

"Wait here. I'll get you a copy." I ran over to Ryan and grabbed a
copy out of his backpack. I also grabbed a stack of articles from the

fact folder. "I just met a nice man selling scary knives who's moving here from Kansas. I'll be done soon." I ran back to Richard's booth, gave him the book, and asked him if he voted.

"Yeah, I'm a Democrat, but I vote for who I think would do the best job. I became a traitor and switched over in 1986."

"Why'd you switch?"

"The Republicans were very frivolous. Their opinions got to where it's not what's good for the people of the United States; it's what's good for the Republicans. I didn't think that was right, so I changed. At least the Democrats want to talk about things. I'm not saying they're any better, but they can't be any worse. Yes, everybody's greedy."

"What do you think about Iraq? Do people ever talk to you about Iraq at gun shows?"

"Oh, yeah!" he said, laughing. "You hear everything. The weapons have been found. Iraqis were on the 9/11 planes. Saddam flew the plane!"

"I've heard the same things! How do you respond?"

"Didn't we help put him in power at one time? Most people don't know the history behind this mess. I disagree with the terrorists. That's wrong, but the money could be used somewhere else. We don't need to be there anymore. Everybody that I personally know says, 'Let's bring our men home.'"

"What message would you send politicians?"

"Bring our men home. End this war and fix the problems we got here at home before it's too late. How 'bout this? Do somethin'. We might not be rich, but we're watchin'."

A few men were interested in buying knives, so I thanked Richard for his time. "Feel free to come back if you get bored."

I decided to walk around the hall one more time before going back to the food area. As I was passing Dave, the man in the wheelchair, he motioned me over. "So tell me about this project of yours," he said. I gave him my spiel and he asked one of the guys in his booth to separate the tables so I could go inside the square. I nervously walked in, wondering why he wanted to talk after our last interaction. "OK, what do you want to know?"

I walked over to the table and grabbed one of the heavy semis, "What do people use these guns for?"

"We live on ranches around here, and we got lots of skunks runnin' around," said one of the sellers.

"They're kinda big for shooting skunks." I grabbed another semi and pointed it toward the ceiling.

"Are these assault rifles?"

"Yeah," said Dave.

"What do people use them for?"

"I don't have no use for assault rifles. But people use 'em for shootin' deer. Two hundred and twenty-three rounds."

"Seriously? People use these to kill deer?"

"Yeah."

"Poor deer."

"Why? There's lots of deer runnin' around."

"Seems kind of extreme for a deer. So could I buy this gun right now?"

"I'd have to ship it to California."

"What if I lived here in Oklahoma? How long would it take?"

"Three minutes."

"Three minutes! Really? How many could I buy?"

"Five."

"Five! What about the background check?"

He grabbed an application form and explained the process. "You fill this out, then we call the FBI. You might pass all of this, but if I have any kind of feelin' that somethin' ain't right, I ain't gonna sell you a gun. If a red flag goes off, sorry sir, you can't buy these guns."

"Does that happen often?"

"No. The outlaws are just as smart as you. So are the dealers."

For the next hour or so, Dave, an ex-Marine who almost always votes Republican, shared his opinions on everything from health care and wages to the military and Iraq. "You're gonna get many casualties. That's just a sad part of life. My number one concern is our boys, not theirs."

"It's not just boys who are being killed. Young women are also on the front lines."

"True."

"Think about all the innocent civilians being killed. If you don't care about them, you might want to read this article about a lieutenant who said the U.S. can't kill its way out of this mess." I pulled a June 13, 2005, *Knight-Ridder* article by Tom Lasseter out of the fact folder. "It's called 'Military Action Won't End Insurgency, Growing Number of US Officers Believe.'" I read this part out loud: "Lt. Col. Frederick P. Wellman, who works with the task force overseeing the training of Iraqi security troops, said the insurgency doesn't seem to be running out of new recruits, a dynamic fueled by tribal members seeking revenge for relatives killed in fighting. 'We can't kill them all,' Wellman said. 'When I kill one, I create three.'"

"Here, I have an extra copy." He folded it up and put it in his pocket.

"I wish I was still young and naive. This war is gettin' to be a very hard thing to swallow," he said. "But those antiwar protesters, they don't support the troops. Jane Fonda should have been shot for treason."

Ouch. This was one of those unexpected moments when I didn't know how to respond, so I ignored the Jane Fonda comment.

"Does the government support the troops by making it difficult to get decent health care when they return? Does the government support the troops by failing to provide them with armored Humvees and the appropriate gear?" I asked.

"I come from a military family. I know what goes on. My grandpa died in a Veterans hospital. I told my wife, 'If I get sick and you put me in a VA, I'll come back to haunt you.' Those boys aren't treated right."

"So why doesn't anyone speak out? I'm seeing the yellow ribbon magnets everywhere. How do you explain it? Look at the voting records. Republicans have a poor record when it comes to veterans' health care."

"It pisses me off. In the end, it's all about money. But no one was drafted. They made a choice. I personally think a boy out of high school should serve for two years. I got two boys. I got a 19-year-old and an eight-year-old. Son is in the National Guard."

"How would you feel if he was sent to Iraq?"

"That's the luck of the draw. Do I want him to go? Hell no."

"And what about the military families who feel like they've been lied to?" I asked.

"Me and my dad argue all the time about this."

"What about the veterans who take part in antiwar marches? Have you heard of groups like Iraq Veterans Against the War?"

"No."

"The group was started by people who served in Iraq. They oppose the occupation. Would you be willing to read some of their stuff?"

"I'd love to. I'm open-minded. Look, Saddam was a threat. I don't feel sorry for the insurgents. I believe it was the right thing to do, but we have problems we need to deal with here at home."

All of a sudden, Ryan appeared. "We need to leave."

"Oh, no. What happened?"

"I took a few photos of a mannequin with ammo straps on her chest and a bunch of paranoid guys with guns showed up saying they were gonna kick my ass. I erased the pictures, but they still asked the security guard to arrest me. We need to leave. Now."

I turned around and looked at the exit area. Five angry men with shotguns slung over their shoulders were staring us down.

"Come with me," Dave said sternly.

We followed him to the door. As I spoke with the event coordinator, a big, burly man looked as if he was about to charge Ryan. "I don't feel safe around this guy," Ryan loudly said to the security guard. "Please keep him away from me." Before the burly guy could do anything, Dave placed his wheelchair between the guys and us. We didn't see this coming. "Let it go. They're with me," he said. The men looked shocked. They stood in silence for five seconds then angrily walked away. We were speechless. We went back to Dave's booth, but decided we should leave because almost everyone in the area was staring. Ryan couldn't thank Dave enough. "Don't worry about it," said Dave. "But next time, leave the camera at home. These guys don't like their photos taken."

"I'm really sorry," said Ryan. "I wasn't taking photos of anyone, but I had to get a photo of that mannequin."

I thanked Dave for inviting me into his booth. "I don't think I'll ever own a gun, but for a few seconds, I had a strong desire to shoot one. Never in my wildest dreams did I think I'd ever want to shoot a gun."

"If you're ever back in Oklahoma, look me up. I'll have ya both over to the ranch for a barbeque and target practice. I really enjoyed talkin' to ya. Funny, I thought all you San Franciscans were tree huggin' liberals."

I smiled and said, "How do you know I'm not?"

He tilted his head to the right, raised his eyebrows, and watched us walk out.

Ryan was clearly shaken up. He was silent until we got into the van, then he explained what happened. He saw the top half of a female mannequin on a table with two strands of ammo covering her chest. It was so ridiculous, he had to take a photo. Within seconds, five guys with rifles slung over their shoulders surrounded him and said, "What do you think you're doing? You're liable to get your ass kicked for taking photos." They called over a security guard and told him to confiscate the camera and have Ryan arrested. He erased the photos, but the men weren't satisfied. He told them he would leave, but he had to find me first.

He was speechless when Dave defended him. "That was amazing. I disagree with him on a lot of things, but he agreed to talk to us. There was a genuine understanding between us. That was big. He didn't have to do that. He charged right over there and he didn't even know what happened," he said as we sat sweating in the hot van. "When you think about it, the whole thing was ridiculous, because all I had was a camera, and I'm surrounded by gun-owning, gun-collecting, gun-wielding nutcases who are filled with fear. What would drive people to be so obsessed with guns and weaponry and defense? They're scared. And they fight their fear by buying more guns. Then they're even more scared because they own so many guns. Then they're scared of their guns, scared of each other, and scared of themselves."

Bull Riding, the U.S. Army, and Hooters

We needed to take a break from politics and cool off, so the next day we went to a water park in Oklahoma City. It was only my second time at a water park, and I'm proud to report that Ryan and I braved the 277-foot-long speed slide featuring a 64-foot free fall. We were the only adults in line, and I'm frightened of heights, so it took me more than five minutes to let go. "You can do it!" screamed the giddy kids behind me. We wanted to see the expressions on each other's faces once we went into free-fall mode, so I watched Ryan scream as he went down, and then it was his turn to watch me. The guy in charge of making sure everything runs smoothly had to give me a little push because I had an even harder time letting go the second time around.

On the way back to the hotel, we passed a protest with people carrying signs that said, "Iraq: Neo-Con Job," "Support Cindy Sheehan," and "Fire Rove." We briefly stopped and met a number of Dennis Kucinich supporters. "It's important to let people know that we're here," said Sharon Ginsler. "There are so many lies and deceptions coming out of the White House. We're doing this every Tuesday. It's our responsibility to have the discussion with others. Once you start talking to people about it, they ask questions." Many passersby honked and gave the group the thumbs up, while others flipped them off and told them to move to Canada.

That night, we went to Bullnanza, an event "featuring the world's top 50 bull riders and the best bucking bulls from around the country." The thought of watching men riding bulls didn't sound very appealing, but in order to truly experience other parts of the country, we promised to immerse ourselves in the culture, so I decided to go wearing my Veggie Heaven T-shirt.

Much to my surprise, the press person I had contacted that morning met us at the front gate and gave us a backstage tour and a pair of

VIP tickets. We had access to the platform directly above the bull pens. The bulls we could see paced around in small circles looking vicious and irritated. Wouldn't you if you were trapped in a tiny square cage? All of a sudden, a guy climbs on your back, someone finally decides to open your cage, and you're let loose to AC/DC blaring over the speakers and a crowd yelling at the top of its lungs. No wonder they kick and twist in a rage of anger. I didn't want to see anyone get hurt, but I was secretly rooting for the bulls. Once the gates swung open, the ride never lasted more than eight seconds, but it was painful to watch the men get thrown to the ground and sometimes even stomped on. Eight seconds is what it takes to win the $100,000 prize.

Because this is a sporting event, I expected to see sponsors like Wrangler, Pepsi, and Coors, but I didn't expect to see Hooters and the U.S. Army. Bull rider number 38 wore jeans under black chaps with yellow fringe hanging from the sides, a black shirt under a black vest, and a black cowboy hat. His clothing was covered in white and gold U.S. Army logos. The front of his vest was covered in the logo and American flags. The back said "U.S. ARMY" on the top and "GOARMY.COM" on the bottom.

Just as I was looking around for someone to ask about the army sponsorship, three heavily made-up young women with similar hairstyles showed up on the platform wearing casual orange pants and skin tight, low-cut Hooters tank tops. The back of the tops said, "Delightfully Tacky, Yet Unrefined." Ryan and I looked at each other. Is this a joke? Turns out Hooters is a major Bullnanza sponsor and the Hooters waitresses were serving cocktails in the VIP room. I have a hard time calling them "Hooters Girls." The platform was fairly small, so there I was in a ponytail, jean skirt, and Veggie Heaven T-shirt hanging out with large-breasted Hooters waitresses. Ryan couldn't resist taking a photo. We got to talking about our trip, and I asked them if they vote. "No," said Leslie. "I haven't made the time to register."

I looked at the others. They shook their heads and smiled.

"Do you follow politics at all?"

"Not really."

Since first hearing about Hooters ten or so years ago, I've often wondered why any woman would want a job that requires her to serve chicken wings in pantyhose, orange short shorts, and an extra-small white tank top with her boobs falling out. I wasn't sure if I'd ever meet a Hooters waitress again, so I asked.

"To pay for college. And I like my coworkers."

"What about the customers? What are the men like?"

"They're mostly pigs. The frat boys are predictable, but the guys who come in with their families are really creepy. When their wives go to the bathroom, they flirt or give us their business cards."

"Guys bring their families to Hooters? I saw a sign advertising free lunches for kids on Sundays when we were in Mississippi, but I thought it was a joke. Let me guess. They come in after church on Sundays?"

"Yeah! I've met a lot of people who come in after church."

As we continued talking, I looked at the sea of cowboy hats in the crowd and noticed that the majority of the men in the nearby bleachers were staring.

Later that night, I visited the website, *army.mil,* to find out more about the bull-riding sponsorship and found photos of bull riders wearing U.S. Army black shirts and black jeans speaking to high school students. One caption said, "James White, an Army bull rider, talks to students at Widefield High School, Colorado Springs, Colo., about being a bull rider and how that parallels with being a soldier." How does being a bull rider parallel with being a soldier? In an April 20, 2004, Army News Service press release announcing the partnership between the U.S. Army and Professional Bull Riders (PBR), Lt. Gen. Dennis D. Cavin, commander of the Army Accessions Command, is quoted saying, "Bull riders embody the tenets of the Warrior Ethos through their commitment to their mission, by never accepting defeat, never quitting and through the camaraderie among them."

Army bull rider, Jaron Nunnemaker, a 30-year-old from Willits, California, said bull riders are a lot like soldiers because "for us, it's a year-round thing too, and we also put our lives on the line; we do it for our families and so do (soldiers); in fact they do it for my family too."

Then I stumbled upon a People for the Ethical Treatment of Animals (PETA) action called "Tell the U.S. Army to Buck the Rodeo!" According to PETA, the U.S. Army spends approximately $2 million annually to sponsor the PBR. "Apparently, the Army's goal is to recruit new soldiers by sponsoring cowboys and providing public relations and 'pageantry support' for rodeos. This means that American citizens' tax dollars are fueling horrific and cruel rodeo events such as calf roping, steer wrestling, and bull riding. Often defended under the banner of tradition, rodeos use normally gentle animals such as horses, steer, and calves and provoke them into 'wild' behavior with the use of spurs, tail-twisting, electric prods, and straps cinched tightly around their abdomens. Even when animals aren't injured—and they often are—they still suffer from fear and pain during these events."

A Truth-Seeker

I met 39-year-old Jerrie Morales, a mother of four who was studying to become a nurse, at Oneighty, a megachurch for Tulsa's young Christians. The hi-tech building looked more like a cross between an Apple store and Virgin Records than a church. Flat panel displays and iPods blaring the latest Christian tunes attracted large crowds of young people, who looked like they just jumped out of a Gap ad. The boys wore ripped-up jeans and T-shirts, and the girls proudly wore spaghetti string tank tops and short skirts.

Jerrie brought her daughter to Oneighty to try out for an upcoming talent show. Like so many people I've met on this trip, Jerrie doesn't fit the "red state" stereotype even though she voted for George W. Bush both times.

"I think gas prices are going to kill our budget, and they don't raise wages when everything else goes up. I'm going to nursing school and am making the same amount I'll make when I become a nurse and we'll just barely make it. I had to get rid of our health insurance in order to pay for school," she said.

"I was surprised by the high cost of everything. Housing and gas cost a lot more in the Bay Area, but food, eating out, and a bottle of water in a gas station is the same."

"I don't know how people survive," she said. "A lot of nurses are leaving California to come here and work. I think we're just now opening our eyes. We need to be aware. We don't know what goes on outside of the United States. I grew up in a military family and lived in Germany, so I have an idea, but it's hard to get information. I'm not sure what I can trust on the Internet."

"What issues do you care about?"

"I want to know how women are dealing with the war. I know what they're showing on TV is just one group of people. They're not showing women like me. Those Iraqi women are like me. They're trying to educate and provide good health care for their kids, just like I am. I remember seeing an Iraqi woman whose baby was dying. She tried to throw herself in the grave with the baby. I was there watching it and bawling. I've read things and watched things. I'm interested to know how those women are doing. I also want to know how the Afghan women are doing."

"You are one of the few people I've interviewed who's expressed an interest in the Iraqi and Afghan women. I've met a lot of people who say we're freeing the Iraqis one minute and we should kill them the next."

"That's a sign of fear. The more the gas prices go up and the more people aren't making enough money and the more they're having problems, the less they're going to care about their fellow men. The average American is stressed out. I try not to let myself go there. I go to work every day and deal with people who are dying and I know they [Iraqis] are going through the same thing. We're supposed to go after one group of people and we get this lady's four-year-old. That could have been my child. We have our own terrorists here. The first terrorist attack was not on 9/11. We had the KKK. We had terrorism when we gave smallpox to the tribes."

"Do you vote?"

"Oh, yes. I homeschooled my kids to teach them about government and the Founding Fathers and the tribes. I want them to see the truth and think outside the box. Don't ever look at anything as black and white because it never is. My kids were coming home from school saying, 'I'm a Democrat,' 'I'm a Republican,' 'I'm a liberal.' I said, 'You can't be a Republican or a Democrat. You have to be an American.' Don't say you're a Republican until you can find ten things wrong with your party and ten things wrong with Democrats. The Republicans here were trying to pull the churches apart because a lot of Christians are Democrats."

"Are you a member of the Democratic or Republican party?"

"No. When I wrote the Democratic Party and the Republican Party asking them for their platforms, the only thing they sent me was their criticisms against the other party; they wouldn't tell me what they believed in. I'm seeing too many flaws. Things are getting so hectic. There is so much you need to know about."

"And the issues people almost always raise during my interviews are gay marriage and abortion."

"Oh yeah, because those are smoke screens. Let's use those issues so we can ignore things that really matter."

"Where do you get your news?"

"I read and research and ask questions. I want to know how people are getting by. The government isn't going to take care of us. People get annoyed with me because I push buttons. When I get out of school, I'm going to spend a lot more time researching and reading the news. It's time to get informed."

From Evangelism to Inclusion

Every time I thought I couldn't bring myself to go to another church, I would get another recommendation that sounded too good to pass up. Several people told me I had to meet the charismatic Bishop Carlton Pearson of Higher Dimensions Church in Tulsa. A fourth generation classical Pentecostal preacher, Carlton had been a rising African American star among wealthy and powerful mostly white evangelicals, including Oral Roberts, Pat Robertson, and Billy Graham. "I had it goin' on. I could pick up the phone and borrow anybody's jet." He preached to more than 5,000 faithful worshipers at Higher Dimensions, the church he founded in 1981. He hosted a weekly television show on the Trinity Broadcasting Network, a popular Christian cable channel. He was asked to pray with President George W. Bush and give political advice to black leaders like former Secretary of State Colin Powell. "I said, 'I don't want to ever see George without blacks around him. You never saw Clinton without blacks.'" Carlton was on his way to becoming an evangelical powerhouse.

In 2002, he had a revelation and the evangelicals who once invited him to preach from their pulpits branded him a heretic. "I started saying that nonbelievers are not going to hell. God loves everyone," he says in a relaxed tone in his office. Carlton is a handsome man with short black hair, a nicely trimmed thin mustache and goatee, and a genuine smile. He's wearing black slacks and a yellowish-orange button-up shirt with sunglasses hanging around his neck.

Carlton always dreamed of being a bishop. He gave his first sermon when he was just five and spoke in tongues at eight or nine. But once he started his own church and his following grew, the pressure to save the world from going to hell became an overwhelming burden. "I did funerals where, based on our doctrine, these people were in hell, not only the ones I was eulogizing, but supposedly most of the people I met in airports, in hotels, on the road, at the mall, these are all people basically hated by God. If He's going to torture them the way I'm taught, He pretty much hated them, but I'm supposed to love them and save them. I said, 'If you really love them, then you forgive them. What's with all this hell stuff? I can't save all these people, God, and I'm tired of the guilt,'" he says, barely pausing for a breath. "I get on these airplanes and I don't want to witness to the guy sitting next me, and I don't think he wanted me to. But I felt guilty. I put my headphones on and laid my head back, so the person wouldn't talk to me, and I'd go to sleep, then feel guilty for not witnessing enough. I realized I wasn't happy. I wasn't content. I was religiously guilty. That went on for years and I was reassessing what that meant."

He began "asking questions and answering the questions and then questioning the answers." That eventually led him to preach the gospel of inclusion. In 2002, he stopped preaching fire and brimstone and started reaching out to everyone, including gays, Muslims, even atheists. Attendance fell from 5,000 to a few hundred per week, and offerings dropped by tens of thousands of dollars a week. "It's cost me just about everything, but at least I'm free."

Free of guilt and the holier-than-thou attitude he once embraced as a conservative evangelical. "We are overly confident. We think we have all the answers. We think we are the answer," he said. "Religion is always telling you, 'You aren't good enough.' We create religions to make us feel better about ourselves. You think God's OK with me today? Well, I don't know, did you pray? Well, yeah, I was praying this morning. Did you pay when you prayed? How much did you pay? I tipped him a 10. You tipped him a 10? Why don't you just give it all to him? Well, I gotta pay my rent. God will help you," he said, laughing and shaking his head.

"What is it about preachers and power?" I asked. "You preached to 5,000 people every week. You had a lot of power."

"Sometimes, we who are in ministry are trying to prove something. We are overly assertive, we are overachievers, we like to be seen and heard. Celebrated. So we build these things around us that feature and focus on us. We stand on the pulpit by ourselves for an hour and a half and everybody's listening to us and taking notes on what we say. And we're the second cousin to God. Marriage is jacked, family is screwed up, private failure, everything else is messed up, but on that platform, he is the giant," he said. "The abuse, the dysfunction, the anger and arrogance and ignorance of religion is profound, and it has produced a generation of very sick people."

Carlton said conservative evangelicals must have someone to hate and, more importantly, they must have something to raise money around. "Most of these guys do it for money. If I scream loud against sin and against liberals, especially as a black, they would love me. That's when I had the backing. I could stand up right now and say, 'I missed God. I made an error in judgment. I was influenced by demons. I'm now back with God. The devil is a terrorist. Islam is wrong. Homosexuality is wrong. Abortion is wrong. America is going to hell,'" he said, raising his voice as if he was on the pulpit. "The money would pour in and so would the people. I know what bells to ring and buttons to push to turn them on. This town would eat me up and so would the country because I would be one of the few outspoken conservative blacks."

Carlton believes the gospel of inclusion will see massive growth over the next decade. "You watch what happens. They who are with us are more than they who are against us. There's gonna be increasing revelations of hypocrisy in the church. They played the Catholic thing down as best they could, but it's in every church. Religion molests people under the guise. We abuse people financially and psychologically."

Wealthy antichoice pastors speak out and march against abortion, but Carlton said they never once supported St. Domenics, a facility he used to run that supported young unwed mothers. "They didn't give us a dime to take care of those girls."

"Did your politics change after you went through this transformation?"

"Somewhat. I still believe that blacks need to join the Republican Party en masse to level the playing field. You can't change that party from the outside. I don't think we should all be Democrats."

Carlton eventually became involved in a variety of movements: he joined the board of Planned Parenthood, and also fights for gay rights. "I so strongly believe in these causes. I'm willing to give it all up and go the direction I'm going 'cause I think it's gonna be more helpful in the long term."

"Isn't that the Christian way?"

"Absolutely. Absolutely."

I was curious to see Carlton in action, so a few days later I attended his Sunday service. The sign outside said, COME AS YOU ARE—LEAVE AS HE IS. There were hundreds of empty chairs on the bottom level and the second level was completely empty, but Carlton didn't seem to notice. He was on fire.

"Our concepts of hell are a form of insanity. It has created in us eternal damnation. I know. I can support eternal damnation in Scripture if I want to."

Carlton enthusiastically preached to the diverse crowd on a red-carpeted stage with a live band and an 11-person choir behind him. He was wearing a long, tailored, shiny gray jacket over matching pants. His podium stood behind a large golden eagle that looked as if it was preparing for take off. Tall columns and two big TV screens lined the wallpapered walls. I wondered what it felt like with 5,000 people in the room. Do the people around me notice all the empty seats? Or are they used to it by now?

"There's a beautiful marvelous change coming. If we can get the psychological neurosis out of our minds that someday God's gonna kill you and destroy you and then torture you. He's worse than Saddam. Can you imagine God in heaven and your favorite alcoholic uncle who always gave you a quarter, always drunk, cussed, and he's in hell now. You'd get him out, but your God won't?"

"All right. All right," said the energetic woman next to me. A short black elderly woman wearing jeans, a white T-shirt, and white baseball cap, she was on her feet throughout most of the two-and-a-half-hour service.

"We are not just dealing with personal issues, we are dealing with cultural abuse. We are dealing with erroneous perceptions of an angry and judgmental God who plans to ultimately punish us for all our perceived imperfections and sins. We're dealing with centuries of religiously inflicted pain. This is hand-me-down, traditional, family, generational, and historical pain."

This was deeper and more profound than anything I'd heard in church until then.

"It's made the human race paranoid. We believe that God is angry. In some ways, the Gods we created are because they've become us. We have become what we've imagined. Remember, you become what you think about. Emotion is the power that attracts. What you fear most you will ultimately experience. We're fighting world terrorism, but the biggest world terrorism that we've experienced is religion. 'Cause religion terrorizes people with this ultimate customized torture chamber that we call hell and a God who's gonna send you there through his devil. God's up there makin' a list, checkin' it twice, find out who's naughty or nice. Find everybody smokes, everybody drinks, everybody lusts, fuss, and cuss. Put 'em all in one. You'd have 'em all. Jesus only wants the saved ones. Not only the ones that he washed, but the ones that stayed clean."

"That's right."

"People all around you are weeping aloud. In many ways, you are, too. The American government is weeping aloud. The Iraqi government is weeping aloud. The governments of the world. The gangs. The angry husbands and wives and children are weeping aloud. You're weeping aloud in your own homes by not talking to each other. You're weeping aloud in your own relationships by carrying gossip and looking to hurt somebody. You're screaming out in a prayer meeting. In a Bible study. Or rushing to a conference and buying someone's tape and tuning into Christian television. We're all screaming this morning by being here. We're in pain for whatever reason. Tell somebody, 'I'm on my way to freedom I didn't know was imaginable.'"

The woman on my right grabbed my hand, and screamed, "I'm on my way to freedom I didn't know was imaginable." Then she shoved her fist in the air.

After the service, I asked a diverse group of people eating together in the lunch room about Carlton's transformation and their personal journeys.

Teresa, a local professor, says she didn't have to struggle with the new message because it just made sense, but it wasn't easy. "We lost just about all of our friends. We associated regularly with quite a few people and most of them left."

"They stopped talking to you?"

"Yeah, we were isolated pretty quickly. If you're in the store and they see you, they go the other way. People we were very close to."

"It was hard, but what Bishop teaches enables me and my family to be less judgmental," added Jennifer.

Seamus, a self-described radical Pentecostal who believes the Republican Party has turned into an autocratic party, said the transformation couldn't have come at a better time. "I was tired of the same old same old. I remember just before I heard him preaching about the gospel of inclusion, I started telling my children that I didn't want to be called a Christian anymore because I was tired of being associated with those kind of people. I wanted to be called Christ-like rather than Christian. And then I heard this and I said, 'That is what I'm lookin' for.'"

"Why didn't you want to be called Christian anymore?"

"There's a lot of hypocrisy right here in the buckle of the Bible Belt. When you come here, you find gay bashers who get caught with men, you find more kids having kids out of wedlock. Christianity and most religions are homophobic. They're led by men who make the rules. They try to quiet women and anybody different from themselves because they don't want anybody to threaten their manhood. If you notice, religions and religious organizations are totally devoid of democracy. That's why I try to disassociate myself. This is the first time I've really been touched by a thought that God really loves all people."

"Some of you have been coming to this church for years, in some cases, decades. I hope you don't mind me being so blunt, but have you been living a lie all that time? I'm just trying to understand why you wouldn't question the Bishop or stop coming if you disagreed with him on such a deep level."

"It's a fair question," said Shelly. "Most of us were raised in the Bible Belt and when you grow up in a church family, you're taught to obey your preacher. Listen, but rarely, maybe never, question. So that stays with you as you age. Everyone you see in this room, deep down inside, they were longing for a different message, but this is all they knew. It's all I knew. Now I question everything. It's like I'm a different woman. I can't tell you how much this transformation has changed the lives of the people here. I wish I could say the same for our friends who've left."

Adventures along the Oklahoma Panhandle

If you want to see what America really looks like, spend as much time as possible on the backroads and in small towns. Otherwise, it all looks the same. Whenever we needed a break from drab hotel rooms, we would spend the evening at Borders. Independent bookstores were hard to find. In small towns, we rarely found anything open past 8:00, but in large cities, we knew we could rely on Borders to stay open until 11:00. Ryan would read, and I would transcribe the day's interviews and call my family and friends to check in. When we were in Tulsa, after practically falling asleep on the table, we stumbled out of the store at 10:45 and forgot where we were. Were we in Tulsa? Or were we in Oklahoma City? The larger towns, especially the strip malls, were beginning to look the same after a long day of interviews.

From Tulsa, we headed north. On the way, we passed all-American front yards displaying various patriotic decor, including a five-foot Statue of Liberty painted gold and a plastic gold eagle mounted on a United States flag that said, "These Colors Never Run." We also spotted a number of religious bumper stickers like, "For Whosoever Shall Call Upon the Name of the Lord Shall Be Saved," and "How Can Ye Escape the Damnation of Hell?" When we stopped for gas in Bartlesville, I met Mary, a 54-year-old housekeeper driving a white car with a bumper sticker on the back window that said, "I Vote by the Bible." She had long brown straight hair with bangs and was wearing glasses, jeans, and a white v-neck T-shirt. She told me she gets her news from the Bible and the 700 Club, the Christian Broadcasting Network's news show hosted by Pat Robertson, the televangelist who concurred with the late Jerry Falwell when he blamed the American Civil Liberties Union (ACLU), "the abortionists, and the feminists, and the gays, and the lesbians," for 9/11.

Mary was a Democrat in her younger years because she believed in "government for the people, by the people, and of the people," but after she was saved, she became a Republican. I asked her what it means to be a Republican.

"Republicans pick the people who believe like we do."

"You mean believe in the Bible?"

"Yes, and godly principles."

A gas attendant approached us, saying I needed permission to interview customers, so I took a photo of Mary and her bumper sticker and we left.

Driving through downtown Bartlesville, you can't miss the Price Tower Arts Center, a nineteen-story, 221-foot-high building designed by Frank Lloyd Wright. We saw a fire station up ahead, and I realized that I hadn't interviewed any city workers yet, so I asked Ryan to stop. He stayed in the van and took a nap. I took a few bites of a power bar, grabbed my recorder, and walked into the garage area. After I introduced myself, five firemen aged 22 to 51 gathered around a table, but at first only a few talked. After 20 minutes or so, they all chimed in and shared stories about working two jobs and living paycheck to paycheck. Bruce, 51, said he "mows a big yard"; Johnny, 31, runs a tire shop; Jerry, 45, works for a plumber; and Jake, 27, does construction.

"We should be able to afford a house and send our kids to school on our salaries," said Jerry. "You get here, go shower, then go to your other job. Your wife doesn't see you for 24 hours. Then she wakes up and goes to work. Your kids don't see you until you get home at night. Then you wake up and do the same thing the next day."

Most of the guys were registered Republicans, but they were fed up with the party. "They [politicians] always talk about business and being for small business owners, but they never talk about the people who keep the community going," said Bruce. "Why don't they talk about the teachers, the trash men, the firefighters, the police officers? They don't know what it's like living paycheck to paycheck."

Johnny said he'd like politicians to spend more time focusing on gas prices, the high cost of living, and jobs, and less time on gay marriage. "That should be the last thing on their list," he said. "The government has no right telling people who they're gonna marry and who they're gonna sleep with," added Bruce. "Who's our government to be telling us that? There are more important issues to deal with. Our economy is about to implode. People are up to their ears in debt. That's more important."

Just as we were about to discuss Iraq, the fire bell went off. The men calmly walked over to the cubbyhole area, grabbed their black hard hats and smoke-filled yellow jackets, jumped on the fire truck, smiled, and waved as they drove off. Before I left, Joe, a young guy who rarely chimed in during the conversation, said, "I can't believe you got these guys to talk about politics. We never discuss those issues at work."

From Bartlesville, we spent the next three days driving west through the Oklahoma Panhandle, formerly called "No Man's Land." A thinly populated strip that seems to go on forever, the panhandle is just south of the Kansas border. I couldn't get over the thick swirling mass of white puffy clouds and the sheer enormity of the bright blue sky that would slowly turn fiery orange as the hours went by. On the way, we passed wheat fields, old oil rigs, and windmills.

Even though we were off the beaten path, it was close to impossible to avoid running into a Wal-Mart. After four months on the road, I still found myself saying, "I can't believe there's a Wal-Mart here." I did quite a few interviews in Wal-Mart parking lots because they are always filled with a diverse range of people constantly coming and going. The people I met who made six to seven dollars an hour told me that while they miss mom-and-pop shops, they wouldn't be able to afford the basics if it weren't for Wal-Mart. The workers I met said they rarely asked for raises or health care because they were grateful to have a job at a time when so many people were struggling to find one. They were afraid they'd be fired if they spoke up or even mentioned the word "union." Hardly anyone followed the controversy surrounding Wal-Mart's business practices, and none knew about the sex discrimination lawsuit filed by six current and former employees in June 2001. The case subsequently turned into a class action representing over two million women, the largest in United States history.

As we continued driving along Highway 64, we were talking about the contrast between the enormous blue sky and the desolate, gritty, and slightly eerie long, flat stretch of road ahead when all of a sudden we entered a swarm of flies. They immediately went into attack mode. They were slamming into all sides of the van, and we couldn't see a thing. It sounded like someone was pelting us with pebbles. We quickly rolled up the windows and Ryan turned on the windshield wipers. They barely moved, and the temperature was still hovering around 97 degrees, so it was not a pleasant experience. In fact, it was awful. It felt like we were trapped in a steamy car wash, only the brushes were bugs.

Fifteen long minutes later, it ended, and we found ourselves in a town called Hooker (population 1,788). Was this a joke? We pulled into the parking lot of the Hooker Gift Shop selling "horny toad" souvenirs and did our best to wipe the bugs off the windows. Inside the shop, we found Hooker shot glasses, Hooker street signs, "Caution: I Brake for Horny Toads" bumper stickers, and T-shirts announcing "Once a Hooker Always a Hooker" and "All My Friends Are Hookers." Ryan bought a white T-shirt with blue lettering that said:

HOOKER, OKLAHOMA

SUPPORT YOUR LOCAL HOOKER

A LOCATION NOT A VOCATION

ALL MY FRIENDS ARE HOOKERS

I had to refrain from laughing when the sweet 70-something woman behind the counter who looked like she had just finished baking an apple pie asked me, in the most innocent voice, why I wasn't buying anything. "You can't come all the way to Hooker and go home empty-handed! Here, this is one of our best sellers." She handed me a Hooker shot glass and smiled when I said I'd buy one for my brother. "He should come back for our streetwalkers festival." On our way out of town, we passed the Hooker Elementary School and saw a sign for the Hooker Horny Toads American Legion baseball team.

Welcome to Liberal, Kansas!

We hopped on Highway 54 and drove north for about 25 minutes from Hooker to Liberal, Kansas. When we spotted Liberal on the map before we left, we decided to visit, even if it was out of the way. How could we not visit Liberal? Ironically enough, Liberal (population 20,218) couldn't be more conservative. In 2004, George W. Bush got 70 percent of the vote. When we arrived, we were greeted by a "Welcome to the City of Liberal" billboard above "Meth Watch" and "POW-MIA" signs. We also saw a garbage can that said, "Help Keep Liberal Clean."

The *Liberal Visitor's Guide* explains how the town got its name. "In the 1880s water was a rare commodity in Southwest Kansas. Travelers and ranchers needed a place to rest their livestock and quench their thirst as they headed to the west, but when water was available it was quite expensive.

"Mr. S. S. Rogers homesteaded in this area and dug a well. When visitors came through the area they asked Mr. Rogers if they could use his well. He obliged their requests, and when they had watered their livestock and restocked their water supply they asked Mr. Rogers what they owed him. 'Water is always free here,' Mr. Rogers would say.

"The surprised visitors would respond, 'That's mighty liberal of you.' In time the area became known as 'The Liberal Well.' As the name caught on, travelers were cautioned to be sure and stop at the Liberal Well. Just a few miles off the southern Santa Fe Trail route, Liberal became an important stop in the history of westward immigration.

"Mr. Rogers added a goods store so people could purchase other items they needed during their travels. Some decided to stay and farm this area and in 1886 Mr. Rogers added a post office to his store, incorporating the small community known as Liberal, Kansas."

Like so many of the small towns we drove through, Liberal was full of faded signs that proudly bore its name; the few businesses that were still open were clearly struggling to survive, even though there was little to no chance after Wal-Mart came to town.

Tanya, a 43-year-old nurse's aid I met at a Laundromat, told me Liberal was hurting. "There are no jobs. Look around. If you're not bilingual, you can't get a job. That's not fair. There used to be a large African American population. Not anymore."

A single mom with three kids, Tanya said she feared for her children's future. The education system was broken, the schools were decrepit, after-school programs didn't exist, the cost of college was constantly rising, and the job market was bleak. "There's nothing for our kids to do but sell drugs and hang out on the corners. It's about their future. I want my kids to leave to get a better life. This world is so messed up. Look at Iraq. We fightin' against each other and for what? Something Bush's dad started. What is he tryin' to prove? He's corruptin' our men. Look how many Americans got killed in this war. Gas prices are high. Oil companies makin' a killin'. We got our problems to deal with at home."

"Where do you get your news?"

"News? It don't take a rocket scientist to figure out the world. It don't take a rocket scientist to figure out what's really goin' on. It don't. I pay attention 'cause I'm in this world, too. I watch CNN, but I'm sick of seein' those lying politicians. They give tax cuts to the rich and keep us poor."

"Are you able to make ends meet?"

"I live paycheck to paycheck."

Before we left, I saw a flyer for a garage sale in a residential neighborhood. We stopped by, and I asked the 50-something woman selling books, lampshades, dresser drawers, a few old bikes, and tools if I could hang around for a few hours and interview people. "Sure, but you can't interview me because I'm a closet liberal," she said smiling. "I'm one of the few."

I thought it would be fun to ask the Republicans in the group what it's like to live in a town called Liberal, but they didn't seem to like the question, so I changed the subject to Iraq. They said they supported the invasion, but believed it was time to bring the troops home. The topic they'd rather discuss was immigration. "The older white people here resent illegals and the border crisis. Just because the illegals need to find a better way of life, they shouldn't be allowed to break laws," said Doris. "Because of the beef plant in town, this town attracts a lot of illegals," added Joe, a 40-something man wearing jeans, a plaid flannel shirt, and black baseball hat. "The Mexicans are takin' over here. People are speakin' Spanish almost everywhere you go. And they have no morals. Crime is up. It's just a mess." Joe had to go because his son was crying and pulling on his pant leg, but before he took off, he asked me for my business card. He looked down at my name for a good five seconds, looked at me, looked down at the card again, and nervously said, "I'm, uh, I'm not racist. I hope I didn't offend you. I have nothin' against Mexicans. It's just that the town is changin' and it's becomin' a real problem."

He assumed I was Mexican. This has happened before. "Oh, don't worry about it," I said with a smile. "I'm not Mexican. I'm Native American. So actually... you're the immigrant." He nervously laughed, nodded his head, and went on his way.

Burning Man Break

On our way out of Liberal, we got a phone call from my friend Aaron. "You guys are working too hard. We have extra tickets to Burning Man. We'll do all the work. We'll bring extra costumes. All you need to do is show up."

Before we left San Francisco, we had briefly talked about going to Burning Man, an annual art festival in the Nevada desert, but because we had no idea where we'd be, we decided to leave it up in the air. It was 22 hours out of our way, but after five months of nonstop interviews, we needed to disconnect, so we went for it.

We spent the next week slowly making our way to the desert. Along the way, we stopped for gas in Wichita, Kansas, and we met Carol, 56, and Bob, 69, a retired couple traveling in an RV that was almost as long as my apartment and got only seven or eight miles per gallon! They couldn't believe that we didn't have air conditioning, so they invited me in for a cold drink while Ryan got gas, changed the oil, and made sure the van was in good shape. Carol and Bob were planning to spend the next three months traveling north toward the Dakotas. We shared stories about our travels, and when I told them about the project, Bob became visibly angry and slammed the steering wheel with his right hand. "I am sick of every politician in Washington, DC. They're all corrupt. We need to get rid of every last one of 'em and bring in new ones." Bob got most of his news from Bill O'Reilly, was most concerned about immigration, and blamed Bill Clinton for our lousy health care system. By that point, I had met many Bill O'Reilly fans, mostly men, and I could almost predict what they were going to say next. They blamed the Clinton administration for just about everything, and they were usually very angry.

I raised my eyebrows, but didn't say anything.

"Are you a liberal? You consider yourself a liberal? Oh, man, I should have guessed. The extremists have taken over the Democratic Party. There's no middle ground."

"Extremists?" I said. "Most of those extremists voted for the war and they keep funding it."

His wife, Carol, smiled at me and said, "Now Bob, don't give her a hard time." Ryan knocked on the RV door to let me know we were good to go. I briefly introduced him to Carol and Bob, but didn't want him to get into it with Bob, so I thanked them for the water and said good-bye.

From there, we visited Indian reservations in Nebraska, passed a 30-foot, 180-ton cast stone depiction of the Virgin Mary called Our Lady of Peace in Pine Bluffs, Wyoming, and hung out with truckers in Little America, Wyoming. When we arrived in Salt Lake City, Utah, we stumbled upon an outdoor Muslim Cultural Festival and an antiwar rally near a busy downtown intersection. We stopped and met several first-time protestors, including many Mormons, holding "Bring the Troops Home" signs.

When we began the long trek toward Nevada, I stared out the window and thought about how fun it would be to bring a few young conservative churchgoers along for the adventure. After a church service at a Tulsa megachurch called Church on the Move, I had asked a group of young women and men how they create community in such a huge church. "Do you ever get together in small groups after the service to talk about the pastor's message?" I asked.

"No, the pastor frowns upon private gatherings outside of the church because that might cause disagreements or debates."

I tried not to interview churchgoers in groups because they responded to my questions with sound bites that felt rehearsed. When we met individually, they seemed more relaxed and willing to speak from the heart.

What would happen if they were given the opportunity to be free of judgment and sin for a week? Free to just be themselves? What would they think of a community filled with people in costumes, music, wild art installations, fire dancers, flashing fluorescent lights, and art cars? What would happen after the culture shock wore off?

It's almost impossible to explain Burning Man to people who've never been. You really have to experience it yourself to truly understand why 40,000 (the numbers are growing every year) people would voluntarily spend a week building a community and camping in the hot and dusty Nevada desert. I've been going to Burning Man since 1998 because of the community, self-expression, creativity, art, and random acts of kindness. It's also nice to disconnect for a week. Depending on one's state of mind and interests, every experience is wildly different.

I feel an instant connection with people at Burning Man—the kind of connection that sadly seems to be missing, even in a city like San Francisco. These days, most people rarely make eye contact on the street or the bus because they're too busy fiddling with their iPods or talking on their cell phones.

One of my favorite things to do at Burning Man is to take off by myself for an afternoon to meet strangers, accept gifts, give gifts, and take in the beauty of it all. Other than ice and coffee, the event is commerce-free.

On one of my most memorable days at Burning Man, a guy holding a huge box of cold crunchy organic carrots approached me and said, "Good afternoon ma'am. Would you like an organic carrot?"

"I would love one, thank you."

I continued on and heard someone announcing, "Mango smoothies, mango smoothies!" I stopped and had a fresh mango smoothie.

Then a bunch of frat-boy types drinking Budweiser invited me in to their solar-powered massage chair camp. As I rested, I was sprayed with lavender water and offered a cup of sake and dried fruit.

After that, I stopped in a Middle Eastern camp and had mint tea and sweets.

Then I got my hair washed and had my face painted in the Hare Krishna camp. I took one last trip out to the edge of the playa, which is a fairly long trek even on a bike, and found a long line of people waiting for a snow cone. I chose the raspberry and grape syrups. After a long day, I returned to my camp and dinner was ready. It's truly a magical playground.

Over 3,000 people work year-round to keep Burning Man going. Like any city, there are roads, street signs, porta-potties that are cleaned on a regular basis, and a medical and information center. Upon arrival, friendly greeters politely tell Burners to "leave no trace" and to "have fun." They also pass out information packets, complete with a city map, a Burning Man sticker, which we put on the glove box, and an events guide filled with activities happening at all hours.

A few hours after we arrived, I met a guy wearing a GOP T-shirt in center camp, an area filled with a café, couches, and stages for music, theater, and spoken word. "Tell your camp that Republicans can have fun, too," he said. "Look, my friend is even wearing a dress." Before we parted ways, the man in the dress told me he had an interview at the White House in a few weeks, but he wouldn't tell me what job he was applying for. "It's top secret," he said.

We had a great time, but I never fully acclimated because I was preoccupied with the trip. I enjoyed taking a break from interviews and the news, but that year, we were too disconnected from the outside world. We didn't know Katrina had happened until three days after the levees broke. A table was set up near center camp with newspaper clippings and a jug for donations. On the night we found out, the Reverend Billy of the Church of Stop Shopping paid tribute to and said a few prayers for the victims. Joan Baez sang "Amazing Grace," and the crowd sang "When the Saints Go Marching In."

We left the next day and stopped in the first hotel we could find. We were glued to the television for hours and couldn't quite comprehend what we were seeing. We learned that 583 Katrina survivors were flown to Salt Lake City, so we left for Utah the next day. A few weeks earlier, I received an email from a guy going to law school in Salt Lake saying he didn't have money to contribute to the trip, but he did have an extra apartment, so we stayed there for the next week or so. As soon as we arrived and settled in, we drove 19 miles south to Camp Williams in Draper, Utah.

The road leading to the camp was lined with American flags and a homemade sign on a military vehicle said, "Welcome to Utah."

The Katrina survivors we met said that after spending a few horrific days in the New Orleans Convention Center, they boarded an airplane in New Orleans bound for San Antonio, Texas, or so they thought. After they took off, they were told they were actually going to Salt Lake City, Utah.

"I never got on an airplane in my life. It was an experience," said 49-year-old Walter Favoroth. "I was hugging my wife saying, 'Baby, are we gonna be all right?'"

He described saving his wife Yolanda. "I'm in water up to here and I had her on my neck. I had to walk like that for five miles. She doesn't know how to swim," he said. "In our house, we were watching the storm. We saw water coming under the door fast. I went to go get a sheet to put under the door and the water just came in. It filled our bathtub and our toilet and water rushed up to the ceiling. In a matter of five minutes, the whole house was full of water."

When I learned that so many people were unknowingly flown to a state that couldn't be more different from Louisiana, I expected to find a lot of angry people, but that wasn't the case. The people I met were happy to be safe and wanted nothing more than to share their stories.

Twenty-year-old Cornell Perkins was in the convention center for four days until a charter bus picked him up and took him to the Louis Armstrong International Airport in New Orleans. How did he feel when he found out he was on his way to Utah? "I felt bad at first. I'm like, what are we doing in Utah? I thought we were going to San Antonio like the National Guard told us. Man, we wound up far away from the south, but I've adjusted and I'm about to start my life over here in Utah."

Every person I interviewed who planned to stay in Utah said they were eager to find work; most made under seven dollars an hour in New Orleans. "Everyone has been nice, but I feel that since I'm out here, I need to do something because I don't have anything," said John Tucker, 26.

At a job fair, 44 New Orleans evacuees were hired and 19 more were called for second interviews. In addition to the job fair, the shelter provided phone and computer services, doctor appointments, prescriptions, free bus passes, and information on housing. One of the signs on the wall in the room where people went to receive services said, "Heads up!! Bad Hair Day? Ethnic Hair Products Due to Arrive at Clothing Supply This Afternoon." Many apartment complex owners in Salt Lake City agreed to both waive deposit fees and cap rents in order to keep living expenses affordable.

At first, I didn't ask people what they thought about the Bush administration's poor handling of the devastation because everyone I met was more interested in sharing their personal stories. When I returned a few days later, I found a few people who were eager to share their opinions on the government's disastrous response.

"If we were in Florida, Bush would have been there the same day, but Bush waited three days and a dollar late. Then he come there like he's some kind of hero. Bush ain't worth a doggone penny," said John Seal, 54. "He's been to New Orleans before. For you to leave us underwater all that time, then you're gonna make like the hero, the Lone Ranger? Hell no. He ain't nothing in my mind. They call him Mr. President or Mr. Bush. The only thing he's Mister of is his house, and his wife might be wearing the pants in there. I think it was mighty lowdown of him to do the things he did."

We thought long and hard about returning to the South to interview people about Katrina, but because things were so chaotic in New Orleans, we assumed we'd probably do more harm than good, so we stuck with our plan and continued on to Montana.

On the way, we stopped in a Wal-Mart parking lot in Idaho Falls—which is in a county that gave Bush 77 percent of the vote in 2004—to ask residents about their reaction to the federal government's response to the hurricane. "I think it was very, very slow. It's sad. Those people didn't have any food for how many days? Five, six, seven days. Not good," said Dorothy Bischoff, 63. "I voted for Bush, so I'm not against him, but this is unacceptable behavior. He really messed up on this one."

"I thought he was doing a really good job after 9/11, but he's too much of an oil man," said Dianne Watts, another former Bush supporter. "His politics have changed, and it's just getting to be more about the politics than the good of the people."

IV

MONTANA

Independence, Change, and American Indians

WE DROVE THE REST OF THE WAY listening to the news, still shocked by the reports of devastation and the poor treatment of the survivors. The people running Camp Draper were incredibly friendly and compassionate, but let's face it: the Katrina survivors we met were airlifted from Louisiana to Utah, an almost entirely white state, and then they were driven to Camp Draper and told to stay in army barracks. And not one person complained.

For the sake of the trip, I had to keep my emotions in check and focus on the next part of the journey. Ryan could tell that I was in a bad mood, so he pulled over and took a photo of the Sandpiper Restaurant sign, which said, HUNTING SEASON IS HERE; BETTER SCHMOOZE YOUR LADY.

He kissed my cheek and we continued the drive to Montana, the fourth largest state in the country (behind Alaska, Texas, and California) with just under 945,000 residents. That's only 125,000 more than San Francisco. Montana has only three electoral votes, has one area code, and is one of only five states with no sales tax. On November 2, 2004, Montana voters received national attention for electing Governor Brian Schweitzer, a proud gun-toting rancher, who also happens to be a pro-choice, populist Democrat. That same day, George W.

Bush beat John Kerry by 20 percentage points, and voters overwhelmingly approved a constitutional amendment banning gay marriage.

While I was intrigued by the state's unpredictable political landscape, I had added Montana to our list simply because I'd always wanted to visit Glacier National Park. The drive reminded me of home. We were surrounded by open space, large farms filled with roaming cattle, and soaring mountain ranges. Over the next few hours, we passed only a handful of cars on the two-lane highway.

Our first stop was in Butte, just five hours north of Salt Lake City. Most of the stores and restaurants in the downtown area were either closed or boarded up. We drove by Club 13, the Blue Ox Tavern, Fat Jack's Casino & M&M Cigarstore, Charlie's New Deal Bar, the Friendly Miners Union Bar, a faded painting on the side of a building advertising "Booths for Ladies" at the Creamery Café, and a billboard that said, "Warning: Montana has the highest alcohol-related fatality rate in the nation. Drunk drivers will be caught & prosecuted!"

Ryan wanted to check out Cavanaugh's County Celtic, an Irish store down the street, so I popped into Bud's Tavern, a workingman's bar filled with former miners. The front of Bud's is covered in a large American flag painting. The front door is in the middle of the red and white stripes. It was almost seven on a Monday evening, and I was the only woman in the place, but I didn't mind. The 50-something men were friendly, and they asked more questions than most. "Where've ya been? What've ya seen? Where ya from? Ya hungry? There's a great Italian place down the road."

I pulled up a stool at the bar, ordered a cranberry juice, and introduced myself to the man to my left, retired miner Michael Rishor. "It's the only thing I think I ever did and I enjoyed it. Twenty-five years of my life. I can't complain. I put a lot of food on my kids' table and got 'em through school. If I had to do it all over again, I'd do the same thing. My dad was a miner. Made some wrong decisions in my life, but I'd do it all over again."

I asked him to give me a brief history lesson about the area.

"In the late 1800s, 100,000 people lived in this town. At least

10,000 miners. Twenty-four hours a day, seven days a week. Now less than 30,000 live here. Nothin' stays the same."

"How was the town affected when the mines closed?"

"It broke its back. There used to be 176 bars in this town at one time. Everything left. Most of the people you see here were born and raised here. Two and three generations. It's a great place to live."

"What did people do after the mines closed?"

"Moved out. They just moved away. Most of the young people either go to the big cities or to the military. There's nothing here for them. Butte still hangs in there. It never gives up. It's the people that make the town."

"Are there many jobs here?"

"Not many, no. It's pretty slow, here especially. The big payin' jobs are all gone."

"What issues are most important here?"

"Jobs. At one time, the mines changed shifts every eight hours. There were as many people on the streets at night as there were during the day. Now it's not like that anymore. It's kinda sad." He looked straight ahead and took a swig of his beer.

"How does the town lean politically?"

"Democrat. Butte always goes Democrat, no matter what. And it always will."

"Are you a Democrat?"

"Oh boy, am I ever."

"What makes you a Democrat?"

"It's a working man's party."

"Do you think it still is? Some people say it's gotten away from the working man."

"Yeah, but it's the only one the working man has. I got out of the military in '67 and turned 21. I've voted Democrat ever since. I'll die a Democrat."

"What message would you send the national Democrats? They rarely come to Montana because you only have three electoral votes."

"Let's get people back to work instead of sending all our money overseas. Bring the troops home. People want to go back to work. I'm sure a lot of these people on welfare would rather be working. Kids gotta eat."

The bartender overheard the last part of our conversation, brought me another cranberry juice, and told me that the daredevil Evel Knievel was born in Butte. "Be sure to include that in your story."

Michael smiled, shook his head, and took another swig of his beer.

From Poverty to Politics

When former welfare recipient, single mom of four, and domestic violence survivor Mary Caferro became a state representative in 2004, it took a while to get used to having health care and a consistent paycheck that was large enough to provide for her family. After many years of struggling to make ends meet, the free food and perks that most politicians take for granted were an unexpected surprise.

"We get a calendar at the beginning of every week, and we get breakfast, lunch, and dinner for free. Sometimes two or three different groups would be having dinners. So when my kids were busy, I'd say, 'I'm gonna pull out my calendar. Where should I go eat?' Of course, I went to the events for stuff I cared about. But for the most part, I thought, really, you would never have to pay for food. It is crazy," she said flinging her long brown hair over her left shoulder. "And health insurance. You get elected, you do a 90-day term every other year, and you get health insurance year round. I've never had that, so I went in and got a physical and thought, wow, this is so fun."

I met Mary at an event called "Hands Up for the Homeless: Neighbors Helping Neighbors" at the Lewis & Clark Fairgrounds in Helena, Montana's state capital. Like many states across the country, Montana is experiencing a rise in homelessness, but unlike New York and California, the homeless in Montana are practically invisible. According to the Montana Council on Homelessness, "Montana's homeless can be found sleeping in cars, tents, abandoned buildings, or staying with family or friends. They might be in motels, hospitals, treatment facilities, jails, emergency or transitional shelters, but most are *not* on the streets. Although traditional street homelessness appears to be growing in Montana, the homeless are often difficult to locate and to quantify." In 2005, there was a significant jump in first-time food bank visits. Some 213,895 Montanans received emergency food from local hunger relief agencies. That's 23 percent of Montana's population. The state is ranked fourth in the nation for the most people working two or more jobs.

"People say, 'Well, what's the problem with poverty?' One of the problems is in 1996, we came up with this wonderful welfare reform program that is not working because poverty has increased. Poverty in Montana increases every year. Our child poverty rate is outrageous. Our uninsured rate is going up. Our wages are low. And we have this wonderful welfare reform program?"

Mary says the Personal Responsibility and Work Opportunity Reconciliation Act, signed by President Bill Clinton in 1996, did nothing to lift people out of poverty. It did just the opposite. "I was living in poverty, working, and trying to go to school at the same time. Then I was told by my caseworker I couldn't count my education as a work activity," she said. "They focus on getting people to work. It's like, take a job, any job, instead of looking at barriers to employment. For me, it was education. I know it's not the answer for everybody, but at the time, the caseworker said, 'You can't count education as a work activity.'"

Then she contacted WEEL (Working for Equality and Economic Liberation), a group whose members believe that economic justice is a basic human right. "They said, 'Of course you can count education as a work activity. Here's the policy manual. Take it and show it to her.' So I did and she said, 'All right, fine.' And I got to count my education as a work activity."

When Mary got word that the state legislature was planning to cut off access to education, she made it her mission to talk with every legislator willing to listen about the bill's limitations and the realities of being poor. "'Please, this is not a money issue. It's philosophical. It's about what we do with our time. Now don't you think that it's pretty valuable that I spend my time going to school so I can leave poverty and welfare once and for all?' And people got it. We ended up stopping that policy change and actually being more inclusive for access to education and how long you could access education."

Mary says the other problem is the system itself. "It provides a low-wage workforce for corporate America and tries to make sure that that workforce is uneducated. Wal-Mart is the perfect example. It's a treadmill."

After Mary became more involved with WEEL, a friend suggested she run for office. "I've always wanted to, but I thought, I don't belong in politics. I don't have the suits. I don't have the money. I need day care. I don't have a partner. And that's the reason I decided to run."

She was outspent by four to one, but she defied the odds and won. "There's 100 representatives for the whole state, so I know how important that seat is. I know I'm there because of all the work other people did to get me there. I also love the access. It was so funny. I called a department one day and they said, 'Oh, we cannot only get you that information, but we'll run it over to you within an hour,' and I'm like, 'What? Are you kidding me?' It was incredible. I'm the same old person, but now I'm Representative Caferro. It just shocked me. And I love being on the floor 'cause I can run around and lobby. They're all right there. Usually I'm outside waiting and waiting. You can turn a bill in two hours."

"It's amazing because races are so expensive and ugly these days," I said. "It's easy to say, 'You can't win. You're an idealist. You don't have the money.'"

"Not only can you run—and maybe this is just a Montana thing—but not only can you run, you can win. Six out of eight of the bills I sponsored passed. But it takes a lot of work," she said. "I have 8,700 people in my district. I went to every door. I had friends go with me door to door. That direct contact with people is what won the election. Even as my opponent had TV and all that media, people said, 'Ya know, I think I'm gonna stick with Mary. I met her.'"

"What was your opponent like?"

"My primary opponent worked for the attorney general and had the old guard supporting him. He was a Democrat, and then I had a

Republican opponent. They both were really nice men. None of them brought up me being a former welfare mom."

"So there were no smear campaigns?"

"As far as I know, there weren't."

"You're lucky, especially in this climate."

"I thought so 'cause I was waiting. I did have a lot of people ask questions like, 'You're a single mom. How come?' People felt comforted that I had my four children while married with the same husband. There was a little bit of that, but not much," she said.

"And like most legislatures across the country, Montana's is male dominated."

"I always saw myself thinking, and a lot of women do this, 'I've got to work my way up the ladder,' instead of thinking, 'I can be in a leadership position.' In the past I've said, 'I'm going to continue with the grunt work and build my experience and name recognition.' My friends said, 'Mary, just do it.' I'm trying to work with other women to get them involved in running for office. I have four women I'm working with right now. All of them say, 'You know, I thought I could be a staffer next session.' No, go for what you think you can do. Do you think you can be a legislator? It takes a lot of reading, a lot of studying, boring meetings. 'Can you do that?' 'Yeah.' 'Then why not just run?' We sell ourselves a little bit short. I kept thinking, I'll run campaigns for another 10 years. Oh my God, I'll be 55. I'll be too tired, so I did it."

"Is there such a thing as a typical Democrat in Montana?" I asked. "In Oklahoma, the Democrats formed Democrats for Life and are afraid to say they're pro-choice. In California, they would be Republicans. In Mississippi, the Democrats finally added a woman's right to choose to its platform."

"It varies. In the House, they are solid on poverty issues and nearly solid on choice. Where it gets tricky is gay and lesbian issues. Sometimes even economic issues. I consider myself a very liberal Democrat. I'm 45. My parents were Democrats. The Democratic Party in Montana has changed. It's become more and more conservative. I'm working on it. I'm organizing a booth at the Indian powwow, and every person I've asked to volunteer has been a new face. I've reached out to young people, to people of color, to gay and lesbian folks. I keep saying, 'If you don't like the party, get involved.'"

"What is your relationship like with House Republicans?"

"Pretty good. My seating for all my committees was between two Republicans and some of the most conservative. So my strategy was to reach out to them and get their support. For example, there's this guy who's terrible on the environment. I asked him, 'Would you cosponsor my Children's Health Insurance Program (CHIP) expansion bill for children's health care?' And he looked at me kind of funny, and I said, 'Think of it this way. All those kids who are getting poisoned by your anti-environment policies will be able to go get health care, and isn't that important to you?' And he laughed and he said, 'I'll cosponsor it.' So he cosponsored it and we had a 50 / 50 split. He was my secured Republican vote for that bill. So I try to reach out to them and educate them, because they have so many misconceptions about social programs. I agree with them. We can do it for a lot cheaper. But you're gonna have to take privatization out of it. For example, take the computer system with CHIP. I can say, 'You know, we can save $15,000 right now.' They respect that I want to save money and that I do it year round. I mean, I study the budget. So I get along fine with Republicans. They don't all like me, but that's only natural. I don't back down."

"What is in store for the future of Montana politics?"

"I think we have to work really hard. We can easily lose seats. We have to be careful about not fragmenting too much within the Democratic Party. Our platform says that we support civil unions, yet four of the top people that ran for state office that were Democrats support the constitutional amendment. So progressives like me are really gonna work hard to make sure that not just Democrats get elected, but people that follow the party's platform."

"What do you want people to know about Montana politics?"

"We have a lot of progressive politicians. Why? Because a lot of constituency groups worked very hard on voter registration, voter turnout, and education. That is something people don't talk enough about. The Montana Conservation Voters and the Women's Vote Project, did tons of the work involved in getting Governor Schweitzer elected. Voter turnout was so high. When people turn out, especially. in this low-wage state, Democrats are gonna win."

"What do you think of the national Democratic Party?"

"I don't like them. I'm a grassroots person. If they want to win, they have to have a grassroots effort. Organize. Howard Dean was on this roll of getting local people out talking to their neighbors. That's what I did. When people talk, you break down so many of the misconceptions. Reach out to people who are not Democrats or first-time voters. Work hard. Look at other strategies. Do everything as if you have no money. So many people said to me, 'You came to my door. That makes me so happy.'"

"Why are you a Democrat?"

"Because I'm a woman, because I'm poor, because I believe in equality, because I believe in the underdog, I believe in the working class. I'm an environmentalist. I'm pro-choice. That's what being a Democrat means to me."

The Only Republican in the Room

Later that afternoon, I met Moe Wosepka, a tall 57-year-old man wearing jeans, a flannel shirt, and a spotless white cowboy hat. After many years of jet-setting around the world as the director of Montana's International Trade Office, Moe felt the need to do something locally. So he became the director of Good Samaritan Ministries, a nonprofit that provides the poor with cash assistance for everything from rent and utilities to medical bills and basic repairs. All the money is raised from the organization's thrift store.

I asked Moe if the job changed his views.

"I grew up in a small town in eastern Montana. It's a world of its own. We don't have poor people. We don't have ethnic people. Everybody's related. During my experience in Vietnam, I was walking around in the rice paddies seeing how people lived, and I just couldn't believe it. People without running water and no electricity and no plumbing. It was unbelievable, but there was a culture. The poor, and the people in the nursing homes, and the people in prison—it's just another culture. It's like a foreign country right here in our own land."

"What is the scope of the problem in Montana?"

"We have a huge problem in this state with meth. Meth is going to cause an incredible amount of problems. In Montana, we're a community that really cares. We don't always agree, but we care. It's the one-on-one involvement with people that need help. It's not just about throwing money at them. Growing up in the West, we're independent thinkers. We're also a lock-them-up society. We don't trust judges. We don't trust government. That's one of our problems."

"How do Montanans deal with poverty and homelessness? Is it talked about or brushed under the rug?"

"Brushed under the rug," he said. "One of the problems we have in Montana is that it's not visible. Most of the poor we deal with aren't visible. There are only a few areas in the state where we have enough population to have services for the poor and the homeless."

"Has changing careers impacted your politics at all?"

"It has. I've become more sensitive to other people's views. I've learned so much from the people I've been called to serve. I have a much broader scope of what needs to be done. I'm one of those people who was a Democrat when I was in college and that's just because that's what I needed to be, and then I became a Republican when I started paying taxes, and now I'm probably someplace in between. We have some caring, dedicated politicians in this state."

"What role do you think the government should play when it comes to homelessness and poverty?"

"I think the government should support the groups here. They're down on the ground and they know the people. The government should support them."

"Do you still consider yourself a Republican?"

"Yes."

"What do you think about the Republicans who use all this pro-family rhetoric, yet they never discuss real issues like living wages, day care, and health care? You know what the reality is for poor people and single moms. You see it every day."

"It's frustrating. Like I said, I'd like the government to support the grassroots groups working on the ground. We need to, as a group, say, this is an issue affecting all of us. How can we make a difference? We waste so much time on abortion and gay marriage. Let's not talk about it anymore. Please. Can we deal with real issues?"

"Why are you a Republican?"

"I believe in small government. I believe in strong defense. I'm not a believer in bombs and bullets. I'm not a believer in the death penalty. But sometimes you have to stand up for yourself. Do I like the war? No, I don't like the war. I don't like any violence. But we have to stand up and say, 'Hey, we're not gonna put up with it.'"

"Put up with what? Saddam Hussein didn't do anything to the U.S."

"Whether Saddam did anything to us directly, the whole region is noticing what's going on. It's affecting the world."

I changed the subject back to poverty. "Are there many Republicans at events like these?"

"I'd say I'm the only Republican here."

"What's it like being the only Republican in the room?"

"They put up with me. We don't talk politics. I don't know if Mary knows I'm a Republican. She's a strong Democrat. We're real good friends. I don't vote Democrat very often, but I don't vote for people that don't have respect for other people."

He wouldn't tell me if he voted for George W. Bush.

Out in Montana

From Helena, we took our time driving along Highway 90 to Missoula, one of the most liberal towns in Montana, and home of the University of Montana and the Jeanette Rankin Peace Center. In 1916, four years before women could vote, Jeanette Rankin became the first woman ever elected to Congress. A Republican, lifelong pacifist, and ardent feminist, Rankin voted against United States entry into World

War I in 1917, saying that "the first time the first woman had a chance
to say no against war she should say it." She lost her seat after casting
that vote, but won another race in 1940. She was the only member of
Congress to oppose World War II in 1941.

We immediately fell in love with Missoula, a walkable city surrounded by towering mountains to the east and west; it has a great
downtown area filled with cafés and funky shops. I was excited to find
Tipu's Tiger, the only vegetarian Indian restaurant in Montana, a few
bakeries offering vegan delights, and the Good Food Store, a veggie
friendly co-op. Once we discovered those gems, we left the cooking
supplies and canned beans in the van. For the first time, we actually
felt like we were on vacation.

It was Friday night, and we wanted to go out and have mindless
fun. A live band. Stand-up comedy. A play. Anything. But no politics.
We needed a break. I asked the woman at the front desk of our motel
if she had any suggestions, but I didn't tell her about the project. I just
said we were in desperate need of a fun night out. She stared at me for
a few seconds, looked down at the desk, then slowly said, "Well, are
you familiar with the Imperial Sovereign Court?"

"Uh, no."

"It's a local group that raises money for various organizations in
town."

"OK." I wondered why she was so nervous. And why was she was
telling me about a fund-raising event?

"It's a group of drag queens," she said, still looking at the desk
while nervously fidgeting with a pen. "There is a drag queen show
tonight."

I thought she was joking. "Are you kidding? Where is it?"

She breathed a huge sigh of relief, changed her demeanor, and
smiled. "I never know how guests will respond when I tell them about
the event. This is a liberal town by Montana standards, but we've experienced some nasty gay-bashing here."

I figured I'd do a few interviews, but we couldn't pass up an opportunity to see a drag queen show in Montana. When we walked
into the decorated hall, the queens were happily posing for photos in

their lavish gowns, exquisite jewels, impeccable makeup, high heels, and fancy tiaras gently placed on their perfectly coiffed hair. Most of the women and a few men wore tuxedos. Ryan and I were the only attendees wearing casual attire, but no one seemed to mind. "You look fabulous," said Donatella, a tall queen with fiery red hair tucked inside a sparkling crown. She told me that it took two hours to get every hair in place. Donatella was wearing two strands of thick faux diamonds, dangling earrings, and a black flowing gown covered in blue flowers and green leaves. "Did you come all this way just to see us? Don't you see this every day in San Francisco?" she said, laughing.

We sat at a table with a mix of people who told us gay Montanans are fighting an uphill battle, but the level of public support is slowly increasing. "One of my coworkers is here to support me," said Jane, a 40-something woman wearing a black pantsuit, "but I wouldn't think of telling everyone at work that I'm gay. We're in redneck country, so for us, it's one step at a time. That's just the way it is." And with that, she bought us drinks and the show began. The women wearing the tuxedos accompanied the queens onto the stage as they performed to some of my favorite dance classics, including "I Will Survive" by Gloria Gaynor, "Last Dance" by Donna Summer, and of course, "I'm Coming Out" by Diana Ross. Jane and her friends welcomed us to their party with open arms, but I could tell that they'd rather dance and enjoy the evening than answer my questions about their struggle, so I put my recorder in my backpack and joined them on the dance floor. Before we left, Emperor X Tim agreed to meet me at one of the state's three gay bars the following day. "It's called AmVets. It's downtown. You can't miss it. Let's meet at noon." AmVets?

The next day, Tim told me that AmVets leased a room to a gay support group a few years before; when the meetings ended, the group would continue the conversation over a few drinks at the bar. The owner needed a steady stream of customers, so he decided to turn AmVets into a gay bar. As you can imagine, not everyone was pleased that a veterans club was transformed into a gay bar, but it seemed to be working. The "Unofficial Website of AmVets Post #3" says, "This bar is an actual Post of the National American Veterans Organization, not the gay bar of Missoula. It has only been with the support of the Board and management that the gay community has been allowed to make this bar part of us. Therefore we strongly urge you to be respectful of these generous veterans of our Armed Forces so that we may continue to enjoy a place where we are free to be ourselves without fear being bashed within the walls. We look forward to welcoming you to the beautiful downtown AmVets Club."

Tim said Imperial Court events, including the yearly drag queen show, raise $20,000 per year for organizations that work with people suffering from AIDS or breast cancer. "We think it's important to help people in need and reach out to the larger community," he said. "The one cool thing about the court is we drew people from Colorado, Utah, Calgary, Washington, even California. It's exciting to show off what we have. They're like, 'Wow, you guys have a gay bar!'"

"What's it like being gay in a state like Montana?"

"You're careful. You're not flamboyant. You're not parading yourself around town. I just try to assimilate," he said. "If you move to San Francisco, Seattle, or Denver, you can have your whole life be gay. You can live in a gay neighborhood. You can even have a gay job. Here, it's different. It's not a complete lifestyle. We have to assimilate into the regular culture."

"Which do you prefer?"

"When I first came out and when I first went to Denver and Seattle, I thought, 'Wow, this is the place to be. I can be gay 24/7.' It was really neat at first, but when you come back here, you really learn to appreciate how both the straight and gay communities learn to cohabitate. At the end of the day, I want people united. People taking care of each other. People being nice to each other. People respecting each other. That's what I value the most."

Out in the Wilderness

A few days later, I attended a panel discussion about hunting and conservation, and, much to my surprise, I met mostly Democrats who told me that not all gun owners are members of the National Rifle

Association. They also criticized national Democrats for essentially allowing Republicans to control the conversation about gun control and for not doing enough to publicize their own pro-environment voting records. They suggested I meet David Stalling, former president of the Montana Wildlife Federation. "If you really want to know about hunting and conservation, David is your man. He's a member of every environmental group you can name." So I called David and the next day we met for coffee at the Bear's Brew Coffee House downtown. He showed up wearing jeans, a green sweatshirt over a gray T-shirt, and a light green baseball hat.

He said one of the main issues Montana conservationists are dealing with is the state's growing tourism industry. "Environmentalists are fighting for the tourism industry, but none of it's sustainable. Most people have lost any connection to the natural world. They fly out here and go to Glacier and Yellowstone [national parks], but they have no idea how tied we are to the land and how everything we do affects the land that sustains us. Clean water. Clean air. People don't seem to get that. I've seen environmentalists come out here driving big giant gas-guzzling vehicles."

David met a number of gas-guzzlers on a recent six-week trip he took to deal with burnout and personal issues. "I hiked from my front porch here in Missoula to Waterton, Alberta. And I only crossed three roads, which was three roads too many. It was about 500 miles. Took me 35 days. I did a lot of thinking and writing and journaling. One of the roads I crossed goes through Glacier and I stopped there, and I saw some people. This one guy heard me talk about how we're losing all the glaciers in Glacier National Park. They're rapidly melting away from global warming. We're seeing a change in vegetation. White bark pine are more susceptible to disease, which affects the grizzly bears. That's a primary food source for them, so since that's not there anymore, they're heading back to the lower country looking for food. They have conflicts with humans, then they're killed, so it's all related. And I was trying to explain that to a guy who claimed to be an environmentalist and he was driving this huge SUV. So I kinda called him on it. He said, 'What can we do about it?' I said, 'For one, we can be more conscientious about how we're living and not drive these kinds of things.' And he was really offended by that. So I headed back into the wild. I'm kind of retreating lately. I've been burned out. Spending more time in the wild. I saw six grizzly bears on my trip. It was a very spiritual experience."

"Are you from here?"

"I grew up in Connecticut. My dad was an avid, passionate bass fisherman. We spent countless all-nighters out on the boats. My dad was more than just a fisherman. We fought to protect estuaries. He taught me a lot about everything else out there. The geese and the birds. I started gaining a real appreciation for the wilderness through straight bass fishing. Then I joined the Marine Corps. And moved to Montana. For the first time, I saw really wild landscapes."

"What are some misconceptions about Montana?"

"People from the outside look at Montana and seem confused. We're a red state that elected a Democratic governor. I think they don't quite get that a lot of us are still closely tied to the land, and there aren't many states left where you are closely tied to the land. Here, Wyoming, and North and South Dakota. Our governor is actually more of a traditional populist than a Democrat. I hope the Democratic Party on the national scale starts examining that and starts changing. I think they've lost touch with the people. I took a vacation and went to New Mexico with Veterans for Kerry in 2004. I spent six years with a special operations unit, yet I would have veterans accuse me of being un-American or communist 'cause I was supporting Kerry. It was bizarre to see. It amazed me. It was frustrating. They listen to Rush Limbaugh and Sean Hannity every day and believe everything they say.

"I have a bumper sticker on my car with a flag and it says, 'Think. It's Patriotic.' I love that. Nobody seems to think anymore. They don't look into issues and come up with their own opinions. That's one of the things I do love about Montana. Maybe it's a product of being out in open space and clean air, but I think people think and are more independent."

"Where do your politics come from?"

"From my parents. My dad died a few years ago and we were really close. He was pretty conservative. When I was a Marine in the early '80s, I loved Ronald Reagan until a bunch of friends of mine were killed in Beirut, Lebanon. I started learning things about Iran Contra and how Reagan had been arming Hezbollah. Then we were involved in some stuff in Central America, and I started thinking, 'Was it right?' So I started coming to my own conclusions, and I got really depressed about it. I started doing a lot of reading. I think they come from my own personal observations."

He then straightened his back and said, "OK, you want to hear about breaking stereotypes? I've had a crazy year. Here I am. I'm a Marine, I live in Montana, and I hunt and kill elk. And I also came out. I'm gay."

My mouth dropped.

"That's been really interesting. That's made me even more left because of the response I get from people in this state that just hate gays. They think it's a choice and you're gonna go to hell. I'm kind of stubborn. When I meet resistance, it pushes me the other way, and I want to fight the bastards. I'm completely out, and I'm going around and speaking on those kinds of issues, too, which creates some tension because I've been a spokesman for the hunting world for a long time, and now some of them aren't real happy about this," he said, laughing. "All of a sudden, some don't want me to be the spokesperson for the hunters. You can't have a gay hunter speaking. Sorry to throw this on you. I'm not sure where this came from."

"No, it's OK. Really."

"I also run into positive things. I was in Red Lodge, Montana, which is a small town, and I was at a gay man's health retreat, and this woman in a toy store asked what I was doing there and I told her. I'm just gonna throw it out there 'cause I like to see what the response is. It turns out, her husband is the Lutheran minister in Red Lodge, and they have a gay son who lives in Spain and is married to a guy. And then they invited us to church the next day. And I'm not a Christian, but I went to the church service just out of curiosity, and a bunch of guys from the retreat went there, and the minister spoke about his son, and he spoke to the whole congregation about how they need to be accepting and take time after the service to chat with us and welcome us and they did. So I've got this weird idea to maybe even leave the environmental movement and try to organize. It'd be fun to go to rural communities and hold forums and get these folks to start speaking out."

I was at a loss for words. All I could come up with was, "Wow," which felt kind of lame.

"I'm an 'earthest.' I believe in what I stand on and what I can see, touch, and feel. For me, my church is out there among the grizzlies and the wolves. I was married for 14 years. My former wife has been incredibly supportive. We're better friends than we've ever been, so it's been really positive. She has a brother who's really religious, and he came by my house to try to save me one day. He started telling me that I'm making a bad choice. That I'm gonna go to hell. Then he started blaming his sister and saying, 'You're not gay. It's my sister's fault.' I feel funny telling you all this stuff, but he actually said, 'You know, men have needs and if your needs aren't being met at home, just look elsewhere, but you're not gay.' I got really mad and I was like, 'I knew I was gay long before I met your sister. I'm just finally facing it. It's not a choice. Why would I make this choice?'"

"How did your friends react?"

"My friends have been great. A lot of my friends have totally changed now, and they admit it. They had all these misconceptions about gays. A lot of them are coming right out and saying, 'Wow, I'm rethinking these things.' I had friends who were opposed to gay marriage who are now reconsidering their positions. It's been cool. That's what we need to do all over the country. So many of the young folks I meet, even in some rural parts of Montana, have been accepting. I've met others who've been beaten up and rejected by their parents. A lot of them move to Missoula because they feel safer here. We have a gay bar in town."

"I know. I went there a few days ago!"

"I was there last night! It's funny. Even among my gay friends, I almost feel like I don't quite fit in because I'm a former Marine and have been putting on this straight act for so many years, but they get a kick out of it in some ways. There's a strong gay community here. The Gay Men's Task Force has been so helpful to me. I came out about a year ago, and I couldn't have done it without them. They hold summits around the state. Guys come from all over: cowboys, ranchers, hunters. The retreats made me feel like less of a freak. I'm like, 'Wow, I'm not alone. There are all kinds of folks like me out there. I'm not the only one.'"

"Wow." I said it again. "Imagine if some of these ranchers went on *Fox News* and said, 'I think gay marriage should be legal.'"

"That's what I want to do! I even thought it'd be fun to have an ad with a rancher or marine and a slogan that says, 'It takes a real man to be gay.' I think it'd be fun."

"You must be relieved."

"I'm glad to finally be out. For years, I struggled with this. I almost killed myself over it. I hated myself. I've gone through suppression and denial. I'm finally feeling good. This trip was about that. On my trip, when I was in Glacier National Park, I ended up sharing a camp with four lesbians from San Francisco, and I kinda suspected they were. They—I found out later—looked at me as some redneck from Montana. And I said, 'So are you guys lesbians?' They said, 'Yeah, why does that bother you?' They were real defensive. I said, 'No, I'm gay.' They said, 'No you're not!' We just really hit it off. They were so funny. Now one of them is trying to fix me up with her friend. And they want me to come down. I've never been to San Francisco. I'm gonna do it."

"You're breaking a lot of stereotypes, even for the San Francisco lesbians."

"It's totally broken stereotypes. One person I know said, 'Well, that doesn't make sense. You couldn't have been gay when you were in the Marine Corps.' OK," he said, laughing. "Actually I want to get involved in that battle, too. See, I get fired up and I love a good fight. I'd love to get the ban lifted on gays in the military. A lot of the young soldiers don't care."

"How did your family react?"

"Dad died a couple years ago. Mom has come around. Most of my family has. It took me 30 years to accept it, so I gotta give them a little while. We went from hunting to gay rights? Wow. My boss, who's been really understanding, is afraid it could affect my work. I'm out there trying to rally conservatives for the environment. If they know I'm gay, they might not work with me. It's not that it comes up as a topic. But really, I'm glad I live here."

On our way out, David told me he recently called a national human rights group in Washington, DC to express interest in becoming their Western point person on gay issues. "They told me they don't work in hostile territory and hung up. Tell your progressive friends that if they keep up that attitude, they'll never win states like Montana."

Going to the Sun

We spent the next few days driving north toward Glacier National Park, one of the largest and most spectacular parks in the country. Almost all the Montanans we met along the way said they took pride in their independent spirit, felt disconnected from Washington, DC politics, and didn't tie themselves to any one political party. I stopped in Withey's Health Foods in Kalispell to stock up on dried fruit, nuts, cereal, and soymilk, and casually told the owner about the project. The long line of customers didn't deter him from loudly telling me he voted for Bush in 2000, but after watching Michael Moore's *Fahrenheit 9/11*, his opinions about the administration drastically changed for the worse, so in 2004, he voted for Green party candidate David Cobb. On the front counter, *American Free Press,* "America's Last Real Newspaper," was on sale next to *Natural Living.*

We spent a few days in Whitefish, a small, low-key, friendly town surrounded by majestic views of the Rocky Mountains. It's also home to the crystal-clear, seven-mile long Whitefish Lake. We found veggie burgers and fries in the Great Northern Bar & Grill downtown and met a number of locals who told us the town's beauty is attracting wealthy people from California and a lot of new development. "We never had glitz, paranoia, or judgment," said Dave, a 40-something contractor. "Now we have all three, plus resentment and expensive restaurants."

"You make the best of it," added Jim, also in construction. "Just tell your California friends there are no jobs here, the pay sucks, and it's real cold. Seriously, there's a lot of work because people are building like crazy, mostly gated areas, so it's a double-edged sword. We want the work, but we don't necessarily want the people."

In Columbia Falls, the "Gateway to Glacier National Park," I met a man at a gas station who said construction is the only steady job in town. High gas prices had caused most of his friends to cut back on the basics and, in some cases, cancel their vacations, but they weren't cutting back on driving. "Kinda tough when there's no public transportation. A man's gotta get to work if he's lucky enough to have a job."

We made it to Glacier just days before the lodges closed up for the winter. We took the Going-to-the-Sun Road, a 50-mile, two-lane highway that literally hugs the side of the mountain, winds through almost every terrain in the park, and offers stunning views of snow-capped mountains, waterfalls, and deep mountain valleys carved by ancient glaciers. It was too cold to camp, so we stayed the night in a cottage at the historic Lake McDonald Lodge, a cozy chalet overlooking the largest lake in the park. As soon as we arrived, we quickly unpacked the van, grabbed our portable cushioned seats, and plopped down on the edge of the lake. We could have spent the rest of our trip just sitting there. Ryan read, and I sat in silence and stared in awe for the next few hours thinking about all the stories I had heard over the past five months. Other than a few ripples, the dark blue glacial lake was calm and peaceful, and the air was pristine.

After dinner, we went to a talk given by a park ranger about climate change and melting glaciers. The number of glaciers in the park has dropped from an estimated 150 in 1850 to just 26 today. If current warming trends continue, park scientists predict that the park will be glacier free by 2030.

On our way out of the east side of the park the next day, I desperately wanted to take a long hike, but we didn't want to leave all of our equipment in the van. So we settled for a short, leisurely walk along the edge of a turquoise-green river. Just five minutes into the walk, we passed a sign that said we were entering grizzly country. "Bears have injured and killed visitors and may attack without warning and for no apparent reason." On our last camping trip on California's Lost Coast, I had forgotten to take a bag of trail mix out of my backpack, and we woke up in the middle of the night to the sound of a sniffing bear. When we saw the bear warning, we looked at each other, and headed back for the van.

Native America

The first town we hit after leaving the park was Browning, home of the 1.5-million-acre Blackfeet Nation, the largest Indian reservation in Montana. The contrasts couldn't be more striking. Despite the bounty of the land and the sweeping views of the park, the people were impoverished and opportunities were scarce. Century-old treaties signed between the tribes and the United States government guaranteed Indians basic services in exchange for their land, but those promises have never been kept. The Blackfeet tribe has 15,200 enrolled members and an unemployment rate as high as 70 percent.

"If you don't work for the tribe, the hospital, the BIA [Bureau of Indian Affairs] or the school district, then all you've got is the convenience stores, Taco John's, and small, part-time, minimum-wage jobs," said 50-year-old Carol Salway-Henderson. "People think we Indians get a check every month and that's not true. Believe me, Indians want to work, but the jobs don't exist. Or they're seasonal. Glacier Park: seasonal. Firefighters: seasonal."

I met Carol at the Museum of the Plains Indian, where she was filling in for a friend who had called in sick. "I'm unemployed at the moment. I got laid off because of the Iraq war. I was in the realty department at the BIA doing land sales. I was the last hired and the first to go when the budget cuts came, so, thank you, Bush. I have yet to be able to find a job here. I'm too overqualified." For the time being, she was doing bead work to make ends meet.

"Did you grow up on the reservation?"

"I spent my summers here, but I was sent to a government boarding school seven miles down the road." Carol's voice cracked when she told me about the U.S. government forcing her mom into a Catholic boarding school at age four. Catholic boarding schools attempted to strip indigenous children of their cultural and spiritual identities by preventing them from speaking their own language and by using religion to "civilize" and assimilate them. Carol's grandmother and grandfather met in one of those boarding schools. "We're still feeling the effects of that," she said, now sounding angry. "Look around this museum. When a child was born into a family, they were given toys that resembled tools they would be using when they were adults. They were given toys that resembled the things their mothers used. They were taught respect for their elders. They were taken out of that environment and put into an environment that didn't resemble anything they knew. You've got these generations now, mine and some behind me, who were not in a family unit, and we lost the ability to parent. It's as if that never happened. No one talks about it."

"What's the biggest misconception you hear about Indians?"

"That we're taken care of by the U.S. government. That we're backward. That we live in teepees. We do have some catching up to do. We finally got paved streets 10 years ago."

I look surprised. "Seriously," she said.

"What do you mean?"

"When I was a kid here, the area behind the school was called Moccasin Flats. There were dirt streets. Just within this past 10 years, they've gone in and paved the streets. And they've named the streets. They've given you a street address. Prior to that, you didn't have a street address. You don't have home delivery for mail or newspapers or anything like that."

"So people didn't get mail?"

"No, you had to use a post office box."

"Why did it take so long?"

"I don't know. I don't know if it was the tribal government or the state. Going back to education, I made sure my three daughters got an education. One of my daughters is a lieutenant in the Army National Guard. Her unit was sent overseas. She was waived because she hadn't finished her classes. She went to Virginia. She lucked out."

"Are many of the tribal members in Iraq?"

"A few of our guys are over there. Why are we there? What does the United States like? Oil. I don't agree with it. I don't want to see my daughter go. She's my oldest and I don't want to see her go. I don't feel we should be over there fighting for oil. You'll find a lot of people on reservations are Democrats."

"Why?"

"I asked my grandpa one time when I was in grade school. We were studying about the government. I said, 'Grandpa, are we Democratic or are we Republican?' He said, 'Oh my girl, we're not rich enough to be Republican. I'm a Democrat.' I think JFK was president at that time."

"Do you see major differences on the reservation when Democrats or Republicans are in office?"

"I see a lot of difference between Democratic and Republican presidents. Reaganomics was bad and then Bush went in. Look how many businesses left the United States. I got a Dell computer. When I have problems, where do I call? India! Come on. They can set up call centers here. During Reagan, you were either wealthy or poor. There was no middle class. Clinton might have did what he did, but he lowered the deficit."

"What message would you send to politicians?"

"Politicians need to start making an effort to go to the areas where there are Natives. I don't mean go to Billings; I mean come to Browning. Go to Rocky Boy. Go to where the Natives are. You'll get a few in the cities, but if you want the Native Americans to vote, you need to go out there and encourage them and talk to them face to face. Oh sure, they can listen to you on TV and the radio. They can read about you in the papers, but if you really want them to know what you stand for, then you need to go where they're at, and let them understand that you do care about what's going on with their culture."

Speaking of culture, Carol said we should drive over to the Teepee

Village Shopping Center and wait for the Indian parade to go by. It was Browning's annual North American Indian Day celebration. We made it just in time to see a number of floats and groups go by, including Indians wearing traditional clothing and headdresses on horses, a small school bus with a large painting of children holding hands under a slogan that said, "We are as one with our ancestors and children— We are as one with our land, culture, and language," a blue jeep covered in red and black balloons and a sign that said, "Together We Can in 2 Different Worlds," and a Head Start float filled with children.

I ran into Village Coin Laundry to put a load of clothes in the wash and met Cheryl Guardipee on my way out. She's a triple major in human services, criminal justice, and hospitality at the Blackfeet Community College. "I don't know what I want to do when I grow up."

"Do you mind me asking how old you are?"

"Fifty-three," she said with a serious tone. "Employment is low here, so I have to keep my options open. It's been that way forever."

"That's what I heard from a woman I met at the museum. So things haven't changed much?"

"Instead of us moving forward, we're moving backward. At one time, we had a couple of meat markets, we had a drug store, we had a show house, we had a few more gas stations. We even had a saddle and boots shop. Now we don't have that anymore. We got one grocery store. A few places to get gas. Gas prices are going up. And that's it."

"Do Indians leave the reservation to work?"

"Racism is bad off the reservation. Racism is really bad in Shelby. I lived in Shelby as a child. We didn't live there that long, but it was bad. My brothers and I had to fight going to school, in school, and coming home from school. Even the teachers were prejudiced. In one classroom, I was the only Indian child in there, and I'll tell you, I paid for it."

"And you're not that dark."

"No, I'm not. My son don't look Indian either, but because he's from Browning, he ended up quitting school. He was in the navy from 1993 to 1996. I'm glad he's out."

"Do you know anyone serving in Iraq?"

"I've had relatives in the service, but luckily none of my family members are over there. We have some tribal members there. Why are our boys over there? Why are they getting killed? What are we doing over there? We should be here. There you go. There's Bush again."

"Do you vote?"

"I just started voting a few years ago. I used to think, 'What's the purpose?' People push [voting] around here. They have vehicles going around if you need a ride. Maybe if more people did vote, we'd get something done."

"What message would you send politicians?"

"Come here. Talk to people. Get to know people. Open your eyes. Come and visit us. This was a tourist attraction at one time for people going to Glacier National Park. Now they just go through. They don't stop. People do stop when we have our Native American Indian days every year. They're amazed that we're here."

While the majority of the Indians I met were very proud of their heritage and their culture, most were at a loss for words when I asked them for solutions to eradicate widespread poverty and alcoholism. Part of the problem, according to Guardipee, is that poverty on Indian reservations is invisible, just like poverty in New Orleans was invisible before Katrina.

I crossed the street and found Cindy and her husband cheering on the Head Start float from the comfort of their brown sedan. Head Start serves children in families living at or below the federal poverty rate, which is $19,350 annually for a family of four. According to SaveHeadStart.org, the program has served 20 million of the country's poorest and most at-risk children and their families since 1965. Budget cuts have forced hundreds of programs across the country to scale back days and hours of operations and support staff. Many programs have also eliminated health insurance coverage for teachers and staff.

Still going strong at 70, Cindy was a teacher for the local Head Start. "I taught for 34 years and then I retired in 2000. I was off for a few months and was asked to come back as a volunteer. So I substituted for a few years, then they hired me back as a permanent sub."

"You must love your work."

"Not a day goes by that I don't find satisfaction in what I do. We're working with struggling and dysfunctional families. Low-income people. A lot of children here don't have three meals a day, but they do get two meals from Head Start, which is important for them. It also gives people an opportunity to be better parents."

Art Deroche, also a Head Start teacher and Browning native, was watching the parade from a chair on the back of his pickup. "I teach the Blackfeet language. There's ten of us. We start with toddlers, ages zero to three. We're trying to get the language back. What do they say? The brown-skinned people without culture. We lose our language and nothing's left."

At 62, Art had the voice of a wise, old village healer, and when he spoke, he looked out into the distance. "Four of us got cut down to six hours a day instead of eight. The federal government and the tribes cut the budget. You gotta hustle out here. If you don't, you'll fall through the cracks. It's tough to be brought up in Browning. A lot of crime. Oh, the crime. Break-ins. Stealing. Drugs. A lot of drugs. It used to be just shacks around here. Dirt roads. No electricity. No pavement. No sidewalks. No street lights. North of here, Indians stayed in Moccasin Flats. Lots of shacks. It's improved, but not that much. There's nothing here for kids. My grandson plays football."

"What are the solutions?"

"Don't know. Been thinking about that for years. Gotta get out there and fight for jobs."

"Do you vote?"

"Maybe once. I voted in a school district election."

"Why only once?"

"It don't do any good. I lost my dad in World War II. My brother went to Vietnam. The politicians are all the same. They're never gonna change."

On the way out of town, we passed a taco shop that said, WE LOVE OUR INDIANS, and INDIANS #1 in red and black lettering on the windows, and a white cement teepee-shaped Espresso House. We decided to drive east and then south toward the Crow Reservation and the

Little Bighorn National Monument. By this time, the weather was drastically changing from mildly warm to extremely cold; because we'd been traveling in the south, we had only summer clothing, so we layered just about everything we brought.

A few hours later, we stopped for gas in Glasgow, and I asked a local guy about the poverty on the Blackfeet Reservation.

"You stopped in Browning? I would never go to Browning. It's too dangerous," was his response. When his friend came out of the gas station mini-mart, he yelled, "Hey Mike, would you ever go to Browning?"

"Hell no!"

We then stopped in a small-town post office to mail a few postcards home. The woman behind the counter looked at me quizzically.

"What's your name?" she asked.

"Rose."

"You're not from around here are you?"

"No, I'm from California."

"I didn't think so," she said with a smile. "You don't look like you live here." She could tell I was confused. "You're a few shades darker than the people who live here."

Turns out she grew up on a nearby reservation and just recently became the town's postmaster. "For the first three months, the locals couldn't believe that an Indian had this job. They're used to me by now, but so many of them said they've never met an Indian before. For all I knew, they think we all still live in teepees. Then I bought a house in town and they were even more shocked because they don't associate with Native Americans."

"Come to think of it," I said, "I haven't seen many non-Natives mixing with Natives, and I've been traveling around Montana for almost a month now."

"That's the way it is here. My daughter studied at UC Berkeley. I went to visit her, and it was such a treat because there was so much diversity. You have no idea. No one gave me a second glance. I fit right in," she said, smiling.

Before I left, I asked her about possible solutions to the persistent poverty on the reservations. "It's all about education," she said. "Unlike most people on the reservation, my parents encouraged me to get an education, and I encouraged my kids to get an education."

Over the next few days, after telling people that we came from Browning and were heading toward the Crow Reservation, we were warned against visiting Indian reservations because "they're too dangerous, especially for women."

The poverty on the Crow Reservation was just as dire. From the highway, you could see dilapidated trailer homes, many with no windows and broken doors, surrounded by junk, rusting cars, and clotheslines hung with tattered clothes. Sixty-two percent of Crow Indians are unemployed, and the 38 percent that are employed live below the poverty line, according to the BIA.

"The problems are so deep here," said an administrator I met at the tribe's community college. "The federal government set up a system that gave us no choice but to rely on them. That led to alcohol and drug problems. In order to make a life for myself, I had to literally walk away from my family because the problems are so bad."

I also met Janine Pease, a Crow Indian and vice president for American Indian Affairs at Rocky Mountain College in Billings. She says racism crops up when she least expects it, but it's not as bad as it used to be. In 1978, she was driving with her grandfather and baby from Browning to Billings on a cold night. Her alternator went out in Valier, a town of about 1,000. It was 9:30 p.m. Everything was closed, so she found a pay phone and called the sheriff to ask for assistance. "I knew I was in bad territory, which is why I decided to call the sheriff. He said, 'I can't call anybody for you.' And I said, 'Is there a place where you would suggest I park? I don't think we'll be able to keep our car warm enough.' He said, 'You're not welcome to park anywhere, except under the light at the Ford dealership, and I will know not to arrest you.' So we stayed there all night."

The next morning, she walked to the nearest gas station, but they refused to help her. She had no choice but to walk. Ten miles down the road, a rancher stopped, took her back to the car, and jumped it. "We were lucky that he happened to be someone who wanted to help

Indians, but when we got to the next town and asked for a new battery, the guys in the station just laughed at us."

"What's it like today?"

"There are areas in Montana you just don't want to go. You just shouldn't go. It's the same way in South Dakota. You have to have a clean car, and you don't want to have feathers or any other Indian stuff hanging from your mirror. Integration has come very slowly to Indian country."

In terms of politics, she said, Democrats have taken some of the leading steps forward for Indian country. "If you go back and study some of the legislation that's been passed, it's happened under Democratic administrations. Jimmy Carter signed the law on tribal colleges. Bill Clinton signed the executive order on tribal colleges and on tribal sovereignty. There just isn't any way you can compare legislation under Republican administrations. I spent my entire dissertation looking into civil rights and education acts, and the leading pieces of legislation that bring what little has happened in Indian country alive have been Democratic initiatives."

Montana's Indians see a glimmer of hope in Governor Ryan Schweitzer. A statement on Schweitzer's website reads, "Montanans need to understand the treaties made between Native Americans and the federal government pre-date the creation of the state of Montana. These treaties state that the reservations are sovereign nations."

Native Americans became United States citizens in 1924, but as late as 1948, they were barred from voting in some states. While amendments have been passed to ensure the voting rights of African Americans and women, a Native Americans' right to vote has never been constitutionally secured.

Going Home

A few days later, we began our journey home. The road to Reno was filled with Highway Patrol writing tickets. I drove in the slow lane to avoid the speeding truckers, and because we couldn't push 60, we weren't concerned. I was more interested in blasting the song "War Pigs" by Black Sabbath.

Up ahead on our right, another officer was issuing a ticket. I was about to pass him, so I slowed down to about 50. I looked in the rearview mirror and noticed him turn his head toward us as we whizzed by.

Minutes later, we saw the flashing lights. What could it be? Was I going too slow? I turned off the music, slowly pulled over, turned off the engine, and grabbed my license out of my purse.

Two well-built, stern-looking men slowly got out of the car. They looked like the guys in *COPS*.

One approached my window. The other one stayed behind. "License, please."

"Sure," I said handing it over. "What did I do? The van doesn't go over 60."

He looked at my license, looked at me, and said, "When an officer pulls someone over on the highway, you're supposed to get in the fast lane when you pass."

"Really? I've never heard of that."

"Yeah, otherwise, you might hit the officer. You have the same law in California."

"Oh, sorry about that. I've never heard of that law, and we rarely drive in the fast lane on two-lane highways because we can barely push 60."

He raised his eyebrows, but didn't say anything. He stared at my license for another 15 seconds, looked at me, and returned to his car. Through the rearview mirror, I watched him speak with his partner and call in my license. His partner then walked over to Ryan's side.

"So you guys from California?"

"Yeah," said Ryan.

"What are you doing in Nevada?"

"We just finished a long road trip."

"Oh, cool," he said leaning in with his forearms resting on the door. "Where'd you go?"

"We started in Texas, spent a few months in the South, then spent some time in Montana," I said.

"Oh, cool. What'd you do?"

"I'm a journalist, and I'm working on an independent project about why people vote the way they do, so we interviewed people about a bunch of different issues."

"What'd you find?"

"Everything. You name it. We found it."

"Cool." He paused. "I'll see what's taking so long." He slowly walked back to his car, stopping to look at the mess of pillows, papers, books, blankets, and duffel bags in the back.

"He seems friendly enough," I said. "Maybe they won't give us a ticket."

Three or so minutes later, the friendly cop returned to Ryan's side and the guy who checked my license was on my side.

"You got a lot happenin' here," he said, looking at the dashboard.

"Yeah, he chose the soldiers," I said with a nervous laugh. "I chose the animals."

"Lots of soldiers. So what do y'all think about the war?"

The war? I paused and looked at the scene on the dashboard, which started with a dolphin. "I think it's horrible that innocent people are dying."

After a few seconds of uncomfortable silence, the friendly cop jumped in. "Do you all have tattoos?"

"Excuse me?"

"You got a tattoo sticker here," he said pointing to the sticker on the glove box.

"That's from a tattoo parlor in Austin," said Ryan. "Yeah, I have a few tattoos."

I wondered where this was going.

"Did y'all take a break from your road trip to go to Burning Man?"

At this point, I realized that the friendly guy must have checked out the van during our last conversation.

"Yes," I said, "we went to Burning Man. I've been going for eight years now."

"Did you guys do a lot of drugs at Burning Man?"

Now I was irritated. "No, we didn't do drugs at Burning Man. We've had two drinks in the past six months. Like I said, I'm a journalist and we're working on a project." I grabbed a business card out of my purse and handed it to the guy on my side. "Here. Check the website."

"Got any narcotics or marijuana back there?" he said looking at the mess in the back.

Ryan could tell I was about to lose it, so he jumped in. "No, we don't have any drugs."

"What about terrorists? You hiding any Middle Eastern terrorists back there?"

Is this some kind of joke? I took a deep breath. "No, we're not hiding any terrorists," said Ryan. "What kind of question is that?"

"We'd like to search the van."

"Fine," I said clearly frustrated. "Search the van. We don't have any drugs." My mind was racing by this point. I thought about what we did have in the back. What if they find our box of political books and articles about Iraq? What if they find Ryan's political T-shirts? The fact that I was afraid we might be arrested because we read political books and wear political shirts made me even angrier.

"Wait a minute," said Ryan. "Do you have probable cause?"

"No."

"What happens if I tell you that you can't search the van?"

"Our big bad boss will probably get mad. Maybe yell."

"Then you can't search the van."

They looked at each other and then looked at us. My hands were tightly grasping the bottom of the steering wheel and were starting to feel clammy. The guy on my side slowly grabbed a pad of paper and wrote me a ticket, only my second since I got my license in 1988. He tore it off the pad, handed it over, lightly hit the side of the van a few times, and said, "Be on your way."

Afterword

THE WEEKEND AFTER returning to San Francisco, I went to the Green Festival, a three-day environmental expo, and felt like I had stepped back in time. The line was long and an activist was handing out flyers about a screening for an anti–Wal-Mart film to a crowd that probably already agreed with its overall message. Across the street at the Giftcenter & Jewelrymart, I noticed a long line of heavily made-up women wearing dresses and high heels. The two crowds couldn't have been more different. I couldn't help but approach the activist and say, "I'm pretty sure this crowd already agrees with you. Why don't you cross the street and give the flyers to those women over there who are in line to go shopping?"

He looked at the line of women across the street, looked at the line at the Green Festival, and said, "Oh, good point. I hadn't thought of that." And off he went.

I had many moments like that when I returned. They made me want to scream.

The trip made me realize how easy it is to get trapped in one's own social bubble and to run exclusively among crowds with similar views. Preaching to the choir is necessary to maintain one's sanity, but reaching out to people who don't necessarily share all of your values is more important. Turn off your computer, get out of your bubble, and talk to people with whom you disagree. Based on what I found, there are many coalitions just waiting to be built and in conservative parts of the country, they need all the help they can get.

Some people simply don't know how to organize. In Jackson, I met a number of pro-choice women who aren't connected. One woman regularly holds what she calls "radical tea parties" for a handful of friends, but she's not involved in any groups because she doesn't know where to find them.

Then there are the people I met who are shattering stereotypes. Several Planned Parenthood directors told me that some of their largest contributors are pro-choice Republicans, yet we rarely hear from them in the corporate media. The same goes for pro-environment Republicans. I was surprised when I found the Republicans for Environmental Protection in Texas. It sure would be nice if the media, rather than reinforce our assumptions, challenged them by giving these activists and groups the microphone once in a while.

From south Texas to northern Montana, I found people who deeply distrust the media, especially the talking heads on TV. One man I met in Kerrville, Texas, said he no longer watches cable news because the pundits, especially the ones who were wrong about Iraq from day one, insult his intelligence. "Why do they still have their jobs?" he asked.

The media's obsession with stereotypes and shallow sound bites about divisive issues has caused the country at large—including many progressives living in Democratic cities—to lose sight of the fact that states like Texas, Mississippi, Oklahoma, and Montana are, in fact, quite diverse in political culture, and inhabited by many more progressive activists than the stereotypes suggest.

I met quite a few news junkies on my trip. Interestingly, the progressives I met get their news from a wide range of sources, and they often listen to and watch conservative talking heads to find out what they're up to. They also read political books and watch documentaries. Many of the hardcore Republicans I met said they don't trust any source other than Fox. Everything else is liberal, and they wouldn't think of listening to NPR, picking up a copy of *The Nation,* or checking out a progressive news website. What does it mean to be informed in this age of 24/7 media in real time? You and your neighbor could feasibly live in two very different worlds depending on where you get your news and information. I'd love to conduct an experiment by drastically altering the media diet of people who get their news from one source and mistrust the rest.

The majority of the low-income people I met don't have time to read news and get information from multiple sources. Most don't read blogs. Many don't even have computers. Then there's the question of what people want from the media. On my radio show, I've interviewed several mainstream newspaper reporters who say coverage of Iraq and Afghanistan has practically disappeared from the front pages and the nightly news because the public no longer cares. But given the conversations I had, I believe that if stories about veteran suicides and military rapes and Iraqi refugees received as much attention as Reverend Jeremiah Wright or flag lapel pins, people would care. I had lengthy conversations about a wide range of issues with people from all walks of life, and many of them said, "It's not every day that I talk about these issues, but I enjoyed it. These issues are important." This trip also taught me about how easy it is to belittle people who live in places that feel foreign to those of us living near the coasts or in progressive cities. After Ryan returned from a three-week camping trip to Utah, he told me that his roommate had a tendency to make fun of people living in small towns. He said if it weren't for our trip, he probably would have agreed with the negative remarks. "I'll be honest. Before the trip, I assumed that people living in small towns were stupid and backward. I denigrated them, but frankly, I didn't know a thing about them. I don't go to church. I live in a city where I don't own a car," he said. "Will I find common ground with a preacher who spews hate? No. But I can find common ground with people who question their pastor. I realized that churchgoers are real people with real problems who turn to religion to feel like they're part of something bigger."

Based on the emails and financial support (more than $5,000) I received from my blog postings, people clearly want to understand the "other side." Adam from Pennsylvania wrote, "I am a 23-year-old gay man, and I cried several times as I read the comments from your interviewees in Texas. Thank you for going out to talk to these people. There will be no peace and no happiness in my life until I can come to understand why there is so much fear, mistrust, and hatred of gays in America, and your work is a comfort to me."

In some cases, they simply want to be understood. Katya, a Democrat from Oklahoma City, wrote, "Thank you for coming to Oklahoma City. We get written off by so much of the country because of our 'red state' status. It's hard for many to understand that there are all types of people here with all kinds of beliefs."

I also heard from curious people living outside the United States. Derrick from Sydney wrote, "It's good that you're letting the interviewees speak for themselves. I'm making all my friends look at your site—especially the lefties with a knee-jerk reaction to the words 'Bush' and 'Republican,' simply because what you have is so much more balanced than what is traditionally available."

J. Clarke from Yukon, Canada, added, "Thanks for your interviews. It gives me hope that there is some tolerance in the United States. Maybe your country is not on its way to becoming a fascist, secular, Taliban, right-wing, Christian monarchy. The heart and soul of the United States is its Constitution and its people. Your interviews show that there's hope."

At the end of the day, it all boils down to the media. Most people don't realize how powerful the media and punditocracy really are. They shape our opinions about everything from Iraq and torture to global warming and tax cuts, and they have the power to make or break a candidate running for office. Perhaps most important, they shape our opinions about each other.

If the corporate media spent more time talking to people of all political stripes—especially to moderate Republicans who aren't afraid of speaking out, or progressives who live in conservative areas—they would find the political climate of this country isn't as black and white as they continue to insist it is. They would also learn that people want more than *infotainment*, spin, and simplistic generalizations; they want a more thoughtful and substantive dialogue about issues that truly matter to their everyday lives. They want the truth. And they want to be heard.

Acknowledgments

This book would still be an idea if it weren't for Ryan. I will always be grateful for your support, encouragement, patience, and silly sense of humor throughout the trip. Even though you got me in trouble and almost ruined my interviews on many occasions, your willingness to embark on a journey with no itinerary speaks volumes about your sense of adventure and desire to better understand "those people." Thank you for everything.

To everyone who so kindly agreed to be interviewed, thank you for sharing your opinions and personal stories with me. I still talk about those of you who welcomed us into your homes without ever asking for my last name or a business card! To the activists working in hostile territory, I don't know how you do it, but I commend you for your courage, for staying true to your beliefs, and for your commitment to equality, peace, and social justice.

Over the course of my journey, I received a number of supportive emails and generous financial support from people who came across my blog. After a long day of doing interviews in the heat, it was such a treat to find your messages, many from as far away as Australia and France. You kept us going.

A special thanks to Peter Richardson, Scott Jordan, Melissa

Edeburn, and everyone at PoliPointPress for supporting a book about real people, and for being so accessible and enthusiastic. Most important, thank you for publishing books you believe in. Thanks to Katherine Silver for your copyediting expertise, and David Peattie and the team at BookMatters for producing this book. You were a pleasure to work with.

Several people greatly influenced me when I was a bright-eyed idealist just starting out. If it weren't for Donna Rosenthal, my first and only journalism professor at St. Mary's College of California, I might have pursued a career in law instead of journalism. Thank you for teaching me about the power of giving people a voice and telling their stories. I'll never forget the day you invited a blind man to class. It was the first time I had ever met a blind person and you said, "No question is a dumb question." I couldn't believe it was possible to make a living by asking people questions and telling their stories. That's when I decided I wanted to be a reporter.

Brian Cooley gave me my first professional on-air gig at CNET Radio in 1996, even though the only radio experience I had at that point was as a news reporter and heavy metal DJ at St. Mary's. Truth be told, my voice was high, and it often generated email complaints from our male-dominated audience. I'll never forget this one: "You sound like a valley girl who belongs in a mall. Your content is good, but your voice is awful." I was crushed. Brian told me to ignore the criticism and exude confidence. "When you're in the studio, pretend like you're talking to your mom and don't forget about the confidence. It's all about confidence." Thanks to your advice, I eventually found my voice and my passion. I wish every young woman just starting out had an encouraging boss like you.

Janet Kornblum, my editor and mentor at *CNETNews.com*, taught me how to navigate the very male world of technology reporting, stand up for myself, and ask for what I'm worth. Thank you for your advice, support, and friendship.

Marilyn Fowler and the wonderful activists involved with the Women's Intercultural Network and the California Women's Agenda are a constant source of inspiration. Marilyn should be relaxing in a hammock on a beach by now; she's been fighting for women's rights since the late 1960s! Instead, she continues to work tirelessly to improve the lives of women and girls around the globe. I hope you know how much I appreciate you and all you've done for the women of my generation.

To everyone at KALW 91.7 FM in San Francisco, thank you for your commitment to global and local independent media, and for making KALW such a great place to work.

A heartfelt thanks to my wonderful family and friends for your encouragement and support, especially my brother, dad, grandparents, aunt Rose, and uncle John. A special thanks to my girlfriends who checked up on me during the writing process and offered helpful feedback: Sue Blankman, Iris Erem (a thousand thanks for the delicious fruit!), Alyssa Landy, Mary McGloin, Marcia Myers, Malihe Razazan, and Dar Wiczek. To my dear and forever friend, Aaron Rabideau, thank you for listening, sharing your creative energy, and encouraging me to tell my story.

Finally, I would not be where I am today without the unconditional love and support of my beautiful mom. When I get depressed about the state of the world, it's comforting to know that you're just a phone call away. Somehow, you always manage to lift my spirits, make me burst with laughter, and keep me hopeful. Thank you for breaking the rules by allowing me to embrace my independence and create my own path. Thank you for being you.

Index

About the Author

ROSE AGUILAR is the host of *Your Call*, a live, call-in, daily radio show on KALW 91.7 FM in San Francisco that focuses on politics, social issues, the environment, and the arts. She also reports for KALW News, writes for *AlterNet.org*, offers analysis on current events for the BBC, and contributed to the book *Red State Rebels: Tales of Grassroots Resistance in the Heartland*. Rose sits on the board of the Women's Intercultural Network, an international nonprofit that links women and girls across cultures. In November 2007, Rose received a "Truth-Teller" award from Flyaway Productions. A California native, she lives in San Francisco.

Other Books from PoliPointPress

The Blue Pages: A Directory of Companies Rated by Their Politics and Practices
Helps consumers match their buying decisions with their political values by listing the political contributions and business practices of over 1,000 companies. $9.95, paperback.

Jeff Cohen, *Cable News Confidential: My Misadventures in Corporate Media*
Offers a fast-paced romp through the three major cable news channels—Fox CNN, and MSNBC—and delivers a serious message about their failure to cover the most urgent issues of the day. $14.95, paperback.

Marjorie Cohn, *Cowboy Republic: Six Ways the Bush Gang Has Defied the Law*
Shows how the executive branch under President Bush has systematically defied the law instead of enforcing it. $14.95, paperback.

Joe Conason, *The Raw Deal: How the Bush Republicans Plan to Destroy Social Security and the Legacy of the New Deal*
Reveals the well-financed and determined effort to undo the Social Security Act and other New Deal programs. $11.00, paperback.

Kevin Danaher, Shannon Biggs, and Jason Mark, *Building the Green Economy: Success Stories from the Grassroots*
Shows how community groups, families, and individual citizens have protected their food and water, cleaned up their neighborhoods, and strengthened their local economies. $16.00, paperback.

Kevin Danaher and Alisa Gravitz, *The Green Festival Reader: Fresh Ideas from Agents of Change*
Collects the best ideas and commentary from the some of the most forward green thinkers of our time. $15.95, paperback.

Reese Erlich, *The Iran Agenda: The Real Story of U.S. Policy and the Middle East Crisis*
Explores the turbulent recent history between the two countries and how it has led to a showdown over nuclear technology. $14.95, paperback.

Steven Hill, *10 Steps to Repair American Democracy*
Identifies the key problems with American democracy, especially election practices, and proposes ten specific reforms to reinvigorate it. $11.00, paperback.

Marks Kouna/akis and Peter Laufer, *Hope Is a Tattered Flag: Voices of Reason and Change for the Post-Bush Era*
Gathers together the most listened-to politicos and pundits, activists and thinkers, to answer the question: what happens after Bush leaves office? $29.95, hardcover; $16.95 paperback.

Yvonne Latty, *In Conflict: Iraq War Veterans Speak Out on Duty, Loss, and the Fight to Stay Alive*
Features the unheard voices, extraordinary experiences, and personal photographs of a broad mix of Iraq War veterans, including Congressman Patrick Murphy, Tammy Duckworth, Kelly Daugherty, and Camilo Mejia. $24.00, hardcover.

Phillip Longman, *Best Care Anywhere: Why VA Health Care Is Better Than Yours*
Shows how the turnaround at the long-maligned VA hospitals provides a blueprint for salvaging America's expensive but troubled health care system. $14.95, paperback.

Marcia and Thomas Mitchell, *The Spy Who Tried to Stop a War: Katharine Gun and the Secret Plot to Sanction the Iraq Invasion*
Describes a covert operation to secure UN authorization for the Iraq war and the furor that erupted when a young British spy leaked it. $23.95, hardcover.

Susan Mulcahy, ed., *Why I'm a Democrat*
Explores the values and passions that make a diverse group of Americans proud to be Democrats. $14.95, paperback.

Christine Pelosi, *Campaign Boot Camp: Basic Training for Future Leaders*
Offers a seven-step guide for successful campaigns and causes at all levels of government. $15.95, paperback.

William Rivers Pitt, *House of Ill Repute: Reflections on War, Lies, and America's Ravaged Reputation*
Skewers the Bush Administration for its reckless invasions, warrantless wiretaps, lethally incompetent response to Hurricane Katrina, and other scandals and blunders. $16.00, paperback.

Sarah Posner, *God's Profits: Faith, Fraud, and the Republican Crusade for Values Voters*
Examines corrupt televangelists' ties to the Republican Party and unprecedented access to the Bush White House. $19.95, hardcover.

Nomi Prins, *Jacked: How "Conservatives" Are Picking Your Pocket –Whether You Voted for Them or Not*
Describes how the "conservative" agenda has affected your wallet, skewed national priorities, and diminished America—but not the American spirit. $12.00, paperback.

Cliff Schecter, *The Real McCain: Why Conservatives Don't Trust Him—And Why Independents Shouldn't*
Explores the gap between the public persona of John McCain and the reality of this would-be president. $14.95, hardcover.

Norman Solomon, *Made Love, Got War: Close Encounters with America's Warfare State*
Traces five decades of American militarism and the media's all-too-frequent failure to challenge it. $24.95, hardcover.

John Sperling et al., *The Great Divide: Retro vs. Metro America*
Explains how and why our nation is so bitterly divided into what the authors call Retro and Metro America. $19.95, paperback.

Daniel Weintraub, *Party of One: Arnold Schwarzenegger and the Rise of the Independent Voter*
Explains how Schwarzenegger found favor with independent voters, whose support has been critical to his success, and suggests that his bipartisan approach represents the future of American politics. $19.95, hardcover.

Curtis White, *The Spirit of Disobedience: Resisting the Charms of Fake Politics, Mindless Consumption, and the Culture of Total Work*
Debunks the notion that liberalism has no need for spirituality and describes a "middle way" through our red state/blue state political impasse. Includes three powerful interviews with John DeGraaf, James Howard Kunstler, and Michael Ableman. $24.00, hardcover.

For more information, please visit www.p3books.com.

About This Book

This book is printed on Cascade Enviro100 Print paper. It contains 100 percent post-consumer fiber and is certified EcoLogo, Processed Chlorine Free, and FSC Recycled. For each ton used instead of virgin paper, we:

* Save the equivalent of 17 trees

* Reduce air emissions by 2,098 pounds

* Reduce solid waste by 1,081 pounds

* Reduce the water used by 10,196 gallons

* Reduce suspended particles in the water by 6.9 pounds.

This paper is manufactured using biogas energy, reducing natural gas consumption by 2,748 cubic feet per ton of paper produced.

The book's printer, Malloy Incorporated, works with paper mills that are environmentally responsible, that do not source fiber from endangered forests, and that are third-party certified. Malloy prints with soy and vegetable based inks, and over 98 percent of the solid material they discard is recycled. Their water emissions are entirely safe for disposal into their municipal sanitary sewer system, and they work with the Michigan Department of Environmental Quality to ensure that their air emissions meet all environmental standards.

The Michigan Department of Environmental Quality has recognized Malloy as a Great Printer for their compliance with environmental regulations, written environmental policy, pollution prevention efforts, and pledge to share best practices with other printers. Their county Department of Planning and Environment has designated them a Waste Knot Partner for their waste prevention and recycling programs.